The Power In/Of Language

Educational Philosophy and Theory Special Issue Book Series

Series Editor: Michael A. Peters

The *Educational Philosophy and Theory* journal publishes articles concerned with all aspects of educational philosophy. Their themed special issues are also available to buy in book format and cover subjects ranging from curriculum theory, educational administration, the politics of education, educational history, educational policy, and higher education.

Titles in the series include:

The Power In/Of Language
Edited by David R. Cole & Linda J. Graham

Educational Neuroscience: Initiatives and Emerging Issues
Edited by Kathryn E. Patten and Stephen R. Campbell

Rancière, Public Education and the Taming of Democracy
Edited by Maarten Simons and Jan Masschelein

Thinking Education Through Alain Badiou
Edited by Kent den Heyer

Toleration, Respect and Recognition in Education
Edited by Mitja Sardoč

Gramsci and Educational Thought
Edited by Peter Mayo

Patriotism and Citizenship Education
Edited by Bruce Haynes

Exploring Education Through Phenomenology: Diverse Approaches
Edited by Gloria Dall'Alba

Academic Writing, Philosophy and Genre
Edited by Michael A. Peters

Complexity Theory and the Philosophy of Education
Edited by Mark Mason

Critical Thinking and Learning
Edited by Mark Mason

Philosophy of Early Childhood Education: Transforming Narratives
Edited by Sandy Farquhar and Peter Fitzsimons

The Learning Society from the Perspective of Governmentality
Edited by Jan Masschelein, Maarten Simons, Ulrich Bröckling and Ludwig Pongratz

Citizenship, Inclusion and Democracy: A Symposium on Iris Marion Young
Edited by Mitja Sardoc

Postfoundationalist Themes In The Philosophy of Education: Festschrift for James D. Marshall
Edited by Paul Smeyers and Michael A. Peters

Music Education for the New Millennium: Theory and Practice Futures for Music Teaching and Learning
Edited by David Lines

Critical Pedagogy and Race
Edited by Zeus Leonardo

Derrida, Deconstruction and Education: Ethics of Pedagogy and Research
Edited by Peter Pericles Trifonas and Michael A. Peters

The Power In/Of Language

Edited by
David R. Cole and Linda J. Graham

WILEY-BLACKWELL

A John Wiley & Sons, Ltd., Publication

This edition first published 2012

Chapters © 2012 The Authors

Book compilation © 2012 Philosophy of Education Society of Australasia

Originally published as a special issue of *Educational Philosophy and Theory* (Volume 43, Issue 6)

Blackwell Publishing was acquired by John Wiley & Sons in February 2007. Blackwell's publishing program has been merged with Wiley's global Scientific, Technical, and Medical business to form Wiley-Blackwell.

Registered Office

John Wiley & Sons Ltd, The Atrium, Southern Gate, Chichester, West Sussex, PO19 8SQ, United Kingdom

Editorial Offices

350 Main Street, Malden, MA 02148-5020, USA

9600 Garsington Road, Oxford, OX4 2DQ, UK

The Atrium, Southern Gate, Chichester, West Sussex, PO19 8SQ, UK

For details of our global editorial offices, for customer services, and for information about how to apply for permission to reuse the copyright material in this book please see our website at www.wiley.com/wiley-blackwell.

The right of David R. Cole & Linda J. Graham to be identified as the authors of the editorial material in this work has been asserted in accordance with the UK Copyright, Designs and Patents Act 1988.

Wiley also publishes its books in a variety of electronic formats. Some content that appears in print may not be available in electronic books.

Designations used by companies to distinguish their products are often claimed as trademarks. All brand names and product names used in this book are trade names, service marks, trademarks or registered trademarks of their respective owners. The publisher is not associated with any product or vendor mentioned in this book. This publication is designed to provide accurate and authoritative information in regard to the subject matter covered. It is sold on the understanding that the publisher is not engaged in rendering professional services. If professional advice or other expert assistance is required, the services of a competent professional should be sought.

Library of Congress Cataloging-in-Publication Data

The power in/of language / edited by David R. Cole & Linda J. Graham.
     p. cm. – (Educational philosophy and theory special issues)
  Includes index.
  ISBN 978-1-4443-6701-0 (pbk.)
    1. Language and education.   2. Discourse analysis.   3. Sociolinguistics.   4. Language and languages–Philosophy.   5. Education–Philosophy.   I. Graham, Linda J. (Linda Jayne)
  II. Cole, David R. (David Robert), 1967–
  P40.8.P685 2012
  306.44–dc23

                                  2011045239

9781444367010

A catalogue record for this book is available from the British Library.

Set in 10/13 Plantin by Toppan Best-set Premedia Limited

Printed in Malaysia by Ho Printing (M) Sdn Bhd

1   2012

Contents

Notes on Contributors

John Baldacchino is currently Associate Professor of Art and Art education at Columbia University's Teachers College. He is the author of five books. His most recent, *Makings of the Sea* (Gorgias, 2010) is the first of a trilogy he is writing on Mediterranean Aesthetics with the other volumes projected for 2013 and 2014. He is currently completing another book, *Art's Way Out: Exit pedagogy and the cultural condition*, to be published by Sense late in 2011/early 2012. His research concentrates on the arts, philosophy and education. Email: avant.nostalgia@gmail.com

David R. Cole is Associate Professor at the University of Western Sydney. He has published widely in journals such as *Prospect, Curriculum Perspectives* and *English in Australia*. In addition, he has edited three books on literacy theory called: *Multiliteracies in Motion: Current theory and practice* (Routledge); *Multiliteracies and Technology Enhanced Education: Social practice and the global classroom* (IGI) and *Multiple Literacies Theory: A Deleuzian perspective* (Sense). He researches in the fields of affective literacy, multiple literacies theory and multiliteracies where he applies Deleuzian theory to open up important social questions in education. He published a novel in 2007 called *A Mushroom of Glass* (Sid Harta, Melbourne). Email: David.Cole@uts.edu.au

Scot Danforth is a Professor in the College of Education and Human Ecology at The Ohio State University. His most recent book is *The Incomplete Child: An Intellectual History of Learning Disabilities* (Peter Lang), a historical analysis of the conceptual and practical development of a science of learning disabilities in the United States. Email: Danforth.10@osu.edu

Sandy Farquhar is a senior lecturer in the Faculty of Education at the University of Auckland, where she teaches in early childhood education with a focus on philosophy, curriculum and policy. She was a recipient of the inaugural PESA scholarship in 2006. She has recently published *Ricoeur, Identity and Early Childhood* (Rowman and Littlefield, 2010). Email: s.farquhar@auckland.ac.nz

Peter Fitzsimons has at various times been a teacher, a professional musician, a radio journalist, a factory manager, and more recently a management consultant in education and health. His PhD focussed on Nietzsche and Education and his recent writing explores the relationship between ethics and social policy. He has published two books and a number of international peer-reviewed journal articles. Email: peterfitz@attglobal.net

Linda J. Graham is an Australian Research Council (ARC) Discovery Postdoctoral Fellow and Senior Lecturer in the School of Education at Macquarie University in

Sydney. Her research interests concern the role of education policy and school practices in the medicalization of childhood and the improvement of responses to children who are difficult to teach. Email: linda.graham@mq.edu.au

Awad Ibrahim is Professor at the Faculty of Education of the University of Ottawa, Canada. He is a curriculum theorist, with special interest in cultural studies, Hip-Hop, youth and Black popular culture, philosophy and sociology of education, ethnography and applied linguistics. He is the editor of the journal *Philosophical Studies in Education*, and (with Samy Alim and Alastair Pennycook) of *Global Linguistic Flows: Hip-Hop cultures, youth identities and the politics of language* (Routledge, 2009). His book, *'Hey, Whassup Homeboy?' Becoming Black: Hip-hop, language, culture and the politics of identity* is to be published by the University of Toronto Press. Email: aibrahim@uottawa.ca

Zeus Leonardo is Associate Professor in Social and Cultural Studies in Education and Affiliated Faculty of Designated Emphasis in Critical Theory at the University of California, Berkeley. He has published several dozen articles and book chapters on race and educational theory. He is the author of *Ideology, Discourse, and School Reform* (Praeger), editor of *Critical Pedagogy and Race* (Blackwell), and co-editor of *Charting New Terrains of Chicano(a)/Latino(a) Education* (Hampton Press). His articles have appeared in *Educational Researcher*, *Race Ethnicity & Education*, and *Studies in Philosophy and Education*. His recent books are *Race, Whiteness, and Education* (Routledge) and *Handbook of Cultural Politics and Education* (Sense). Email: zeusleonardo@berkeley.edu

Jane Mulderrig (PhD, Lancaster University) is a Lecturer in Applied Linguistics at Sheffield University. She is on the editorial boards of *Glossa*, *Discourse*, and *Journal of Critical Education Policy Studies*. Her main research interests are in applying corpus-based critical discourse analysis to investigate questions of identity, power and personality in a range of discourse contexts. Her publications use this approach to investigate New Labour 'spin', discourses of the knowledge economy in UK education policy, and most recently to develop a linguistic approach to the analysis of 'soft power' in contemporary governance. Jane has also published in the area of disability and gender policies, and equality and human rights. She is currently investigating public discourses of ageing. For details of other activities and to download publications see: http://www.shef.ac.uk/english/staff/mulderrig.html. Email: j.mulderrig@sheffield.ac.uk

Jessica Ringrose is a Senior Lecturer at the London Institute of Education. She is currently researching young people's digitized sexual cultures and subjectivities. Her research on classed and raced femininities and competitive, heterosexualized aggression and (cyber)bullying can be found in *Feminism and Psychology*, *Feminist Theory*, *Girlhood Studies*, and *British Journal of Sociology of Education*, among others. Jessica's new book: *Postfeminist Education? Girls and the sexual politics of schooling* will be published by Routledge in 2011. Email: J.ringrose@ioe.ac.uk

Foreword

This monograph in the *Educational Philosophy and Theory* series brings into sharp focus the power of language and the many different ways discourse can dominate or liberate. *The Power In/Of Language* edited by David R. Cole and Linda J. Graham takes up its challenge from Zeus Leonardo's remarks on 'white privilege' which he suggests is often perpetuated through discursive strategies and tactics.

This collection is thematically integrated by the fact that contributors reference the work of Foucault, Deleuze and Gramsci (among others) across a range of themes and subject areas: disability science, post-colonial theory, critical discourse analysis and critical race theory to name a few of the prominent examples. Given the linguistic and discursive turns of educational and cultural theory, this emphasis on the 'power of language' is a welcome one and the penetrating analyses by renowned scholars will be of great service to those in the field working to analyse and unseat race, gender, class and cultural privilege.

Introduction

DAVID R. COLE and LINDA J. GRAHAM

This monograph examines discursive strategies of domination and resistance used within the educational context.

In his 2004 essay 'The Color of Supremacy: Beyond the discourse of "white privilege" ', Zeus Leonardo (2004, p. 137) argues that 'white racial supremacy revolves less around the issue of unearned advantages, or the *State* of being dominant, and more around direct processes that secure domination and the privileges associated with it'. In relation to the issue of 'white privilege', he claims that in failing to engage with the active strategies and tactics employed by some groups to gain and maintain dominance over others, scholars end up perpetuating 'an image of domination without agents' (p. 137). Leonardo challenges those interested in marginalisation to direct critical attention beyond the status of dominance or marginality towards the structural, political, social and economic forces that allow them to be so.

In taking up Leonardo's challenge, we noted that strategies and tactics of domination are often discursive – hidden beneath layers of everyday language, ways of speaking about others and, interestingly, also about 'ourselves'. Because we think we are speaking only of ourselves, whether that be in racial, nationalistic or cultural terms, we fail to acknowledge or accept how speaking of ourselves is in fact a way of defining and subjectivating others – who we can then position as unlike 'us'. Language is thus a powerful weapon but, like other weapons, language can both hurt and defend. We are interested not only in the discursive tactics used to position the 'other', but also in the subversive effects of creative, determined and sustained responses to those tactics. For there are responses, even though they may eventually be ignored, vilified or victimised. So whilst, as Butler (1997) argues, 'a name tends to fix, to freeze, to delimit' (p. 35), the act of speaking to or speaking of also opens a space for linguistic return – an opportunity for the subjected to retort and subvert. This right of reply to address provides radical opportunities for the marginalised to speak themselves differently and, in so doing, engage in purposeful resistance.

To bring these broader issues into sharper focus within the educational context, this book features scholarly works that outline strategies and tactics of domination and resistance in and around (or 'outside') places of teaching and learning

1

The Actions of Affect in Deleuze: Others using language and the language that we make ...

DAVID R. COLE

Introduction

Gilles Deleuze inextricably ties up the ways in which power works through and in language with affect. The problem that confronts us is therefore: What is affect, and how does it relate to language and power? Deleuze suggests that we get different answers to these questions depending upon whom we ask, and as such resists outlining a clear definition of affect anywhere in his oeuvre. In this paper, I have constructed the two ways in which affect is approached in the writing of Deleuze in terms of a model (please refer to Figure 1) to aid comprehension of the idea, though this does not represent a unified theory of affect. The point of the Deleuzian scholarly synthesis and reinvention of these thinkers through his studies (Hardt, 1993) is not to become confused by the ways in which affect has been deployed to support different philosophical outlooks, but to realise that affect is a philosophical tool that helps to build perspectives. For example, Spinoza used affect in his system of ethics to connect desire with reason; language therefore takes on a powerful ethical and joyful cadence as it communicates deeply felt emotions. Nietzsche used affect as a basis for sensation in his understanding of the will to power and the eternal return. Language, as such, assumes power as it is combined with the ways in which the repetitions of time and the energies of the will may drive one's life. Bergson, on the other hand, made affect part of his conception of *durée* and the *élan vital*, so that language may be imbued with the many subtle nuances of the continuities in time, memory and creativity, and these may constitute power. One should not therefore try to teach the truth of affect, nor rationalise it into a coherent or unified 'affect theory' but instead use it to develop theory that will help to sustain and modify one's views with empirical evidence and the fluctuations that may be contained in this evidence.

In contrast to Deleuze's focused scholarly studies, his joint publications with Félix Guattari on *Capitalism & Schizophrenia* (1984, 1988) do not bear down on specific philosophical systems. This writing is populated by conceptual figures such as rhizomes and the machinic phylum that synthesise and distribute the arguments as they occur. Affect appears as a connective element in this argumentation that takes particular ideas

The Power In/Of Language, First Edition. Edited by David R. Cole and Linda J. Graham.
Chapters © 2012 The Authors. Book compilation © 2012 Philosophy of Education Society of Australasia.
Published 2012 by Blackwell Publishing Ltd.

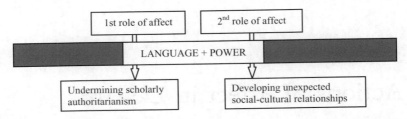

Figure 1: The two-role model of affect from Deleuze[1]

and points of intensity and makes them open to reabsorption and usage in novel ways. For example, Deleuze & Guattari (1984, 1988) are critically concerned about pre-figuration in primitive communities that has in many ways given rise to war machines and the modern development of the state. The historical lineage and analysis of this situation is dispensed with in favour of a moving confrontation with pre-figuration. The ideas and analyses are nomadic, affect is used as a conceptual weapon and an organising principle that links certain players and moments in history with their realisation in today's globalised society. Deleuze & Guattari's (1988) writing provides a connection between the creative uncon-scious, where the ideas and analyses are synthesised, and the plane of becoming that impinges immanently on everything that we do now (Cole & Throssell, 2008). In terms of the power of language, affect sits in the unconscious in systematic and organised ways, for example in the libido, which may be realised in advertising campaigns or the scripted speeches of politicians. Our society has made a huge investment in education, and this point of intensity is imbued and distributed with affect through teacher-talk and educa-tional research. There is an enormous interconnected field here, through which educa-tional affect makes things happen in the lives of teachers, academics and students, who may develop responses to power and language in unconscious and sentient ways.

Talking with Unconscious-affect

When Freud (1953) discussed affect in the interpretation of dreams, he was talking about a 'mood or tendency that is a determining influence on the dream' (p. 627). He analysed various dreams that patients related to him, examining the symbolic and metonymic figures that these dreams represented. Affect appears in all these dreams, not as constituent parts or as a comprehensible whole, but as a means to join together the expression of the patients with their particular emotional states. As such, anxiety, pain or paranoia could permeate the dreams as affect without being named by any of the patients. In the role of the analyst, Freud took it on himself to name the affect in the dreams, and to discuss the various ways in which the patients have articulated affect in their monologues. This situation could be designated as a parallel case to the analysis at hand of education and the power of language. It should be stated that there are potential blockages, neuroses and misunderstandings with respect to articulating the power of language in education. These problems spring from the fact that education, subjectivity and power in language are not unified or indeed cohesive units of analysis. This was perhaps Freud's point of introducing the Id, Ego and Super-ego as a distinctive layering in the analysis. These factors are representative of disunity that is also a mode of abundance that always exceeds disciplinary regimes or any discourses of control or limitation such as definitions of the self. We therefore must expand the range of unconscious affect from devices that serve to make the subconscious analysable, and include the social plane on which contemporary educational practices work with power and language.

To find such a strategic deployment, we need to turn to the second role of affect in Deleuze & Guattari (1984, 1988) and the ways in which this has been taken up in, for example, contemporary feminism. This is because poststructural thinkers such as Elizabeth Grosz (1994) or Elspeth Probyn (2004) have disavowed the psychological basis of affect, and endeavoured to make affect mobile and without the dualism of the analysed-analyst (Cole, 2007a). Deleuze & Guattari (1984) have also worked to remove the Oedipal and Elektra interpretive templates from the dreams of the analysed subject and in contrast to the power of the analyst. As such, when we look for affect in the power of language in education, we cannot place ourselves in the role of examining the emotional moods or tendencies of a particular student or cohort or institutional discourse. Rather, we should firstly examine our own emotional proclivities, and articulate the ways in which they are factors in any analysis of the phenomena involved with the study. So, for example, if we observe a grade nine painting class with students disengaged and seemingly using the colours and brushes to make random splodges of colour and graffiti, what are we expressing, taking into account unconscious language-affect, when we endeavour to write up the report? The affect of rebellion expressed through the creativity of the group action should be included as a 'voice' in the discussion, as should the dissonance and factors of control that are perhaps already present in the school and have contributed to the expression of affect by the students. The discursive mode of the report must take into account peer relationships and power games that might be shaping the articulations of the class at any moment. There must be room in the writing for the dynamic and changing lived experience of the subjects, such as home life influences or the power of the media. The report should also be inhabited by the writer's understandings of their reception and relationships with the research context, and the ways in which the group have reacted to the extra presence. In summation, the report should not be a diagnosis of 'a lack of fulfilment of curriculum goals' caused by behaviour management problems or malad-justed students, but, according to the second role of affect, an earnest attempt to understand the complicated ways affect populates this situation through becoming:

> Becoming, [while happening in a gap], is nonetheless an extreme contiguity within [the] coupling of two sensations without resemblance, or, [it could be figured as] a light that captures both of the resemblances in a single reflec-tion ... . It is a zone of indetermination, as if things, beasts, and persons endlessly reach that point that immediately precedes their natural differentia-tion. This is what is called an affect. (Deleuze & Guattari, 1994, p. 173)

The important point here is that becoming is not only about the ways in which changes coalesce and emerge in the educational context, or the outcomes of becoming that education can be reduced to. The second role of affect is about the complex and often hidden processes included in the becoming. In a similar way to Peter Clough (2002) who has used affect as constitutive of the social context of learning through the writing of educational narratives, the aspect of becoming that we may take from the second role of affect in Deleuze will include fictional elements and the narrative re-creation of life. In other words, the second role of affect does not determine becoming as a wholly factual or psychological account of events that aims towards teleology. The second role of affect in Deleuze presents events as processes of complex material unpickings and entangled situations. In consequence, what emerges is a type of minor philosophy of education (Gregoriou, 2004) that attends to the movements of desire in language and power. Whenever one speaks in an educational context new connective apparatuses appear that will communicate unconscious affect that spreads on turbulent planes that depend on the learning that occurs. One must therefore analyse the teaching and learning educational plane and make sense of the two-role model of affect from Deleuze in terms of the language of pedagogy.

Teaching and Learning with Language-affect

The educational complex opened up by attending to the philosophy of Gilles Deleuze involves context and practice. Context is important as affect is grounded in the situational points of intensity under scrutiny. Practice is thoroughly connected to language by the affect that one may produce due to the synthesis, analysis and representation of any repetition of an action (Albrecht-Crane & Slack, 2007). The Deleuzian analysis at this point relies heavily on the work of socio-linguists such as William Labov (1971) who had discovered that some of the rules of language, that he called 'variable rules' can generate systematic, endogenous or 'grown from within' variation (p. 21). For example, in small urban communities, social networks may develop that use language as a 'badge of identity' (De Landa, 1993, p. 14). These identities circulate around the community and define power relationships, allegiances and structures that maintain and transform the local dialect. In effect, Labov's (1971) research forms a potential bridge or undifferentiated plane where power relationships that could potentially undermine the circulation of social meaning in a system are stabilised.

Teaching and learning therefore critically involves a combination of the first and second roles of affect. The word of the teacher is principally about the first role of affect. The teacher's language will transmit power according to Deleuze as a function of its affect. If the teacher has researched his or her subject well, and speaks with passion and sincerity, these affects will permeate the atmosphere of the class, the learning context and the subsequent educational practice. This however is not a unidirectional or intentional relationship. This is because the second role of affect is also connected to teaching and learning due to the ways in which the socio-cultural context of the classroom funnels and plays with language, power and meaning. There will be an undifferentiated plane in the educational context between the students that will draw in parts of their social lives and perhaps not actively involve the teacher. This plane will also define power relationships, language and affect (Cole & Yang, 2008). The teacher cannot step into this plane from the outside, but must actively look for ways in which to connect with this plane through understanding the socio-cultural systems that are present in a cohort, but without trying to ape or become part of them in an artificial manner.

Another example to illustrate the two-role model of affect in teaching and learning that we may derive from Deleuze could be of a teacher investing time and energy writing up his or her excellent classroom practice and sending off the account to an educational academic. The first role of affect is important in terms of the validity and accuracy of the account and the power of the language used by the teacher, the second role of affect takes place in the description of the teaching and learning context as an understanding of systematic endogenous variations in the lesson will add to the plausibility of the 'best practice' as it should be possible to repeat this one off great piece of pedagogy. In other words, the teacher will not only have to think about the formal impact of his or her writing style, and the suitability for academic consumption, but also the ways in which the writing deals with the specific desires and power relationships as constituted by the body of the class and how these may be transformed from within (Boler, 1999; Bourdieu & Passeron, 1977). This teacher would also want to explain the collective practices of teaching in his or her school, and the ways in which they relate to this particular instance of teaching and learning. He or she should pinpoint the ways in which the students have learnt according to the specific pedagogic approach under analysis and also the responses and understandings of the students to the pedagogy at this point. The meaning of the report of best practice therefore comes about due to the two roles of affect and the processes that are inherent within the language of the collective teaching context, or as Deleuze and Guattari have put it:

> ... there is no simple identity between the statement and the act. If we wish to move to a real definition of the collective assemblage, we must ask of what [do] these acts [consist of] immanent to language [and] that are in redundancy with statements or that constitute order-words. (Deleuze & Guattari, 1988, p. 80).

This movement towards a definition of the collective assemblage takes us further in understanding the educational complex that is defined by the two-role model of affect. According to the definition of the collective assemblage of Deleuze & Guattari (1988) the problem that causes an educational system to buckle and misfire is the production of order-words, or redundant instructions and directives that sit between the act and the statement. These order-words are incorporeal transformations (pp. 108–9) that take on board power and life and circulate around institutions and places of education like the routing of electricity in plasterboard walls. The most obvious example of this is the language involved with behaviour management issues. Teachers may spend much of their time repeating instructions or telling students off, when the real problem is often a basic lack of engagement with the teaching and learning activities (Woolfolk & Margetts, 2007). The first role of affect is present through the sound of the voice of the teacher, and the stress that this sound will invariably transmit. The second role of affect will be manifest in the reactions of the students, perhaps through mimicry or laughter, off task conversations, or any cynical and resigned reactions to being reprimanded. The collective experience of such classrooms may be fragmented and hostile.

Collectivity also involves the transmission of modes of working between different parties involved with the educational action. This transmission is itself a practice of communication that is open to the two-role model of affect. Any transformed practice will have to be represented and understood through language and the context of the learning. Here Schatzki's account of practice is useful to supplement the two-role model of affect I outline here. According to Schatzki (1996, 2001, 2002) in an important sense, practices prefigure individual actions. In other words, for him, practices precede particular actors and actions, and work to shape their performance as well as supplying its meaning and significance in the particular context. So while any transformed practice is no doubt novel, it remains bounded by its relationships that it may develop between itself and the representation of other practices that are according to Deleuze structured and figured through affect. Schatzki (2002) views social activity as 'composed of a mesh of orders and practices', where orders are 'arrangements of entities e.g. people, artefacts, things' and practices are 'organized activities' (p. 27) and both of these are present in Deleuze & Guattari's conception of 'order-words'. As such, the order-words rely heavily on the first role of affect that is determined by the power and tone of the teacher's voice, and subsidiary factors such as body language and institutional identification and representation of pedagogy. The second role of affect is also implicated in practice as the social relations that are developed through teaching and learning are subject to constant variations in immanence and redundancy. Any indiscreet and throw-away lines of the teachers or students may be picked up and recycled in different contexts, strange relationships and jokes may be intuited by the students from the teacher's choice of content to illustrate a point (Brown, McEvoy & Bishop, 1991). The control and discipline of the teacher and institute may be enacted due to the second role of affect in ways such as the acting out of scenes with exaggerated or cruel punishment, inter-personal violence and sexuality, the order-words being transformed through these practices and the ways in which affectivity is contagious. Deleuze does not give us a neat solution to the free movement of desires, but asks us to follow it, and in particular through the use of figures such as the rhizome or the machinic phylum to understand how desire flows. To this extent, it is worth pursuing the machinic phylum from *A Thousand Plateaus* in order to examine how this idea relates to the two-role model of affect and the power in/of language that can be found in the writings of Deleuze.

The *Machinic Phylum:* Power and Language in Context

According to Deleuze, affect in education makes relationships happen between learning and practice. Furthermore, the language and power that one uses to describe practice and the ways in which learning undergoes transformations in context, and in turn alters the affect that is produced in teaching and learning (Semetsky, 2006). All of these multi-faceted arrangements of affect, language and power may be fed into the machinic phylum of Deleuze & Guattari (1988) to understand the ways in which power is represented through education. For Deleuze & Guattari novelty emerges from within systems, rather than being imposed from without, i.e. through hylomorphism or the doctrine that primordial matter is the first cause of the universe and combines with forms to produce bodies. This is illustrated through the example of metallurgy. For a blacksmith 'it is not a question of imposing a form upon matter but of elaborating an increasingly rich and consistent material, the better to tap coincidentally intense forces' (p. 411). As De Landa (1997) puts it, for Deleuze & Guattari 'the blacksmith treated metals as active materials, pregnant with morphogenetic capabilities, and his role was that of teasing a form out of them, of guiding, through a series of processes; heating, annealing,

quenching, hammering, the emergence of a form, a form in which the materials themselves had a say ... he is less realizing previously defined possibilities, than actualizing
virtualities along divergent lines' (p. 4).

In expounding their notion of novelty emerging from within systems, Deleuze &
Guattari deploy the key concept of the 'machinic phylum'. As De Landa explains,
the machinic phylum serves to 'conceive the genesis of form in geological, biological and
cultural structures as related exclusively to immanent capabilities of the flows of
matter-energy-information and not to any transcendent factor, whether platonic or
divine e.g. the hylomorphic schema' (De Landa, 1997). In terms of the two-role model
of affect, the genesis of form shows how affect works as a transformative element in
expressions. This element works 'from within to transform from without' (Cole, 2005, p.
4). For example, the teacher's language can, according to the first role of affect, develop
blips and stutters that signifies the otherness and separation that a teacher may experience in their power-related job standing at the front of the class. In the second role, the
transformations of affect develop due to social and cultural forces, potentially taking the
expression of any collective along divergent lines. These expressions may be charted
according to the order-words. The concept of the 'machinic phylum' can be further
clarified by considering the terms 'machinic' and 'phylum' separately.

'Machinic' refers to the combinatorial diversity of the elements of a system. The more
diversity and heterogeneity there is the greater the potential for novelties to emerge. As
De Landa (1997) expresses it, 'a crucial ingredient for the emergence of innovation at
any level of reality is the "combinatorial productivity" of the elements at the respective
sub-level, that is, at the level of the components of the structures in question. Not all
components have the same "productivity" ' (p. 2). De Landa illustrates the last point in
this quotation by contrasting the low productivity of sub-atomic particles, yielding only
about one hundred different kinds of atoms, with the prodigious productivity of the next
level up where combinations of atoms yield seemingly uncountable numbers of different
molecules. This combinatorial richness, which favours the emergence of novelty, is
enhanced by both heterogeneity of components and by the presence of processes that
enable heterogeneous elements to combine. For Deleuze & Guattari, 'what we term
machinic is precisely this synthesis of heterogeneities as such' (1988, p. 435). In terms of
the two roles of affect in education, the top level of educational process is often characterised by policy documentation and scientific analyses of empirical studies of populations. Yet the greatest heterogeneity happens at the base level, where actors coincide and
may innovate on form and content, sometimes by enacting the top level of educational
policy. Deleuze & Guattari (1988) therefore point to a reversal in educational organization, whereby the two-role model of affect could be locked into the organizational
structures of education through the machinic phylum. This action of reversal synthesises
and prioritises the language of pedagogy in terms of the two roles of affect as an
immanent feedback system between all elements involved in the context of practice.

The second term of the Deleuze & Guattari concept of the 'phylum' connotes the
processes of self-organization or the idea of a common body-plan, which through
different operations, for example, embryological foldings, stretchings, pullings, pushings,
can yield a variety of concrete designs for organisms or systems. For instance, while there
is a huge diversity of actual body instantiations in the animal kingdom, these are variants

on a common body-plan head, limbs, torso, etc. But it could also be said that Deleuze & Guattari are proposing something even more general than this. De Landa (1997) comments that it is '[a]s if one and the same material "phylum" could be "folded and stretched" to yield all the different structures that inhabit our universe.' So they envisage an 'all-purpose' phylum. The concept of the 'machinic phylum' conjures up ongoing novelty but with recognisable continuity like ever more intricate variations on a theme. In terms of the two-role model of affect in education, pedagogic and collective enuncia- tions of power and language circulate around the system, perhaps without any unifying direction but the coincidence that one may ascribe to order-words. The work that needs to be done through the phylum or plane of immanence, as Deleuze & Guattari (1988) elsewhere term it (pp. 266–7) is in terms of tracking and developing relationships between these enunciations that retains their novelty and at the same time helps to develop potential in terms of the two roles of affect in teaching and learning situations. One way to achieve such 'convergent-emergence' is through erotic language-affects and their application in education.

Erotic Language-affects

The machinic phylum is a useful figure that one can take from Deleuze & Guattari (1988) and apply to the routing of desire through power and language in education. However, it does not deal with the potential intensification that this process implies. In terms of the example of the language of the classroom practitioner, or the writing up of 'best practice', the machinic phylum is akin to a Chinese box that we may feed these processes through to understand how power may evolve through language and out of these situations. Yet it is also not a completely mobile system. The two-role model of affect therefore needs an extra level of impulse to enable a flexible mode of application. Following on from the positioning of unconscious-affect, erotic language-affects are a possible way in which to create a plane of becoming for the two-role model of affect. These affects are plural as they imply multiple becomings. It could be said that two of the most vital factors to make education work that we derive from the investigation of affect are time and the force of the practice (Fiumara, 2001). This is true in an intensive as well as extensive sense as the subjective time of the imagination needs to be dealt with as well as the objective time of the learning experience. If one uses the example of a teacher who is achieving great advances with their students using expressive, transactional and poetic language in a complex way (Britton, 1970), this says something profound about the intimacy and subjective sense of time (Martindale, 1990) that the teacher has produced with this group, as well as the subsequent group force. This type of behaviour may be apparent when the teacher has the students for long periods of time, and the representational projects that the group set out to achieve are messier in terms of exact timing and the group consensus and assessment of outcomes. What one needs in terms of the two-role model of affect working in education are strong bonds between participants in the learning process in order to keep creativity and collective enunciation fluid, vital and alive.

It could be suggested that these bonds might be created, preserved and moulded through use of erotic language-affects. One perhaps flinches somewhat when mentioning such an idea, as erotic language-affects have rarely figured on the educationalist's horizons, and it could be stated that there are moral and social taboos around bringing up such a topic in a teaching and learning context. Yet erotic language-affects fit into this article and exposition of the two-role model of affect and the power in/of language in terms of:

Firstly, the philosophy of education that one may derive from the two roles of affect, erotic language-affects locate and strengthen the central, bonding elements of the thesis by creating the conditions whereby contiguity and the ways in which this continuity is represented (Irigaray, 1985) may be achieved and the will to resist interference from administration and instrumental reason may be heightened. This is important for the two-role model of affect as power may be drained through attention to the minute detail of theoretical construction of an argument for affect in education, or its exact conse-quences in terms of operation. Deleuze suggests that we enact the model in terms of putting philosophy to work (1994a, 2001) and erotic language-affects are one way of doing this. Furthermore, it should be noted that erotic language-affects are not a move in the direction of educational humanism (Maslow, 1970; Suler, 1980) or of completing a sense of the whole or unified self in education that learns in holistic ways, but these affects indicate the subjective principles associated with pleasure and enjoyment that may build upon the closeness imbued by using language with power and the inner or intuitive sense of time that one may derive from developing this ability (Noddings & Shore, 1984).

Secondly, erotic language-affects work on the level of viewing, understanding and deciding what to do with the power of language once it has been recognised. In terms of language analysis, systemic functional linguistics has used this idea in terms of an appraisal system (Martin & White, 2005). This system offers a typology of the lexico-grammatical resources available to both construe and realise interpersonal dimensions of experience at the level of discourse semantics. This leads to a type of prosodic realisation that can be saturating, intensifying or dominating. It also fits in well with the intention and direction of applying Deleuze's two roles of affect in education and making desire work to the benefit of students and teachers and places of learning.

The third meaning of erotic language-affects in this context refers specifically to the Deleuzian philosophical notion of affect as it has been derived from Spinoza. Philoso-phers such as Lloyd (1989) have taken this idea to infuse the mind with sexuality, as the Spinozist positioning of *affectus* with power leads one away from desexed, disembodied ideas. In fact, everything that the mind can think is tied to the body in this figuration of bodily ideation, so, for example, Deleuze & Guattari's (1984) body-without-organs reflects a body locked up and self-replicating in terms of producing streams of internal thoughts without external release. In education, this body may be conceived through closed systems, punishment and the walls of the classroom. The coded language of teaching manuals and professional practice reproduces the body-without-organs because they may drain the sprightly sexual body of emergent life through internalisation and the potential subjectification to inflexible regulation (Cole, 2007b). Erotic language-affects give us a way of talking about these connections, and applying the two-role model of affect to the transformations of the body that the education system enables and main-tains, these changes in form may be sexual or power driven, or a subtle mixture of tacit learning tendencies.

It should be possible to draw a line through the ways in which erotic language-affects take us towards an understanding of speaking with language and power in education from Deleuze. Yet the unification of these three strata of erotic language-affects is an analytic and synthetic process that shows how Deleuze's ideas are to a certain extent resistant to summary and simplification. In many ways, this is the first role of affect working and playing with the meaning that one might get from the three parts of erotic language-affects. The plane of becoming for education that these affects sit upon is therefore not a surface-effect (Colebrook, 2004) but part of the diagrammatical under-standing that one may achieve with regards to language and power from the philosophy of Deleuze (the social cartography). Speaking with the affects that are connected with eroticism creates a tone and atmosphere whereby power flows freely, yet could also be misunderstood. This is in line with Deleuze's preoccupation with the nature of desire and examples of language production that he uses to illustrate his ideas such as 'stuttering' (Deleuze, 1994b). A teacher using erotic language-affects is closing the gap between his or her self, the knowledge and concepts under scrutiny, and the learner-subjects or the collective. Yet he or she is also taking a risk and leaving themselves open to moral inquiry in terms of enacting or projecting the erotic element of this pedagogy, and that is a clear breach of power and not using language to make desire flow in education.

Conclusion

In conclusion, one could state that this two-role model of affect derived from the work of Deleuze has the potential to open up education to the extent that it maybe applied in real teaching and learning situations, as well as to the study of these situations. Just as Foucault's ideas about discourse may be deployed to develop a powerful and consistent methodology for examining power and language in education (Graham, this issue); Deleuze's two roles of affect gives us a way of making sense of the passage of power from speaker to the spoken-to and vice versa in the collective educational environment. Order-words flow through this situation in terms of the power concerns of the institute and governance under question and the ways in which these forces have been interpreted by teachers and students alike. For example, the ethos of the school and the school rules that may appear in school publications may be analysed using the two-role model of affect outlined here. One might use the first role of affect in order to question the appropriate nature of the rules and regulations as they specifically apply to the ways of working of the class. If the teacher and students merely reproduce these rules, the resultant affect will not be usable as an emergent quality. On the other hand, if institu-tional rules are integrated into the everyday practices of the class through practice and context, the regulations and exterior power concerns may become an unstable affect that will work with the imagination and force of the group to help it progress (Foucault, 1980). This is where the second role of affect may be applied and the group will practice teaching and learning through language and power that is wholly owned and directed by complex local dynamics.[2]

Notes

1. I have designed this model to aid comprehension of the ideas that will be explained in this article. Deleuze does not name such a model in his work.

2. This paper has come about due to two papers published by the Philosophy of Education Society of Australia's national conferences. I would like to thank Dr Robyn Glade-Wright (University of Tasmania) and Professor Paul Hager (University of Technology, Sydney) for their contributions to the two initial papers.

References

Albrecht-Crane, C. & Slack, J. D. (2007) Toward a Pedagogy of Affect, in: A. Hickey-Moody & P. Malins (eds), *Deleuzian Encounters: Studies in contemporary social issues* (London, Palgrave Macmillan).

Britton, J. (1970) *Language and Learning* (Harmondsworth, Penguin Books).

Brown, W. H., McEvoy, M. A. & Bishop, N. (1991) Incidental Teaching of Social Behaviour, *Teaching Exceptional Children*, 24:1, pp. 35–38.

Boler, M. (1999) *Feeling Power: Emotions and education* (New York, Routledge).

Bourdieu, P. & Passeron, J-C. (1977) *Reproduction in Education, Society and Culture* (London, Sage).

Cole, D. R. (2005) Learning Through the Virtual, *CTHEORY*, 1. Available at http://www.ctheory.net/articles.aspx?id=445

Cole, D. R. (2007a) Teaching *Frankenstein* and *Wide Sargasso Sea* Using Affective Literacy, *English in Australia*, 42:2, pp. 69–75.

Cole, D. R. (2007b) Virtual Terrorism and the Internet E-Learning Options, *E-Learning*, 4:2, pp. 116–127.

Cole, D. R. & Throssell, P. (2008) Epiphanies in Action: Teaching and learning in synchronous harmony, *The International Journal of Learning*, 15:7, pp. 175–184.

Cole, D. R. & Yang, G. Y. (2008) Affective Literacy for TESOL Teachers in China, *Prospect*, 23:1, pp. 37–45.

Colebrook, C. (2004) The Sense of Space: On the specificity of affect in Deleuze and Guattari, *Postmodern Culture*, 15:1. Available at: http://muse.jhu.edu/journals/pmc/v015/15.1colebrook.html (retrieved 3 January 2008).

Clough, P. (2002) *Narratives and Fictions in Educational Research* (New York, McGraw-Hill Education).

De Landa, M. (1993) Virtual Environments and the Emergence of Synthetic Reason. Available at: http://www.t10.or.at/delanda/delanda.htm (retrieved 4 August 2008).

De Landa, M. (1997) The Machinic Phylum. Available at: http://www.t10.or.at/delanda/delanda.htm (retrieved 15 September 2008).

Deleuze, G. (1983) *Nietzsche and Philosophy*, H. Tomlinson, trans. (New York, Columbia University Press).

Deleuze, G. (1991) *Bergsonism*, H. Tomlinson & B. Habberjam, trans. (New York, Zone Books).

Deleuze, G. (1992) *Expressionism in Philosophy: Spinoza*, M. Joughin, trans. (New York, Zone Books).

Deleuze, G. (1994a) *Difference & Repetition*, P. Patton, trans. (London, The Athlone Press).

Deleuze, G. (1994b) He Stuttered, in: C. V. Boundas & D. Olkowsky (eds), *Gilles Deleuze and the Theatre of Philosophy* (London, Routledge).

Deleuze, G. (2001) Dualism, Monism and Multiplicities (Desire-Pleasure-Jouissance), Seminar of 26 March, 1973, D. W. Smith, trans., *Contretemps*, 2:May, pp. 92–108.

Deleuze, G. & Guattari, F. (1984) *Anti-Oedipus: Capitalism and schizophrenia*, R. Hurley, M. Steem & H. R. Lane, trans. (London, The Athlone Press).

Deleuze, G. & Guattari, F. (1988) *A Thousand Plateaus: Capitalism and schizophrenia II*, B. Massumi, trans. (London, The Athlone Press).

Deleuze, G. & Guattari, F. (1994) *What is Philosophy?* H. Tomlinson and G. Burchill, trans. (London, Verso).

Fiumara, G. C. (2001) *The Mind's Affective Life; A psychoanalytic and philosophical inquiry* (Hove, Brunner-Routledge).

Foucault, M. (1980) *Power/Knowledge: Selected interviews/other writings* (Brighton, Harvester Press).

Freud, S. (1953) The Interpretation of Dreams, J. Strachey trans., in: J. Strachey (ed.), *The Pelican Freud Library Volume 4*, (Harmondsworth, Penguin Books).

Graham, L. J. (this issue) The Product of Text and 'Other' Statements: Discourse analysis and the critical use of Foucault, *Educational Philosophy and Theory: Special Issue–The Power In/Of Language*.

Gregoriou, Z. (2004) Commencing the Rhizome: Towards a minor philosophy of education, *Educational Philosophy and Theory*, 36:3, pp. 233–251.

Grosz, E. (1994) *Volatile Bodies: Toward a corporeal feminism* (Bloomington and Indianapolis, IN, Indiana University Press).

Hardt, M. (1993) *Gilles Deleuze: An apprenticeship in philosophy* (London, UCL Press).

Irigaray, L. (1985) *Speculum of the Other Woman* (Ithaca, NY, Cornell University Press).

Labov, W. (1971) *Sociolinguistic Patterns* (Philadelphia, PA, University of Pennsylvania Press).

Lloyd, G. (1989) Woman as Other: Sex, Gender and subjectivity, *Australian Feminist Studies*, 10, pp. 13–22.

Martin, J. R. & White, P. R. R. (2005) *The Language of Evaluation: Appraisal in English* (Basingstoke, Palgrave Macmillan).

Martindale, C. (1990) *The Clockwork Muse: The predictability of artistic styles* (New York, Basic Books).

Maslow, A. H. (1970) *Motivation and Personality*, 2nd edn. (New York, Harper and Row).

Noddings, P. & Shore, P. (1984) *Awakening The Inner Eye – Intuition in education* (New York, Teacher's College Columbia University).

Probyn, E. (2004) Teaching Bodies: Affects in the classroom, *Body & Society*, 10:4, pp. 21–43.

Schatzki, T. R. (1996) *Social Practices: A Wittgensteinian approach to human activity and the social* (Cambridge, Cambridge University Press).

Schatzki, T. R. (2001) Introduction: Practice theory, in: T. R. Schatzki, K. Knorr Cetina & E. von Savigny, *The Practice Turn in Contemporary Theory* (London & New York, Routledge).

Schatzki, T. R. (2002) *The Site of the Social: A philosophical account of the constitution of social life and change* (University Park, PA, Pennsylvania State University Press).

Semetsky, I. (2006) *Deleuze, Education and Becoming* (Rotterdam, Sense Publishers).

Suler, J. R. (1980) Primary Process Thinking and Creativity, *Psychological Bulletin*, 88, pp. 144–165.

Woolfolk, A. & Margetts, K. (2007) *Educational Psychology* (Sydney, Pearson Education Australia).

2

Manufacturing Consent: A corpus-based critical discourse analysis of New Labour's educational governance

Jane Mulderrig

Introduction

My aim in this article is to demonstrate the rhetorical novelty displayed by New Labour in its governance of education. This special issue of EPAT begins from the premise that strategies of domination are often hidden beneath (and reified through) everyday language. The ways in which we routinely define ourselves individually and collectively position us and others as social subjects (Foucault, 1971), thereby structuring social relations of power and domination. This article presents selected findings from a historical analysis of change in the discursive construction of social identity in UK education policy discourse. My chief argument is that through its linguistic forms of self-identification the government construes educational roles, relations and responsibilities not only for itself, but also for other educational actors and wider society. More specifically, I argue that New Labour's distinctive mode of self-representation is an important element in its hegemonic project, textually manufacturing consent over its policy decisions, and helping to articulate its self-styled 'enabling' model of governance. As evidence for these claims I discuss two prominent trends in New Labour's education policy rhetoric, which I characterise as 'personalisation' and 'managerialisation'. Respectively, these relate to the discursive representation of social identity and social action.

Discourse, Education, and the Capitalist State

The findings presented in this article stem from a much larger project[1] that examined patterns of historical change in how government discourse represents and legitimates the distribution of power and institutional organisation (thus governance) of UK state education (Mulderrig, 2009). This study employed corpus linguistic methods in a longitudinal critical discourse analysis (Chouliaraki & Fairclough, 1999; Fairclough, 2003) of education policy texts dating from the Heath government of 1972 to that of Blair in 2005. To contextualise the study I used neo-Marxist state theory (Jessop, 1999; 2002), Colin Hay's more localised account of the British political context (Hay, 1996, 1999), and educational sociology (e.g. Dale, 1989; Tomlinson, 2001; Trowler, 2003). During the time period examined Britain adopted a range of strategies to *respond* to and, importantly, *help to shape* a number of major political, economic and cultural changes.

The Power In/Of Language, First Edition. Edited by David R. Cole and Linda J. Graham.

These include an overall shift from an industrial to a so-called 'knowledge-based' and globalised economy; from a welfare to what has been dubbed a 'workfare' approach to social policy (Jessop, 1994; 2006); as well as the emergence of new forms of governance (Newman, 2001), and the increasing political emphasis on creating a lifelong 'learning society' (Dale & Robertson, 2006). Particularly important were demands for privatisation, marketisation and welfare retrenchment.

In education, this period saw structural and ideological pressures to align education more closely with economic policy goals. Indeed, the 'vocabularies of motives' (the discourses that articulate the goals and values of education) were changed, redefining the nature and purposes of education (Dale, 1989).[2] This discursive shift prepared the way for further 'modernisation' programmes by a reinvented Labour party that put economic competitiveness at the centre of its political agenda. The chief aim of this study was to take policy discourse as the lens through which to explore the dynamics and tensions of education policy-making in this context of profound political and economic change, and specifically to explore the extent to which economic concerns do in fact infiltrate the discourse of educational governance (see Mulderrig, 2008, for an analysis of economic discourses from Thatcher to Blair). Critical discourse analysis, in dialogue with political economy and educational sociology, is ideally suited to such an investigation, since it is premised on the socially embedded nature of discourse. This allows us to argue that education policy texts do not exist in a social vacuum, but have a complex, historically changing, and mutually constitutive relationship with their social context.

A critical analysis of policy discourse explores and assesses the sociological significance of the textual strategies that emerge from this dialectical relationship. The main focus of analysis was on the textual strategies by which shifting relations of power in educational governance were negotiated and legitimated during this period. The social theorist Nikolas Rose (1999) commented that a key factor in successfully negotiating governmental legitimacy is the institutional identity it projects to the public. Therefore the government's social identity was one of the main points of inquiry in the linguistic analysis, the findings of which were then interpreted in relation to a sociologically informed understanding of the historical context. In this sense the primary focus was on how the government represents and legitimates its own 'acts of governing' (Mulderrig, forthcoming a), as well as how it represents education (including its functions) (Mulderrig, 2007; 2008) and its actors (Mulderrig, 2003b; 2007).

Corpus-based Critical Discourse Analysis

Critical discourse analysis (CDA) is a problem-oriented interdisciplinary research tradition within the social sciences, subsuming a variety of approaches, each with different theoretical models, research methods and agenda (see Fairclough, Wodak & Mulderrig, 2011 forthcoming for an overview). Unlike some forms of discourse-based research, CDA does not begin with a fixed theoretical and methodological stance. Instead, the research process begins with a particular topic—here, the governance of education in the 'post-Fordist' era—and the theoretical and methodological tools are then developed as the object of research is progressively refined. Corpus linguistics is a computer-based method for analysing large bodies of textual data (McEnery &

Wilson, 1996). Its incorporation in CDA has been a relatively recent development (e.g. Koller & Mautner, 2004; Mautner, 2005; 2009; applied to educational research: Mulderrig, 2003a; 2003b; 2008; forthcoming a; forthcoming b). The choice to combine them in this study was motivated partly by a wish to develop a systematic and thus *replicable* form of critical discourse analysis. Furthermore, I wished to investigate patterns of change over a significant period of time. Robust findings could thus only be generated by examining a very large corpus of data (500,000 words), which in turn requires the use of corpus software tools. There is also a heuristic value to this combined approach in directing the analyst's gaze in unexpected and often fruitful directions. For example, I have elsewhere used 'keywords'[3] analysis to investigate the historical rise and fall of the most prominent political discourses in relation to UK education (Mulderrig, 2008).

The corpus analysed comprises 17 digitised policy consultation documents ('White Papers'), which were subdivided into four periods to allow comparison over time. Corpus software tools were used to direct the preliminary search for patterns of self-representation; I then progressively added layers of interpretation to the findings by drawing on Fairclough's approach to CDA (1992; 2000; 2003; 2005), and Van Leeuwen's sociosemantic model of social action and legitimation (1995; 1996; 2007). In the first stages of the analysis I ran concordance searches for the two most prominent (in terms of 'keyness') forms of self-representation used by the government: *we* and *government* (respectively, around 2600 and 2000 occurrences). I then used systemic functional grammar (Halliday, 1994) to code each instance according to action-type[4] and the degree of agency represented for the government. Two key trends in the corpus emerged from this stage of the analysis, both of which appertain to the New Labour government: 1) the emergence of an increasingly personalised, inclusive identity represented for the government, and 2) evidence of an increasingly managerial identity constructed for the government, and in particular a relatively regularised linguistic realisation of managerialism in the form of a particular type of action and power relation that I term 'managing action'. I discuss each trend below.

'Personalisation'

Following Van Leeuwen (1996), the choice of the term *the government* impersonalises the representation through 'institutionalisation' (abstractly representing a group of people by means of their institutional belonging), whereas the use of the personal pronoun *we* personalises it, foregrounding +human[5] semantic properties.[6] While this pronoun is rarely used by the previous governments,[7] under New Labour it eventually displaces the term 'government' altogether. Moreover, as the graph below illustrates, there is a dramatic surge in the overall textual prominence of the government[8], almost doubling the figure for the preceding period, with an average figure of 1.34% compared with 0.74% under Major.

As Figure 1 clearly shows, New Labour is not a retreating government. Undoubtedly, the Blair government represents a dramatic and unequivocal shift in self representational style: of the 2654 instances of *we* throughout the entire corpus, 91% of them (2421) occur under Blair. In fact, this pronoun is the second highest keyword under New

Labour. In any genre, for a common grammatical word like *we* to be the second highest keyword is really quite remarkable and suggests that under New Labour[9] this pronoun is a significant strategic element in building a more inclusive political identity. The increasing use of the pronoun 'we', along with other discursive strategies, is part of a general trend in recent decades towards the 'personalisation' of public discourse (Fairclough, 1992; Habscheid & Knobloch, 2008; Petersoo, 2007). This can beviewed as a symptom of the increased economic importance of language in the Post-Fordist era (for a discussion, see Fairclough *et al.*, 2011 forthcoming). In a context where commercial (and political) profitability and success increasingly rely on the 'face' institutions present to the public, this increases strategic concern with design, presentation and communication techniques. More generally, it may signal what Fairclough (1992) terms a process of 'democratisation' of discourse, of which one aspect is a tendency towards more informal language and the removal of explicit textual markers of power asymmetries.

I would argue that in the realm of politics it has particular significance; by collapsing the distinction between the government and the people, this mode of representation draws citizens into the very processes of governing, thus implicating them in policy decisions. When adverts or commercial organisations adopt this 'personalised' collective identity, the effect is not the same. It may generate greater affinity and identification with the brand or company in question (as it is doubtless intended to), but it does not draw us into the governance processes of that organisation. In New Labour discourse the pronoun *we* may be favoured over *the government*, with its authoritarian tone, in order to create a discourse more consonant with its claims to participatory democracy, and a 'stakeholder' vision of citizenship. However, as Fairclough (ibid.) observes, democratised discourse can in fact simply be a means of disguising power asymmetries, rather than removing them. Moreover, because *we* potentially includes the reader (which at times in the data it does), it allows the government to claim consensus on its vision of things, thereby removing the space for dialogue and alternative voices which one would expect of policy consultations, thereby having a de-democratising effect.

The Meaning of We

The collective pronoun *we* is semantically complex. Its meaning can be 'inclusive' (including the reader/hearer) or 'exclusive' (excluding them; thus referring only to the

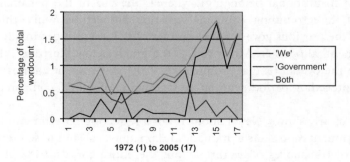

Figure 1: Textual prominence of the UK New Labour government

government). I coded every occurrence in the data according to these categories. However, the distinction between them is in fact not always clear. The variability in meaning and use of *we* is not merely a technical issue, but of considerable analytical significance. This is particularly true in political discourse. Representational choices play an important role in constructing collective identities and the allocation of roles and responsibilities within and beyond the state. They are therefore a key textual mechanism for (re)drawing lines of inclusion and boundaries of political responsibility. Thus in my analysis I explicitly include a third category of ambivalent cases, given their highly significant role in New Labour's mode of governance and legitimatory rhetoric. Figure 2 is a sample extract from the concordance[10] findings from the data. Each instance is coded as [I] inclusive, [E] exclusive, or [?] ambivalent. The surrounding text in this extract provides some evidence of the way each type is used. The cases of exclusive *we* are making promises or statements about the government's own actions. Cases of inclusive *we* make evaluative statements about the nation's activities, while many of the ambivalent types are modalised (expressing obligation, possibility or likelihood). In fact, these functional patterns represent a highly systematic and distinctive rhetorical pattern under New Labour.

The Functions of We

Having analysed the clausal environment of every instance of *we*,[4] I found marked patterns in the functional distribution of each type. To summarise, exclusive *we* represents the government's own past, present or future actions; in particular there is a systematic correlation between exclusive *we* and boasts about the government's actions. Cases of inclusive *we* frequently make comparative or evaluative statements about the nation's activities, often in competitive terms. Ambivalent types tend more frequently to be modalised (expressing some sort of need or obligation) as in the last two examples above.

Concordance Results for 'We'
The Skills Challenge and How [E]We Will Meet It. Skills for Employers,
portion of skilled, qualified people[?]We will not achieve a fairer,
a fairer, more inclusive society if [?]we fail to narrow the gap between the
  skills rich and the skills poor.
    is a contribution to the work [E]we are engaged in with our European
partners
er the long term. To achieve that [?] we need to act in five key areas
  the Union, where it is vital that [?]we identify best practice and share
ice and share our experiences. [I]We all know that skills
We all know that skills matter. But [I]we also know that as a nation we do
But we also know that as a nation [I]we do not invest as much in skills as
e do not invest as much in skills as [I]we should. Compared with other
  Compared with other countries [I] we perform strongly in some areas
  such as higher education. But [I] we have major shortfalls in
eet differing consumer demands [E]We are under no illusion about
are clear about their contribution [?] we can make much faster progress
  towards the shared objective. [?] We must put employers' needs
respond directly to those needs[?]We must raise ambition in the demand
  for skills

Figure 2: Sample extract from the concordance findings from the data

Inclusive We *and the Logic of Competitiveness*

Although comparatively few in number, clearly inclusive cases of *we* more frequently occur in policy documents jointly published with the Department for Trade and Industry, whose remit also includes economic and social policy in general, rather than solely education. Examples typically draw comparisons between Britain and its international competitors or the Britain of today and that of the past (e.g. *we lag behind our competitors, we have a workforce with worldclass ICT skills, we are part of a global environment, we have some first class schools, we have particular skills gaps, we compare well at the HE level, if we are to sustain our place as a leading global economy*). The last example illustrates the role of assumptions in claiming a commonly held neoliberal value system. It contains a conditional semantic relation 'if X then Y', and contains a significant degree of tacit information. First, it assumes that we would indeed wish to sustain our place as a 'leading global economy'. This is in addition, of course, to the presupposition that we *are* a leading global economy (on presuppositions, see Chilton, 2004). This is an example of what Martin (1991) terms 'buried reasoning', whereby the reasoning involved in some statement is hidden through abstraction. Here the evaluative premises that constitute the logical scaffolding of the statement are hidden. Unpacking the example, we can recover this and other information lost in the different generalising transformations it has undergone:

(*If we are to sustain*) NG[[*our place*] as [a *leading global economy*]]

This clause is structurally dependent on what comes next in the text (an evaluative statement about what we 'must' do in order to 'sustain our place'). The goal of the process (sustain) is contained in the nominal group (NG), which contains a number of assumptions. Firstly, it contains an embedded evaluation which we might 'unpack' as: *we have a place as a leading global economy*. This potentially refutable assertion is turned into a fact-like attribute *'our place'* through the grammatical choices made. As a result its deniability is reduced—as Halliday and Martin observe, 'you can argue with a clause, but you can't argue with a nominal group' (Halliday & Martin, 1993, p. 39). Secondly, a further embedded nominal group functions as the qualifier: *a leading global economy*. The subject of the clause *we* is thereby constructed as the equivalent to the entity *economy*. I would argue that equivalence draws on the logic of a neoliberal value system, which is also triggered by the attributes *leading* and *global*. These help construe a positively evaluated state of affairs which we would 'naturally' wish to sustain.

Through this type of evaluative statement, a nation state is represented as equivalent to its economic system, and then ascribed characteristics whose value is intertextually derived. The attributes *global* and *leading* do not semantically encode a positive or negative value in the same way as lexis whose chief semiotic function is evaluation (for instance *splendid* or *terrible*). In the above extract, a *global* economy is one which is valued on the basis of the scale on which it is able to operate. The value triggered is one of power relative to other economies, achieved through geographical 'reach'. Similarly, the predication *leading* again values the entity in terms of power, this time its ability to direct and affect others. These two dimensions of evaluation are coherent only within the structural framework of competitive activity, the basic form of social relation around which capitalist economic activity is organised. Taken together, I would therefore argue that the evaluative components of this clause are derived intertextually from a neoliberal discourse of competitiveness—promulgated notably by the EU (Muntigl *et al.*, 2000)—wherein countries' economies are represented as less confined to national territory, but rather operating across an increasingly transnational or 'global' competitive terrain, and where national economic success is measured in terms of relative market position.

Ambivalent We *and the Legitimation of Policy Injunctions*

The most frequent use of ambivalent *we* (75% of the time) is to represent exhortations with varying degrees of explicitness. Thus, under New Labour there is an increased tendency to obfuscate social responsibility, in respect of both the obligations and desires that constitute the rationale for policy proposals. In an argumentation strategy typical of this genre, the government outlines the problems it is attempting to address when it comes to formulating policy in a problem-solution textual pattern. This causal relation between policy problem and policy solution is represented in terms of social necessity. Policies are thereby represented as meeting some form of shared need, where the (grammatical) subject of that need is the ambivalent *we*. The necessity is of two main types: a duty to act in some way (*we must do X*), or a particular felt need (*we need X*). In both cases the government effectively acts as a spokesperson, making statements on behalf of an unspecified collective. This is a strategy associated with socially powerful actors: 'like the "power of prediction", the power of making statements on behalf of others, or indeed on behalf of "all of us" … Is a power which has an uneven social distribution, and is important for identification' (Fairclough, 2003, p. 171). The actual modalizations involved contain high degrees of deontic commitment (obligation)—thus, *we must do* versus *we might do*. In effect, therefore, the textual patterns found in the New Labour data represent social imperatives, not possibilities. The ambivalence of the subject (*we*) serves to mitigate any face threat by spreading the responsibility across a collective social subject.

The verbs *ensure* and *make sure* are frequently used in New Labour policy discourse to construct a managerial role for the government, steering others' actions. They form part of a larger 'grammar of governance' that plays a significant part in constructing a so-called 'enabling' modality of governance (Mulderrig, forthcoming b). They are similarly used in this hortatory context. In all but two cases, the remainder of the clause thus represents a managed actor or actors engaged in some process. The following are typical examples: [*we must ensure that*] all [pupils] *have the skills and capabilities; people learn how to be creative* and *all schools deliver high standards.*

The Hegemonic Role of We*: Inclusion and Shared Responsibilities*

The success of the strategy of 'personalisation' in legitimating policy rests on semantic slippage across the different types of *we*. Often this slippage works simply by juxtaposing various statements containing the different forms of *we*. This extract illustrates how the strategy can be used to legitimate a neoliberal model of citizenship through the assumption of a shared consensus.

> Beyond these subjects, we[?] need to be confident that everyone leaving education is equipped to be an informed, responsible, active citizen. In an ever

more complex, interdependent world, where an engaged population is crucial to the health of our society, we[E] continue to put citizenship at its heart too. And we[?] need real confidence that our schools and colleges really do give young people the skills they need for employability. (DfES, 2005, *14–19 Education and Skills*)

In the extract ambivalent *we* textures a hortatory evaluation about the role of education in socialisation. The second sentence paints a picture of the global economic context for education policy in which individual responsibility is paramount. The next sentence juxtaposes this citizenship argument with an economic responsiveness discourse of education, where the emphasis is on the acquisition of skills to enhance individual employability. While not explicitly conflating them, this textual arrangement construes a close association between employability and citizenship. Significantly, where such work-farist discourse is evoked the agency of the evaluation is absorbed in an ambivalent *we*. Throughout the Blair data the semantic slipperiness of *we* helps construct an apparent consensus on the nature of the world we live in and the inescapable responsibilities this creates. In turn, this supposedly inexorable context of global economic competitiveness is used to preface and legitimate policy proposals made by the government. Through this rhetorical device, government policy decisions effectively become harder to criticise since their legitimacy rests on global economic forces apparently beyond the government's control. The legitimation is implicit, triggered only by juxtaposing: 'we (I) live in a changing world', 'we (?) must respond with X activity', and 'we (E) will provide the following policy solution'. Moreover, given the way this device exploits the semantics of the pronoun *we*, the political effect is that we are now all implicated in the rationalisation and legitimation of policy. In this way, political consensus is assumed, not jointly produced.

'Managerialisation'

Turning to a second key trend identified in the data, I found that the traditional authority and control of the government has progressively given way to a more managerial form of institutional identity. This also extends to the activities represented for the government, which are increasingly concerned with controlling and monitoring the activities of an ever-wider range of actors. The concept of 'governance' has come to occupy a prominent place in academic inquiry over the last two decades. In part this is a reflection of substantive changes in the way advanced liberal states predominantly organise their economic, political and social activities. We might characterise this as a move away from the rigid hierarchies of bureaucracy, towards a new form of 'soft power'—or persuasive power (Nye, 2004)—involving the coordination of complex networks of self-governing actors.

In the last quarter of the 20th century, the decline of the post-war bureaucratic regime and its centrally regulated industrial economy gave way to the gradual emergence of a new 'diagram' of relation between government, expert and citizen. It is characterised by technologies of self-governance, audit, and appraisal (Rose, 1999). A key figure in this new style of governing is the active citizen-consumer, empowered and responsibilised to make choices that further their own interests or those of the 'community'. Importantly, this requires a shift in power relations: citizens must have greater agency over their own actions; the government less direct control. As Rose puts it, 'the social state gives way to the enabling state' (1999, p. 142). We might posit that such an 'autonomising' model of democracy would be capable of absorbing potential conflict by instead offering choice, opportunity, possibility, and so forth. With greater reliance on individual volition, this form of 'soft power' would seem to be less coercive and more intrinsically democratic. However, I will argue that the discursive forms this takes, do not so much remove coercion as mask it in more subtle forms.

As discussed above, I used systemic functional grammar to analyse each instance of *we* and *the government* according to action-type. In general, this revealed an increasingly managerial identity constructed for each successive government through a variety of verb forms (e.g. *lead, direct, consider, discuss, evaluate*) and textual collocates (e.g. *appraisal, benchmark, delivery*) which seemed to confirm the rise in public sector managerialism posited in the literature (Clarke & Newman, 1997). What the literature could not predict, however, was the proliferation under New Labour of a particular linguistic construction which helps enact this managerial model of governance in a very subtly hegemonic way though a specific type of action and power relation. Drawing on both sociological theory and the empirical data I call them 'managing actions'.

Managing Actions

As the name suggests the term 'managing actions' refers to a set of lexicogrammatical resources for getting people to do things. Typical examples are *ensure, require, expect, support* and *help*. Rather than the direct agent of processes, the government is the instigator or controller of others' actions. Some cases involve causative-type verbs like *enable* or *allow* followed by a managing action realised in various forms. However, not all examples involve causative structures or even verbs at all. For example, in some cases the managing action may be nominalised. In fact managing actions overlap with a variety of surface forms. Moreover, systemic functional grammar fails to capture their sociological significance, thus following Van Leeuwen's approach (1995; 1996) I formulated a sociosemantic typology for these actions. I then analysed their distribution and function throughout the data.

The increase in 'managerialism' is closely associated with more general trends in governance since the late 1980s (Clarke & Newman, 1997; Newman, 2000; 2001). As this model of governance progressively displaces others, it necessarily involves the rene-gotiation of power relations. Thus, my typology attempts to move beyond the purely textual level in order to capture the important role of social power in the discursive representation and enactment of management. In the example *We will take powers to allow schools greater freedom to innovate*, power relations are semantically encoded in the lexical forms *allow* and *freedom*. In other cases, they are assumed, as in examples representing the government's expectations of others, where the successful instigation of others' actions is vested in its institutional authority. Thus, forms of managing vary in coerciveness and intersect with the power relations between the participants. It follows that these relations may in part be reproduced or transformed through the forms of management represented. For example there is a tendency for more explicitly coercive forms of management, as encoded in the semantics of the verb (*expect, require*) to be textured with institutional actors whose power and influence we know to be in decline, namely LEAs (Dale, 1989; Trowler, 2003). Conversely, actions which semantically encode greater freedom and/or less coercion (*enable, allow, encourage*) tend to be textured with schools, which accords with the principle of school autonomy in the creation of an educational market of 'independent state schools' (Blair, 2005).

In the typology below (Figure 3) managing actions are grouped into three subcategories, (tendentially) ranged along a cline of coercion,[12] and named according to the type of managerial role they construct for the government. In descending order of coerciveness, they are Overseer, Leader, and Facilitator. To the extent that managerialism is becoming an increasingly significant aspect of the art of governing, these categories help provide a more detailed picture of the type of managerialism the government employs, in what domains and with what people.

The Overseer is the most coercive role, where the manager is in control of the managed actor's behaviour, seeing it through to completion. In other words, they encode the meaning 'without X, Y wouldn't do it'. Completion of the activity is assumed semantically. The Leader role assumes the manager's authority to instigate others' actions, but the future orientation encoded semantically means there is no assumption of their completion. Finally the least coercive is the Facilitator role. Here the manager's authority over the managed actor is assumed, but completion of the action is not necessarily assumed. They encode the meaning 'without X,Y couldn't do it', for want of either ability or permission/opportunity. Here, the coercion works by assuming the managed actor is willing to act and as such, although on the surface the least coercive, is nevertheless a particularly hegemonic formulation.

General Findings

I used this typology to examine the use of these managing actions throughout the data. The results indicate a huge surge in their use from just 9 instances under Thatcher, to 43 under Major, to 358 under Blair. By 2005 they account for 20% of all verbal collocates[13]

[1] **Overseer** *Ensure (that) -- does, Make sure (that) -- does*

[2] **Leader** *Require – to, Expect – to, Look to – to, Want – to, Envisage that – should, Urge – to, Encourage – to, Ask -- to, Invite -- to, Promote* [+ nominalization meaning 'the doing of X by MA']

[3] **Facilitator**

a) Ability

Support – (to/in doing), Help – to, Facilitate – to, Let – do, Allow – to, Enable – to, (Transform/Enhance) the capacity of– to, Make it easier (for--) to,

b) Opportunity

Free –to, Give –(greater/more) freedom(s) to, Provide/Increase/widen the) opportunities for -- to, Provide for – to

Figure 3: Typology of managing actions: managing actions in three subcategories, ranged along a cline of coercion

of the government. Under Blair there is also a proliferation in the linguistic forms by which they are represented. The data for the governments prior to New Labour in fact contain very few managing actions, and are mainly semiotic (*require, expect, look to*), constructing a 'leader' role for the government, delegating responsibilities to various actors. Under Thatcher this is mainly used to remove powers from the Local Education Authorities, in an important move that prepared the ground for a more deregulated and market-based state education system. Under Major this 'hollowing out' of power from LEAs continues, alongside the use of managing actions to allow the government to oversee a wide range of actors and activities in securing greater economic competitiveness (see also Mulderrig, 2008 on the discourse of competitiveness under Major). Thus, the government will: 1) *require LEAs to increase delegation to their schools;* 2) *expect LEAs to continue to make appropriate provision for such pupils;* 3) *encourage higher education institutions to make available information about the employment of new graduates, by subject, including if practicable details of average starting salary.*

The most coercive action *require* permits little scope for resistance and is tantamount to an imperative. Conversely, rather greater compliance appears to be anticipated when it comes to LEAs continuing to provide for pupils with disabilities and special educational needs (example 2). In the third example, a median level of coercive effort is put into the attempt to stimulate the marketisation of universities. The next sentence in the document makes it clear that this is the purpose: *This will help potential higher education students to make better informed decisions.* The assumption is that what constitutes better information in selecting a university education is the long-term monetary returns it is likely to yield.

Despite the government's claims to '*offer an active, enabling government*', it is interesting to note that its most textually prominent role, and by some margin, is actually that of the traditional manager. It uses its Leader role to oversee, benchmark and monitor others—types of activities that involve fewer freedoms for educational actors than the government makes claims to. Where for Major the emphasis was on competitiveness, under Blair this shifts to the strategy for securing it in a knowledge economy, namely skills—the highest-ranking keyword under this government.

Blair the Overseer: Strategic Economic Planning and Modelling

The single most frequently used managing verb is *ensure*, which constructs a steering role over both economic and educational practices. It does so by guaranteeing an abstract vision of excellence and success in both spheres. In an expansive, positively affective discourse, the government offers ever-widening opportunities for improvement, access, information, and participation. Thus [*we will ensure that young people*] *develop knowledge and skills to take their place in society; achieve National Curriculum level 5; have some good quality engagement with employment; obtain the learning and skills they need to take on new challenges at work, or learn how to be creative and enterprising to generate ideas, products and innovations.* The most frequently managed actors are young people or people generally, both of whom are steered into lifelong learning practices. These are construed as the keys to full participation in both work and society, illustrating the central role of educational practices in New Labour's Third Way alignment of social justice with economic participation. A wide range of actors and actions are managed by *ensure*, ranging from securing competitiveness in UK businesses to guaranteeing the rights of school governors to dismiss incompetent staff. In terms of contemporary governance, *ensure* thus appears to be a prominent textual mechanism for coordinating increasingly complex networks of activity across larger political and social spaces.

Blair the Leader: Delegating and Coordinating

In its leader role, the government is represented as institutionalising and orchestrating joined up governance. It thus manages actors who are represented in terms of their organisational properties or functional remit. These include middle-tier governmental and non-governmental organisations, partnerships and other more-or-less abstract networks of actors (*Education Action Zones, Regional Development Agencies, Learning and Skills Council, Sector Skills Development Agency, Local Forums, Local Strategic Partnerships, and the Skills for Business Network, LEAs*). Such institutional actors are *expected, asked* and *invited* to engage in predominantly semiotic middle-management activities. Under Major prominent attention was given to the macro level economic goals, its leader role mainly shifting educational controls towards a hollowed out model, removing powers from the middle tier. The Blair government builds on this, elaborating a specifically skills-based growth strategy, developing new roles, relations and institutions of a networked or 'joined up' model of governance. This extends also to LEAs who, compared with the previous governments, are somewhat less coercively managed in new, different roles. To the extent that we can call the flows of power under Major a 'hollowing out' of the state, we might therefore characterise those under Blair as 'filling in'.

Blair the Facilitator: Enabling Neoliberal Change

The facilitated actors are institutions (*schools, universities, colleges*) occupationally represented actors (*learners, heads, teachers, workers, employers, parents, trainers*) or the sectorally defined *business*. The most frequent form of facilitating is *support*. While a variety of actions are managed by it, a recurrent theme is that of skills. Businesses are helped to succeed by focussing on the skills of their workforce, while learners and young people are supported in developing them, as are heads and middle managers. Thus, in what is in fact the most textually and politically prominent theme of the Blair data, the government *supports* a variety of actors to *upgrade, acquire, develop, renew: (key, core, basic, advanced, professional, work-related) skills*.

Meanwhile schools are helped to take on an increased range of responsibilities for securing both excellence and social inclusion. The government's facilitation of schools is textured with both a discourse of competitive marketisation and a more pastoral discourse of needs and social problems, construing a central role for schools in securing social inclusion. Thus on the one hand they will be helped to *raise the quality of teaching and learning; deliver greater flexibility; meet the needs of talented and gifted children; develop further to become Centres of Excellence*. While on the other hand, they will be helped to *become healthy schools* (this refers to *pressing public health problems* including smoking, drug and alcohol abuse) and *meet the needs of children with special educational needs*. Finally, *we will* [P] *help schools* [M] *deliver this* [M] *focused* [P] *support* (for *young people* who are struggling to reach, by age 14, the required standard set for them in government targets).

The represented actions in this example help texture a pastoral discourse [P] with the managerial [M], so that support and social inclusion become a matter of meeting external targets, even while still at school.

Summary

In terms of contemporary governance, *ensure* appears to be a prominent textual mechanism for coordinating increasingly complex networks of activity across larger political and social spaces. While this permits greater governing at a distance, it doesn't necessarily imply a weakening of power, simply a change in how it is applied, for example by monitoring performance and emphasising desired outcomes. In terms of the evolution of managerial models of governance a distinctive pattern emerges from this analysis. The first two periods include very few managing actions. Under Thatcher they are used to remove powers from LEAs, suggesting a structural diagnosis of a problem in the existing bureau-professional model for governing education. Under Major, a broader economic and organisational vision of competitiveness is articulated through its Overseer role, alongside a continued removal of LEA powers. Under Blair, both the proliferation of managing actions and the way they are textured suggest that this economic vision of competitiveness has moved from the planning stage to its strategic enactment. And at the heart of this strategy are skills, which are represented as the central formula for both economic and social success. So central in fact, that the term is the highest-ranking keyword in this period, occurring 1473 times. Indeed, in so far as skills represent a key element of labour power in a knowledge-based economy, under Blair education's role as the main producer of capitalist labour power is rendered more explicit than ever.

Conclusion

Many political economists and educational sociologists have commented that New Labour's policies contain strong ideological continuities with the preceding Conservative governments (Brivati & Bale, 1997; Campbell & Whitty, 2003; Hay, 1999; Jessop, 2002; 2006). In this article I have explored these neoliberal lines of continuity while at the same time illustrating its distinctiveness at the level of political rhetoric. As evidence for this claim I have provided a (necessarily schematic) overview of two key trends identified in New Labour's discourse of educational governance: 'personalisation' and 'managerialisation' (for a fuller treatment see Mulderrig, forthcoming b and forthcoming a respectively). Both relate to the government's mode of self-representation, respectively constructing its social identity and its social actions and power relation with others. Together, I argue, they help construct a more subtly hegemonic and managerial style of governance. Through close textual analysis of its policy discourse, informed through a political economic understanding of the historical context, it becomes apparent that New Labour displays a striking novelty in its policy discourse.

Despite the supposed shift towards a more devolved model of educational governance, this is clearly not a retreating government. In fact a marked point of comparison in the whole corpus is the huge surge under Blair in the textual prominence of the government; statistically it becomes the most prominent actor. This prominence is, however, masked to a considerable degree through its inclusive style of self-representation. This is by no means a neutral or insignificant textual choice, since the semantics of this pronoun allow the government to elide its own identity with that of the public, and thereby make claims on behalf of the entire nation. Indeed, the semantic slipperiness of this pronoun is systematically exploited in such a way as to implicate every one of us in the legitimation of government policy decisions. This government also displays the greatest linguistic inventiveness in enacting a managerial style of governing that affords far fewer freedoms than its own rhetoric would suggest. It was stated at the outset that the ways in which we routinely define ourselves individually and collectively position us and others as social subjects, thereby structuring social relations of power and domination. To the extent that the role of education policy is to negotiate the future of education on the basis of its imagined relationship with the wider socioeconomic order, and to (re)draw lines of individual and collective responsibility, I would argue that New Labour enacts this through a much more subtle form of hegemony.

Notes

1. I am grateful to the ESRC for funding this doctoral research.
2. For a fuller account of the political economic context of this study, see Mulderrig, 2007; 2008.
3. In corpus linguistics, 'keyness' refers to the statistical significance of a word's frequency relative to some norm.
4. Following Halliday's social semiotic approach (1978; 1994) we can classify the elements of a clause according to its Participants, Processes and Circumstances. Generally realised as verbs, Processes are sub-divided into sub-types, which map onto the three main realms of human activity doing, being, and sensing. Thus, they can be categorised as Material, Existential, Relational, Verbal, Mental, or Behavioural. The representation of the government's actions in the data is in fact frequently very complex, abstract and metaphorical. The analysis process itself therefore fed back into the development of descriptive tools, with additional models of description overlaid onto the analysis as it progressed. Thus, as I encountered classificatory problems using systemic functional tools, I drew additionally on Van Leeuwen's alternative model of representation (1995, 1996), and Graham's treatment of abstraction and metaphor in policy discourse (2001).
5. In the linguistic study of lexical meaning, words may be analysed into a series of binary semantic features like ADULT/NON-ADULT, MALE/FEMALE. For example, the word *man* could be analysed as ADULT, HUMAN, MALE, while *woman* could be analysed as ADULT, HUMAN, FEMALE. These semantic components are conventionally presented as + or—the relevant feature (e.g. the word *bull* would be +ADULT, -HUMAN, -FEMALE).
6. For a more extensive analysis of 'personalisation' under New Labour, see Mulderrig, forthcoming b.
7. The only significant exception is the data for Thatcher, where the pronoun does make an appearance, albeit comparatively infrequently.
8. 83% of cases of the pronoun refer specifically to the government itself, thus lending evidence to the claim that the government has become a significantly more prominent figure in education policy discourse (the most textually prominent actor by a considerable margin).
9. This result may also indicate the increased prominence of this textual strategy in public discourse more generally. Nevertheless, the stark contrast with the discursive style of the preceding government suggests that this is an important feature of New Labour discourse in particular.
10. In corpus linguistics, 'concordance' lines display in a vertical list all occurrences of a particular search word in their textual environment. Here the search word was, of course, the pronoun

we. These lines can be expanded to display more of the surrounding text; this step is necessary to analyse each occurrence in more detail.

11. Using systemic functional grammar (Halliday, 1994), I categorised each instance according to the type of process (the verb) that *we* is responsible for—see note 4 above for more on this method.

12. It is important to note that this typology has been derived in order to characterise the findings in the data examined; it is not intended as a universally applicable context-free grammar. Thus, for instance, the specific power relations underlying the social practice examined here were factored into the analysis. It would, however, be interesting to 'test' its interpretive capacity in other social contexts. Note also the typology only contains verbal collocates of *we* and *the government.* Thus other possible surface forms like nominalisations have been omitted.

13. 'Collocates' are words that co-occur. Thus the verb co-occurring with *we* or *the government* is a managing action in a fifth of all cases under New Labour.

References

Blair, T. (2005) Press Conference, 24 October, BBC 1.

Brivati, B. & Bale, T. (eds) (1997) *New Labour In Power: Precedents and prospects* (London, Routledge).

Campbell, C. & Whitty, G. (2003) From New Right To New Labour: What's new in English education policy? *Anglistik und Englischunterricht*, 65, pp. 101–122, Special edition: *Britain under Blair* (Heidelberg, Winter Verlag).

Chilton, P. (2004) *Analysing Political Discourse: Theory and practice* (London, Routledge).

Chouliaraki, L. & Fairclough, N. (1999) *Discourse in Late Modernity: Rethinking critical discourse analysis* (Edinburgh, Edinburgh University Press).

Clarke, J. & Newman, J. (1997) *The Managerial State* (London, Sage).

Dale, R. (1989) *The State and Education Policy* (Buckingham, Open University Press).

Dale, R. & Robertson, S. (2006). The Case of the UK: Homo sapiens Europaeus vs. homo quaestuosus Atlanticus? European learning citizen or Anglo-American human capitalist? in: M. Kuhn & R. Sultana (eds), *Creating the European Learning Citizen* (New York, Peter Lang Publishing).

Department for Education and Skills (2005) *14–19 Education and Skills*, White Paper (London, HMSO).

Fairclough, N. (1992) *Discourse and Social Change* (Oxford, Blackwell).

Fairclough, N. (2000) *New Labour, New Language?* (London, Routledge).

Fairclough, N. (2003) *Analysing Discourse: Text analysis for social research* (London, Routledge)

Fairclough, N. (2005) Critical Discourse Analysis, *Marges Linguistiques*, 9, pp. 76–94.

Fairclough, N., Wodak, R. & Mulderrig, J. (2011 forthcoming) 'Critical Discourse Analysis', in: T. Van Dijk (ed.), *Discourse Studies: A multidisciplinary introduction*, 2nd edn. (London, Sage).

Foucault, M. (1971) *L'Ordre du discours* (Paris, Gallimard).

Graham, P. (2001) Space: Irrealis objects in technology policy and their role in a new political economy, *Discourse and Society*, 12:6, pp. 761–788.

Habscheid, S. & Knobloch, C. (2008) (eds) *Discourses of Unity: Creating scenarios of consensus in public and corporate communication* (Berlin, De Gruyter).

Halliday, M. A. K. (1978) *Language as Social Semiotic: The social interpretation of language and meaning* (Baltimore, MD, University Park Press).

Halliday, M. A. K. (1994) *An Introduction to Functional Grammar*, 2nd edn. (London, Edward Arnold).

Halliday, M. A. K. & Martin, J. R. (1993) *Writing Science: Literacy and discursive power* (London, Falmer Press).

Hay, C. (1996) *Re-stating Social and Political Change* (Buckingham, Open University Press)

Hay, C. (1999) *The Political Economy of New Labour: Labouring under false pretences?* (Manchester, Manchester University Press)

Jessop, B. (1994) The Transition to Post-Fordism and the Schumpeterian Workfare State, in: R. Burrows & B. Loader (eds), *Towards a Post-Fordist Welfare State?* (London, Routledge).

Jessop, B. (1999) The Changing Governance of Welfare: Recent Trends in its Primary Functions, Scale and Modes of Coordination, *Social Policy and Administration*, 33:4, pp. 348–359.

Jessop, B. (2002) *The Future of the Capitalist State* (Cambridge, Polity).

Jessop, B. (2006) *From Thatcherism to New Labour: Neo-Liberalism, workfarism, and labour market regulation* (Lancaster, Department of Sociology, Lancaster University) at: http://www.comp.lancs.ac.uk/sociology/soc131rj.pdf (accessed 2 April 2006).

Koller, V. & Mautner, G. (2004) Computer Applications in Critical Discourse Analysis, in: A. Hewings, C. Coffin & K. O'Halloran (eds), *Applying English Grammar* (London, Arnold).

Martin, J. R. (1991) Nominalisation in Science and Humanities: Distilling knowledge and scaffolding text, in: E. Ventola (ed.), *Functional and Systemic Linguistics: Approaches and uses* (Berlin and New York, Mouton de Gruyter).

Mautner, G. (2005) Time to Get Wired: Using web-based corpora in critical discourse analysis, *Discourse & Society*, 16:6, pp. 809–828.

Mautner, G. (2009) Checks and Balances: How corpus linguistics can contribute to CDA, in: R. Wodak & M. Meyer (eds), *Methods of Critical Discourse Analysis* (London, Sage).

McEnery, T. & Wilson, A. (1996) *Corpus Linguistics* (Edinburgh, Edinburgh University Press).

Mulderrig, J. (2003a) Learning to Labour: The discursive construction of social actors in New Labour's education policy, *Anglistik & Englischunterricht*, 65, pp. 123–145, Special edition: *Britain under Blair* (Heidelberg, Winter Verlag).

Mulderrig, J. (2003b) Consuming Education: A critical discourse analysis of social actors in New Labour's education policy, *Journal of Critical Education Policy Studies* 1. Available at: http://www.jceps.com/index.php?pageID=article&articleID=2

Mulderrig, J. (2007) Textual Strategies of Representation and Legitimation in New Labour Policy Discourse, in: A. Green, G. Rikowski & H. Raduntz (eds), *Renewing Dialogues in Marxism and Education* (London, Palgrave Macmillan), pp. 135–150.

Mulderrig, J. (2008) Using Keywords Analysis in CDA: Evolving discourses of the knowledge economy in education, in: B. Jessop N. Fairclough & R. Wodak (eds), *Education and the Knowledge-Based Economy in Europe* (Rotterdam, Sense Publishers), pp. 149–170.

Mulderrig, J. (2009) *The Language of Education Policy: From Thatcher to Blair* (Saarbucken: VDM Dr Muller Verlag).

Mulderrig, J. (forthcoming a) The Grammar of Governance, *Critical Discourse Studies*.

Mulderrig, J. (forthcoming b) The Hegemony of Inclusion: Constructing the subjects of Third Way politics, *Discourse and Society*.

Muntigl, P., Weiss, G. & Wodak, R. (2000) *European Union Discourses on Un/employment* (Amsterdam, John Benjamins).

Newman, J. (2000) Beyond the New Public Management? Modernising public services, in: J. Clarke S. Gerwitz & E. McLaughlin (eds), *New Managerialism, New Welfare?* (London, Sage).

Newman, J. (2001) *Modernising Governance: New Labour, policy and society* (London, Sage).

Nye, J. (2004) *Soft Power: The means to success in world politics* (New York, Public Affairs).

Petersoo, P (2007) What Does 'We' Mean? National deixis in the media, *Journal of Language and Politics*, 6:3, pp. 419–436.

Rose, N. (1999) Inventiveness in Politics, *Economy and Society*, 28:3, pp. 467–493.

Tomlinson, S. (2001) *Education in a Post-welfare Society* (Buckingham, Open University Press).

Trowler, P. (2003). *Education Policy*, 2nd edn. (London, Routledge).

Van Leeuwen, T. (1995) Representing Social Action, *Discourse and Society*, 4:2, pp. 193–223.

Van Leeuwen, T. (1996) The Representation of Social Actors, in: C. R. Caldas-Coulthard & M. Coulthard (eds), *Texts and Practices: Readings in critical discourse analysis* (London, Routledge), pp. 32–71.

Van Leeuwen, T. (2007) Legitimation in discourse and communication, *Discourse and Communication*, 1:1, pp. 91–112.

3
'Relative Ignorance': *Lingua* and *linguaggio* in Gramsci's concept of a formative *aesthetic* as a concern for power

John Baldacchino

> Time, space: necessity. Fate, luck, events: all the snares of life. Do you want to be? There's this. Conceptually it isn't. Being needs to be trapped in a form, and for a while it needs to end up like that, here or there, in this or that way.[1] (Pirandello, 1971a, p. 85)

In Luigi Pirandello's *Uno Nessuno e Centomila (One, No One and a Hundred Thousand)*, the main character, Vitangelo Moscarda, finds himself in an existential crisis, triggered by what he considers to be a facial defect when one morning, looking at the mirror, he discovers that his nose is bent to the right! Moscarda's accidental epiphany throws him into a crisis that turns his life—and that of others—upside down. He sets out to inflict his torment on everyone else. Ironically he tries to resist what he perceives as an unravelled life by fixing the act of *being* into *form*: 'Everything, as long as it lasts, brings with it the verdict of its form, sentenced to be like this and unable to be otherwise ... . As with forms, goes the act' (Pirandello, 1971a, p. 85).

I would say that in Pirandello, formation can only be assumed as a recurrent inauguration, where what is known *now* has to be nailed down and fixed forever—even when the truth is that this fixedness is contingent and short-lived. This is why Moscarda goes into crisis. While he states, 'when an act is done, that's it; it never changes' (1971a, p. 85), he is fully aware of the irony of this state of affairs. If life were to be fixed in *form*, it would fall into the predicament of causality where nothing is ever fixed. The only way one could escape from such predicament is to read *formation* through an aesthetic, rather than a causal, lineage. Here the relationship between form and act would take a *dialectal* instead of a *dialectical* turn, where relational grounds are transformed into expressive horizons. Here, representation takes a prominent position within the problematic of truth. Taking this from hermeneutic and aesthetic positions, truth as representation moves beyond the foundational formation of ontology. Instead, truth becomes an *event* of what Gianni Vattimo calls 'the access to the positive *chances* which for the sake of man's very essence, are found in the conditions of post-modern existence'; an access that is only possible 'if the outcomes of a "destruction of ontology" are taken seriously' (1999, p. 20).

The Power In/Of Language, First Edition. Edited by David R. Cole and Linda J. Graham.
Chapters © 2012 The Authors. Book compilation © 2012 Philosophy of Education Society of Australasia.
Published 2012 by Blackwell Publishing Ltd.

Vattimo goes on to say that:

> As long as man and being are thought of metaphysically, platonically, in terms of stable structures that would task thought and existence with 'founding' itself, with becoming established (through logic and ethics) within the domain of becoming by reflecting itself in the whole myth of strong structures in all fields of experience, it would be impossible for thought to live positively through that true and proper post-metaphysical time that is post-modernity. (1999, p. 20)

This is where the whole question of formation—read from the widths of a representational horizon—would have to negate the strictures of the nostalgia for fixed grounds. When Vattimo speaks of metaphysics, he pays particular attention to those 'emblematic' philosophical traditions that include Marxism's 'vocation' of the recovery of use value and its normative implications. (1999, p. 30) Vattimo sees this recovery as a structural turn of fixedness.

It is with such a critique in mind that this essay starts by revisiting Antonio Gramsci's original reading of the relational constructs of base and superstructure. In this context, this reading bears in mind the assumptions made through the agonistic character of both a formative approach to life, as well as a concern for power. I would argue that this concern for power is inherent to formation as read from Gramsci's discussion of the politics of aesthetics (in his discussion of *catharsis*) as well as the notion of struggle as being formative, when he discusses the distinction between *lingua* and *linguaggio*, where, as I will elaborate later in this essay, *lingua* captures and articulates quotidian occurrences while *linguaggio* enters these occurrences into the realms of grammar that Gramsci almost always reads through the power relations that they sum up. Thus a concern for power through formative struggle comes by not simply as an aesthetic 'moment' that is politicised, but as a recurrent political *dialect* that comes out of forms of *speaking* that reflect the quotidian engagement with life as a grammar of struggle. It goes without saying that this remains firmly couched in the linguistic *agôn* that lies at the foundation of any form of hegemony.

This is why rather than an *epistemological* hierarchy between base and superstructure, Gramsci insists on a *gnoseological* point of view,[2] when he argues that the proposition in Marx's *Preface to a Contribution to the Critique of Political Economy*, 'that men [and women] become aware of structural conflict on the ground of ideologies, must be considered as a statement that has gnoseological and not purely psychological or moral value' (Gramsci, Q10.II, 1975a, p. 47).[3] A gnoseological stance accommodates a fluid concept of base and superstructure, where the 'necessary reciprocity' with which these conceptual edifices are qualified, is 'in fact, the real dialectical process' (Gramsci, Q8, 1975a, p. 48) by which anything could be effected politically. This reciprocity makes base and superstructure equivalent. In so doing, Gramsci inherently negates the hierarchical structures by which Marxian orthodoxy has stagnated the very notion of power that ultimately posed aesthetics and language as mechanical 'effects' of what were seen to be economic 'causes'.

The political scaffolding that has traditionally sustained Marxian structuralism was mainly intent on 'objectively' reversing the alienation of value as operated by capital's exploitation of human labour. However, as a philosopher Gramsci pays closer attention to the interplay between social and political formation and the cultural and 'historical *peaks*' ('*punte* storiche') that mostly emerge as aesthetic and linguistic ruptures within hegemonic narratives; and where rather than revolutionary assaults on the economic structure of alienation, he looks elsewhere for a 'solution'. As Laclau & Mouffe (1985) have argued, 'for Gramsci, political subjects are not—strictly speaking—classes, but complex "collective wills"; similarly the ideological elements articulated by a hegemonic class do not have a necessary class belonging' (p. 67). Here, Gramsci's philosophy effectively anticipates what Vattimo calls the aesthetic and rhetorical experience of truth (1999, p. 20).

Though Vattimo speaks of aesthetic and rhetorical experience as a consequence of what he calls the *koiné* between hermeneutics and nihilism (1995), it could be argued that Gramsci's position, though not nihilist or hermeneutic, has opened a similar intellectual horizon. This is indicated by Gramsci's unique, some might say peculiar, philosophical attention to a wide and plural horizon of events, narratives and histories that he was never keen to synthesize in one system. His close attention to Benedetto Croce's pragmatic philosophy cannot be ignored. It is no surprise that Gramsci's philosophy is laden with sensitivities that indirectly defy the structuralist scaffolds of Marxian political economy and its ensuing theory of power, given that his foundational approach to Marx is directly informed by the works of Antonio Labriola (1971) and Croce (2001), both of whom have offered unusual takes on historical materialism. It was Croce's work that particularly exposed Gramsci's philosophical interests to an array of linguistic and cultural intricacies in which he invested robust philosophical weight in his endeavour to understand the world. This is more pronounced in his continuous and highly informed attention to local knowledge as it emerges from common sense, or as he would later call it 'the folklore of philosophy'. Likewise specific forms of art and literature take centre stage in his study of society; and specific authors like Luigi Pirandello, whose existential immersion in the narratives and being of the South and its wider 'Mediterraneanism', undoubtedly gave Gramsci a vantage points of originality, especially in how he read Central European philosophers like Kant and Hegel.

With the intent of highlighting such a rich philosophical texture, this essay pays specific attention to Gramsci's 'Kantian' reading and its direct consequence on how *after Gramsci* the notion of formation takes a route that sidelines the 'strong structures' emphatically critiqued by Vattimo. Likewise one finds that unlike most Marxist philosophers, Gramsci's work seldom entertains a guaranteed 'reversal' of the alienation of human value. As for the *present*—where such reassurances retain an indiscriminate suspicion over any form of reassurance, even when expressly made as a critique of philosophical reassurance—this essay suggests that Gramsci's work might still offer other ways of re-reading our formative possibilities without having to subscribe to 'newly' strengthened structures. And this, I would add, is especially the case when such readings retain some of the genial idiosyncrasy with which Pirandello's anti-heroes—like Vitangelo Moscarda, and more so the better known character, the 'late' Mattia Pascal[4]—begin to address those innermost aspects of human learning.

Catharsis as a Formative Aesthetic

Not surprisingly, when Gramsci reads Marx he does not stop with a dialectical reciprocity between political economy and ideology. Writing on *catharsis*, he returns to the base-superstructure argument with a twist that may sound irrelevant to its original context, but which (perhaps more now than ever before) makes very interesting reading for those who see in Gramsci's work a continuous and growing relevance to current state of affairs. Though rather brief, Gramsci's reflection on catharsis is rich and varied in its philosophical, cultural and political implications. These comments are found in Notebook (*Quaderno*) 10.II, which he wrote as a political prisoner in fascist Italy. In the Riuniti Edition of the *Quaderni del Carcere* (Prison Notebooks) this passage is found in *Il Materialismo Storico e la filosofia di Benedetto Croce* which is the first in a series of six, thematically edited, volumes. Interestingly the Riuniti editors place the catharsis passage between his comments on the base-superstructure theory (found in Q10.II and 8) and a longer commentary on 'The Kantian "noumenon" ' (also written in Q10.II). One cannot ignore a certain thread of argument between these discussions.

To start with, Gramsci's take on *catharsis* is unusual. He argues that:

> One could employ the term 'catharsis' to point to the course [that is taken] from the merely economistic (or selfish-passionate) to the ethico-political moment; that is, the superior development [*l'elaborazione superiore*] from base [*struttura*] to superstructure within human consciousness. This would also entail the course taken from 'objective to subjective' and from 'necessity to freedom'. (Q10.II, 1975a, p. 48)

In view of Gramsci's argument that the base-superstructure dialectic has a *gnoseological* value, his treatment of the dialectical ground for catharsis must also imply that knowledge pertains to the question of *Truth* (as a gnoseology) rather than a structure of *Sciences* (as *epistemology*). At the risk of oversimplification, one could briefly describe this distinction as follows: while *gnoseology* examines knowledge's intrinsic relationship with the Truth, *epistemology* studies knowledge from its fundamental criteria of validity. This also implies that in the course taken from object to subject, knowledge (as gnoseology) partakes of truth as a claim for *freedom*. More importantly, perhaps, is that gnoseology allows the play with the political 'dialect' that permeates Gramsci's close analysis of hegemonic power through the occurrence of speech as *lingua* and what appears as a philosophy of common sense, captured in the larger grammar of *linguaggio*. At this stage I would highlight what will later in this essay become central to the discussion of power in terms of such occurrences and grammatical assumptions—particularly when the whole question of catharsis cannot be simply taken out of the political contexts by which an aesthetic positioning in Gramsci is never neutral.

One cannot ignore how Gramsci uses a term (*catharsis*) that is normally found in aesthetic theory to indicate more than a poetic mechanism of Tragedy. Aristotle famously centres his attention on catharsis when he defines tragedy as 'a serious complete action, which has magnitude, in embellished speech, with each of its elements used separately in the various parts ... accomplishing by means of pity and terror the catharsis of such emotions' (*Poetics*, 1449b 25, 1987, p. 7). Gramsci takes the notion of 'complete action' in Aristotle's definition of tragedy significantly further. He argues that 'the base [*struttura*] provides an external force that crushes man, assimilates him with itself, renders him passive; it is transformed into a means of freedom; an instrument for a new ethical-political form, at the origin of new initiatives' (Q10.II, 1975a, p. 48).

This inverts the traditional (Marxian) tenets of the base-superstructure argument. Instead of arguing that the economic base would ultimately liberate men and women from the ideological superstructure that reflects capitalism, Gramsci's argument suggests that the base still has the propensity to turn freedom and a new ethical political form into an instrument of its economic and selfish-passionate character. In other words, the expected liberation from capitalist forms of production would not happen unless the base-superstructure dialectic is fundamentally transformed—and somehow *flattened*. This does not mean changing the economic base because the source of oppression is not found simply at the base but within the *relational* character of base and superstructure as *gnoseological* constructs—i.e. as constructs that come into being, and ultimately change, according to our assumptions of freedom and truth—never forgetting that the latter (as suggested in my parallel reading of Gramsci with Vattimo) is more often than not experienced aesthétically and rhetorically. This also means that even when the 'base' is new and innovative it would not alter the fact that its mechanism remains instrumental unless the constructs of structure and super-structure are recognized and ultimately surpassed. Here one could also see how Gramsci breaks off with what Vattimo perceives as Marxism's objective of a recovery of use value and its normative implications (1999, p. 30). And I would hasten to add that the main reason for this breaking off with Marxian structuralism comes directly from Gramsci's reading of power through the formative character of aesthetics and rhetoric, bearing in mind that like Nietzsche, Gramsci's philosophical apprenticeship was in philology.

This might explain why for Gramsci, the moment of catharsis is other than a mechanistic overthrowing of economic infrastructures, and even less of a possibility of recovery. In effect, catharsis forms part of human consciousness from which the concept of change (that is akin to it) cannot be externalised. In his usage of catharsis as a concept of change Gramsci regales it with an ethical foundation that goes further than Aristotle's controlled context of poetic tragedy. He expands this poetic mechanism to the totality of our critical practices, the summation of which becomes the 'philosophy of praxis'. One could say that the notion of catharsis is extended to that of a formative *aesthetic*. Because of its formative essence, and in view of its *aesthetic* terrain, catharsis cannot be limited to an operative moment within a simulated state of affairs. Yet as an aesthetic moment it is also susceptible to manipulation from the part of specific economic structures even when catharsis is proposed as a mediator of change or progress. This is why Gramsci does not simply equate catharsis with a psychological moment of economic revolution. From this reading of catharsis one could also discern how Gramsci considers the aesthetic dimension as a critical form of action that counters the dualisms of object and subject, contingency and necessity. Ultimately catharsis expresses a concern for power, because it has to do with a dialectic that is rooted in the complexities by which language—*qua* rhetorical praxis—operates within the polity.

> It seems to me that the establishment of the 'cathartic' moment becomes the point of departure for all the philosophy of praxis; the cathartic process coincides with the chain of syntheses that are the outcome of dialectical development. (Gramsci, Q10.II, 1975a, p. 48)

As a point of departure for 'all the philosophy of praxis', catharsis is a juncture between the contingencies that imply necessities and the necessities that signify freedom. Catharsis, then, is not simply a moment of synthesis, but a moment where the dialectical onus of social and individual existence is signified by the personal testimony of social change—a change that fulfils all the social potentials by which we discern history. Parenthetically, Gramsci remarks that: 'no society would perish before it would have expressed all its potential content' (*ibid.*).

Noumenal 'Grounds'

As in his discussion of catharsis, Gramsci offers another take on yet another philosophical canon: Kant's *phenomena* and *noumena*.[5] Unlike his Marxist colleagues, Gramsci never rejects *phenomena* and *noumena* as idealist distractions. His approach is distinctly Crocean in that it follows a pragmatist reading of history that takes a different course from Kant's or Hegel's.[6] While Croce is seen to bring significant advocacy of Hegel's philosophy into Italian scholarship, at the same time he presents philosophy with his own take on history and historicism. Gramsci follows Croce's lesson and instead of dismissing the concept of *noumena* he locates it on historical grounds.

Bearing in mind that Croce regards philosophy as gradually maturing into 'absolute historicism' (*storicismo assoluto*) (1945, p. 13), one must not disregard the (equally 'historical') urgency by which Kant dedicates his work to the restoration of metaphysics in direct response to Hume's 'problematical concept' (Kant, 1990, §29, p. 71). In this context it would not be contradictory to argue that Kant's restoration of metaphysics from the agnostic mechanisms of empiricism is marked by history. Gramsci's reading seems to imply that there is an historical reason why Kant labours on the (often contradictory) relationship between metaphysics as a science on one hand and the force of common sense on the other. Kant's work emerges from the historical urgency that makes his philosophical assumptions fundamental. It does not take much to sense a feeling of urgency:

> Metaphysics must be science, not only as a whole, but in all its parts, otherwise it is nothing; because, as a speculation of pure reason, it finds a hold only on general opinions. Beyond its field, however, probability and common sense may be used with advantage and justly, but on quite special principles, of which the importance always depends on the reference to practical life. (Kant 1990, p. 147)

Kant's philosophy suggests a *social* character to the notion of consensus as *sensus communis* where 'common understanding' is recognised as 'a touchstone to discover the mistakes of the *technical* use of the understanding'. This is how, Kant tells us in his *Logic*, we orient ourselves *in thinking* 'when common understanding is used as a test of judging the correctness of the speculative one' (1988, p. 63).

In Gramsci's reading, Kant's historic urgency complements the pragmatic affair of what mediates fact with truth. In its pragmatic contexts, mediation takes on various roles—pedagogical and political; cultural and scientific; aesthetical and ethical, linguistic and *praxial*. By ways of his own reading of mediation as a series of plural and pragmatic roles, Gramsci does not limit mediation to grammar or metaphysics. He assumes for metaphysics an equally pragmatic context, where knowledge and experience not only operate on the realistic planes of the present but are also projected into the possibilities of the future. This is evident in Gramsci's questioning of Marx's critique of *noumena*:

> In [Marx and Engels's] *The Holy Family* it is argued that reality is exhausted within phenomena beyond which there is nothing; which certainly is a fact. But there is no easy way of showing this. What are phenomena? Are they something objective, existing within and for themselves? Or are they qualities which man has preferred as a consequence of his practical interests (the construction of his economic life) and his scientific interests? That is, the necessity to find a new order in the world and to describe and classify things (a necessity which is also linked to practical interests set now and in the future)? (Gramsci, Q10.II, 1975a, p. 48)

Gramsci explains that our interests and needs emerge from those 'non-definitive philosophies', where 'it would be difficult to avoid thinking of something real beyond these forms of consciousness'. This is well distanced from 'the metaphysical sense of a "noumenon" '. Rather, a noumenon must be read through a recognition of 'the concrete sense of a *"relative ignorance"* of reality ["*relativa ignoranza" della realtà*] as something still "unknown" [which] one day could be known with the perfection of human "physical" and intellectual instruments' (Q10.II, 1975a, p. 48, my emphasis). Gramsci's option is to turn a technical question into a technical solution. He adopts a Crocean assumption of historical progress as a springboard from which knowledge leaps from an unknown present into a knowable future. In this way Gramsci avoids Marx and Engels's empiricist shortcomings, where 'one could make a historical forecast that simply consists of a thought projected in what is to come as a process of development like that which until now, has been verified in the past'. (Gramsci, *ibid.*)

This proposes a radically different reading of Kant's attempt to reconcile subject with object. Taking a lead from Croce, Gramsci does not follow suit in a materialist mechanisation of critical discourse. Gramsci's critique already anticipates (by half a century) what has now been labelled as a Post-Marxist reading of critical theory.[7] In Gramsci, the *noumenon* becomes a *simple* thought—perhaps, a desired anticipation—that forms part of a process of incremented verification where need and meaning are facts of language and grammar as well as facts of economics, science and ultimately political power. On a closer look, one sees that this is not far removed from Kant's original intention. Once the mediation between the noumenal and phenomenal referents of the understanding are recognised in their historical urgency, one could also appreciate why (and how) Kant makes it his personal duty to bridge reason with that of duty and freedom, the true and the good. Kant's political positioning may not be as forthcoming as Gramsci's, but nevertheless it remains there—which is where we need to constantly remind ourselves that Kant's enthusiasm for the Enlightenment was not simply a case of sympathetic spectatorship, but a philosophical praxis rooted in radical politics.

Kantian Interludes

There are at least five reasons why we should pay attention to Gramsci's Kantian *interludes*; and more so in view of his reading of Kant's notion of *noumenon* vis-à-vis the historical '*relative ignorance*' by which human beings arrive at the achievement of apposite 'intellectual instruments' of knowledge and ultimately, at adopting effective praxes for political change:

I. The first is to do with Gramsci's search into the definitional spaces of the noumenon. The first thing he does is to place noumena within the sights of historical possibility. He does this because he wants to link noumena with the question of knowledge—which in Gramsci's terms must be read as gnoseologically charged and thus strategically effective in terms of the praxis that must emerge from the expectation of new polities. This has a profound effect on how one *learns* the noumenon as: (a) something *other* than a mere appearance, and (b) as something *else* from a mere fact. This sense of anticipation also implies that in the relative ignorance by which the noumenon implies a future knowledge, women and men are empowered with the ability to anticipate what rationally remains unclear, because it is yet unknown. Basically, this means that women and men can learn while arguing their way through something that still has to become fact. (Which is why Marx's materialist instincts rejected noumena as mere speculation.)

The same question prompts us to wonder why Gramsci sought another way of placing the noumenon within history and science. I would venture to think that this is where one finds a link to the speculative nature of learning and argument, which is made possible through aesthetics and rhetoric. Gramsci adopts the noumenon as a form of historical possibility with the *proviso* that such a possibility is not discursively presented, but is cast in the immediate whereabouts of the self and the social (with all the shortcomings that the notions of *individual self* and *social being* would bring). As *possibility*, the noumenon is also a *want*; a need of something beyond one's self; an 'ignorance' of fact that retains facticity; and perhaps more importantly a form of creativity—i.e. an ever-renewed *presentation*, in the sense of a perpetuated *neue Darstellung* (Negri, 1991, pp. 12ff). Most of all, this discussion of possibility takes us straight into Gramsci's approach to the relationship between knowledge as a fact of language and common sense. If there is something strikingly original in Gramsci's approach, it is found in how he precludes positivist shortcuts, and how he assumes possibility as something that may be put on hold by the fact of future consciousness, even when it remains central to human creativity.

II. The second reason for this Kantian interlude is raised by a need to read Gramsci next to Jean-François Lyotard. This is in part related to the conditional contexts of 'postmodernity' which both Gramsci and Lyotard 'shared'—if we go by Lyotard's definition of the postmodern as modernity in its nascent form (Lyotard, 1989). More importantly I would like to draw the reader's attention to Lyotard's definition of the postmodern *vis-à-vis* pedagogy and law as narratives of a *performative* kind. Without a Kantian intervention, it will be difficult to make connections between Lyotard and Gramsci. This connection is not prompted by academic or political expediency, but because like Gramsci, Lyotard shares a wrestled background with the fallacy of a Marxian 'certainty',[8] and like Gramsci, Lyotard managed to emerge from this by attending to those other criteria that human beings continuously 'invent'. As Lyotard states in *Au Juste* with respect to Kant's notion of the 'ability to judge' (which, according to him, Kant 'left mysteriously hanging'):

> The ability to judge does not hang upon the observance of criteria. The form that it will take in the last *Critique* is that of the imagination. An imagination that is constitutive. It is not only an ability to judge; *it is a power to invent criteria* (Lyotard & Thébaud, 1994, p. 17, my emphasis).

Here I do not want to read Gramsci *after* Lyotard or even dare to suggest a Kantian juggle between them. Rather, I am interested in a parallel positioning of issues. This could be done because Gramsci and Lyotard share a common *manner* by which they give priority to the historical character of philosophical 'urgency' and perpetuate this state of affairs as if it were put on hold by Kant's judgmental decree (and 'mysterious suspension').

III. The third aspect relates to Kant's definitions and perusal of *sensus communis*, understood as *common sense*—i.e. as a common understanding on one hand, and as a spirit of the common in its universalist implications on the other.

This may lure the Gramscian scholar's attention to the use of *senso comune* (common sense) and *buon senso* (good sense), which in their linguistic formation and application raise the issue of causality as opposed to the kind of metaphysical answers that emerged in 17th and 18th century theocentrism (Gramsci, Q10.II, 1975a, pp. 29ff). However this link is only useful insofar as the Kantian contexts that introduce it are clarified and secured in Gramsci's discussion of the noumena and the relative ignorance that they suggest. In Gramsci's words, this is not an easy task:

> If reality is how we know it, and our knowledge is in constant change. If, in other words, no philosophy is definite but historically determined, it is difficult to imagine how objective reality could change with our own ways of changing, and to admit this is not only difficult for common sense but also for scientific thinking (1975a, p. 48).

IV. Fourthly, the Kantian intervention of common sense (and how Gramsci reads it) provides a possible avenue to a further understanding of the cultural ground that informs philosophy's historical urgency. I regard the notion of a *'formative* aesthetic' as insepa-rable from one's engagement with how the idea of *being* relates to *practice* in a critical way. Long before post-structuralism came about as a *visible* narrative, Gramsci provides the right tools by which we attain a philosophical understanding of the world without conscripting knowledge into the false certainties of meta-narratives. This understanding begins with Gramsci's invitation to pay specific attention to the peculiarly folkloristic roots of our thinking (what he calls the 'folklore' of philosophy—such as religion and superstition as crude world outlooks that await elaboration and enlightenment [Q11, 1975a, pp. 3ff]). This is also why Gramscian analyses lean heavily in favour of philosophy as a *form* (rather than an *instrument*) of creativity.

V. Set apart from the Kantian argument, Gramsci's personal prelude—the memory of his childhood as his source of survival during the latter end of his adult life—strikes us with a form of language that is embedded in a *local* form of knowledge. This is frequently (some may say, *constantly*) signified by distinctly Sardinian references. References of this kind do not merely signify an accidental regard to the dialectal force of Sardinian as a language. For sure, Gramsci's Sardinian *idiom* is not a play of words or a fanciful twist. It marks Gramsci's political roots with what originates from *Gramsci-the-individual*.[9] As an individual, and as someone whose personal life is intrinsically linked to his public role, *Gramsci-the-individual* is never alien to *Gramsci-the-political-prisoner* or *Gramsci-the-intellectual*. By closely attending to the *origin* of his private-public intellectual intentions Gramsci comes across as being intimately linked to the idea of knowledge as culture, and of culture as formation, culture as philosophy, culture as truth, culture as education ... etc.

Gramsci's work offers the possibility of taking a number of philosophical lineages into the essence of what we deem as *formative* to make it a moment that is synonymous with the moment of art. Here we are not simply referring to 'art' as a specific genre of 'art making', but as that realm that implies the consciousness of *doing* by which we *speak of* the world as well as *make of* the world a possible representation of our intentions towards it. This is what I mean by Gramsci's *formative aesthetic*. This method is not far removed from how Gramsci regards Kant's noumenon as a preoccupation with the imperatives of reason within history. It is also not that removed from how Gramsci speaks about his life and makes of this speech a political discourse that intervenes into everyday life by the sheer will that becomes political praxis. Unlike many of his contemporaries Gramsci reads history on a *personal* level without ever entertaining any social-functionalist generalisation. As we see in his appraisals of Pirandello's work, Gramsci presents human possibility as an *in-your-face* approach with no punches held; as a form in the manner of which, action ensues.

Gramsci's intellectual artistic and cultural interests make no apologies for being an intrinsic part of *Gramsci-the-individual* whose day-to-day survival in a fascist prison is no accident but a significant point of intellectual origin. I consider this as a very important *given* that has to be kept in mind in any discussion that makes reference to Gramsci's work. This *given* is further clarified when one keeps in mind two important aspects of how a personal 'origin' operates within the public and critical spheres:

a. One needs to identify the *distances* set as distinctions between person, discourse, and decision.
b. One must also pay attention to *how* and *where* one finds the person's *descent* from decision to discourse. How this is done remains open to our ability to judge (and therefore, to re-cite Lyotard, how we 'invent criteria').
c. Perhaps more significantly this has to do with how *lingua* and *linguaggio* are made distinct, how they work together and how they relate to the decisions we take as individuals—as the protagonists of language as *lingua* and *linguaggio*.

Private, Individual, Social

The relationship between the *private*, the *individual* and the *social* relies on a widening of possibilities in our notions of history, art and knowledge. While clearly the private and individual are *protagonist* acts, the notion of *the social* needs some explanation, especially when it comes to refute the accusation of relativism. An opening of the social dimension of the *formative* grounds by which we come to play the aporetic games of knowledge would mean that our perspectives of 'the social' might be partly expressed in how history is reflected in the aesthetic imagination and the cultural imaginary. This highlights a distinction between the aesthetic dimension (in the sense of its *everydayness*) and those historical forms of cultural life by which we identify our formative projects with the acts and desires of society. As a way into this state of affairs I suggest that we consider this passage from Gramsci's critique of Pirandello:

> Pirandello's importance appears to have an intellectual and moral character, which is more cultural than artistic. He sought to introduce the 'dialectic' of modern philosophy into popular culture, against the Catholic-Aristotelian ways of conceiving the 'objectivity of the real'. He has done this in the ways of the theatre and in the only way with which Pirandello could do it. This dialectical concept of objectivity presents itself to the public as acceptable in how it is impersonated by characters of exception—in romantic vest—in a paradoxical struggle against common and good sense. But could it be otherwise? Only in this way could Pirandello's drama show less of a character of 'philosophical dialogue'—which nonetheless it has enough of, since more than frequently, the protagonists have to 'explain and justify' new ways of conceiving the real. On the other hand Pirandello does not always escape from a true and proper solipsism, since in him the 'dialectic' is more sophistic than dialectical. (Gramsci, Q6, 1975b, p. 55)

It is important to note how Pirandello himself is not excused from the predicaments of the literary imagination. The fine thread between sophism and the dialectic that runs through his work does not stand for a deficiency of objectivity. It prompts the recognition of the subjective domain by which the private Pirandello often appears through the diaphanous membranes of his public narrative. Pirandello provides us with an exciting arena where the narratives of the objective confront the decisions of objectivity. In his work the domain of the personal operates as a synthesizing ground on which protagonists are expected to ' "explain and justify" new ways of conceiving the real'.

Pirandello gives expression to these multiple 'dialects' as a diverse mass of possibilities crossing between the *dialectical* and the *dialectal*. This axis of possibility is presented to the public as a plurality of consents pooled together and continuously *re-cognised*. Pirandello makes the objective possible by what is *acceptable* and *expected*, rather than by what is simply *known*. In its invented criteria, the prospect of human thinking is given to us as inter-legible.

Gramsci argues that in Pirandello the literary and the quotidian express a recollected 'sociality' of the *acceptable* (and *known*) by which we engage with the *familiar* as a reconstructed range of 'characters of exception [...] in a paradoxical struggle against common and good sense'. But Gramsci does not stop there. He goes on to argue that Pirandello's work also runs on the understanding that paradox is the backbone of a quotidian dialectic that remains akin to the dialectal.

This may disappoint anyone still claiming that what we need is a dialectic that would resolve everything in a benign way. As we have seen in Gramsci's definition of catharsis, the dialectic does not resolve itself linearly within a fixed synthesis. Rather he suggests a chain of syntheses, which seem to imply that the process neither seeks, nor sees, a specific end. Pirandello's world presents us with a world that proffers incongruent conditions for common and good sense—which, anyone familiar with the Italian South would confirm as a norm and not an exception (Baldacchino, forthcoming). Here any formation takes place in a realm that appears more and more *aesthetical*—i.e. expressive of a dialectal condition that prefigures a kind of dialectic without a necessary synthesis. In this condition even the extents of the objective world could not support the optimism of an amnesiac (or indeed *pastoral*) benignity in culture, literature, art, or education. Thus catharsis becomes a *continuous*—rather than a *teleological*—condition. It is also because of this condition that the *aporia* of history, knowledge and the social could be assumed; and it is because of this condition that the games of an aporetic history are played to full fruition.

Formative Struggle and Legislative Grammar

This is where the construction and wording of any theoretical and practical decision emerge as a space of cultural activity. But here the activity is not necessarily bound by pre-defined contexts. Rather, it is characterised by the junctures to which works of art and literature like Pirandello's would alert us. This will make no sense unless we read culture (as *Bildung*)[10] in its dual nature of *formative struggle* and a corresponding *legislative grammar*.

(i)   By *formative struggle* we define culture's pedagogical portents as the struggle for the possible against the fallacy of accountable measure.

(ii) Within a corresponding *legislative grammar*, the legitimacy of a *formative struggle* is expressed by a state of affairs where knowledge and history are narrated in their respective *aporiei*. This is also related to what Lyotard terms as the 'agnostics of language'.

Gramsci never talks about practice *in vacuo*. He assumes practice as a *critical activity*—as denoted by the word 'praxis'. Gramsci defines cultural and artistic praxes as forms of struggle. More than a form of political activism, the idea of struggle in art and culture is intimately linked to that of reality as apprehended (and learnt) in negotiation with 'possibility'.

> To struggle for a new art would mean to struggle for the creation of new individual artists; which is absurd, because artists cannot be created artificially. One must speak of the struggle for a new culture, that is, for a new moral life which can only be tied to a new intuition of life until it becomes a new way of feeling and seeing reality, and thus a world intimately made natural with 'possible artists' and 'possible works of art' (Q 23, 1975b, pp. 8–9).

The parameters of a formative struggle assume possibility as a relation (not creation) of makers and doers. These parameters exclude the Culture and Education industries' attempt to standardise creativity, since creativity is a *negotiated* structure of possibility. (Once knowledge is standardised into a curriculum, any further possibilities are proscribed.) Within the realms of possibility, the condition for a 'new intuition of life' depends on the grammars of struggle as 'a new way of feeling and seeing reality'.

This has a direct bearing on the how the Cultural and Educational industries' institutionalised forms of knowledge have been mortgaged into the fallacy of accountable and measured standards. The fallacy of creating a new art by assumed formulae of exclusive merit is prescribed by systems of *mimetic* knowledge by the very same artistic institutions (like schools, theatres, cultural centres ... etc.) that are meant to promote and sustain the arts.[11]

So-called 'liberal democracies' and their respective meritocracies also consider the apprehension of reality—whether by feeling, seeing or knowing—as an intellectual production that is reminiscent of Taylorism. By selecting epistemological hierarchies and their corresponding standards of practice, the Education and Culture industries continuously pre-empt knowledge by their own forms of legitimacy. This amounts to the preclusion of *known* possibilities and it comes about when the standardization of knowledge ignores a fundamental pedagogical and cultural prerequisite in art—that of paradox.

What the curricular engineer and the cultural manager forget is that formative knowledge only comes about when, and *only when,* our pedagogical and cultural constructs are allowed to perceive possibility as a paradoxical approach to truth. Curricular and standardized polities also tend to forget that culture and pedagogy are forms of dispute. (Baldacchino, 2008) Likewise in the processes of our cultural and aesthetic forms of learning, *formation* must be seen as equivalent to *struggle*. As a form of struggle, the process of formation speaks and plays by enacting itself as a *fight*:

> [T]o speak is to fight, in the sense of playing, and speech acts fall within the domain of a general agnostics. This does not necessarily mean that one plays in order to win. A move can be made for the sheer pleasure of its invention: what else is involved in that labor of language harassment undertaken by popular speech and by literature? Great joy is had in the endless invention of turns of phrase, of words and meanings, the process behind the evolution of language on the level of *parole*. But undoubtedly even this pleasure depends on a feeling of success won at the expense of an adversary—at least one adversary, and a formidable one: the accepted language, or connotation. (Lyotard, 1989, pp. 10–11)

This idea of an agnostics of language should not make us lose sight of the second principle, which stands as a complement to it and governs our analysis: that the observable social bond is composed of language 'moves' (Lyotard, 1989, pp. 10–11).

Taylorism and Post-Taylorism

An 'agnostics of language' is key to a better understanding of learning and culture as forms of dispute. Dispute operates on the ground of form and the elaboration of its constituents. When I say *form* I do not mean an outer shell that accommodates whatever we find convenient to it. The definition of form is related to the Platonic definition of the idea (*eidos*) where the essence, rather than the shape (*eidolon*) of the world is apprehended in a number of acts and intentions by which we as human beings make sense of existence.

Form also moves from formation to *in*formation and onto *con*formity. We do not assume the essence of the world as a fixed quantity of ideas that we increasingly come to know. We act upon the world and therefore inform the world in continuous relationship with it, by which we also conform to it. Thus we *humanise* the world: although pollution and war are also human activities and they play an equal role in the world's *humanisation*. This is why we should retain an agnostic view of form and how we inform the existing world. Form and formation are unified as acts of performance. But performance is also cultured, schooled and aesthetized. The idea of play comes to us as a *pre*formed set of criteria.

An 'agnostics' of language moves between person, discourse and decision to sanction the paradox of the possible as form. If any, this is where one could conjure up a 'ground' for history's possibilities.[12] For struggle to be formative, it must be open to playfulness. Socially, the playful is that 'observable bond' by which Lyotard invites us to the agnostic world of exchange—which is where we must revisit Gramsci's classical critique of Taylorism.

Gramsci argues that in a Taylorist set-up, the distance set between the manufacture of labour and its 'human content' gives rise to the 'invisibility' of production (the making of objects) (Gramsci, Q22, 1975c, p. 467). In a Taylorist form of production value is taken out of context and wealth disregards the common origin that it shares with what makes the object. The contemporary tales of measured accountability have their origin in this invisible market, where knowledge is not immune to the rules of exchange. The distance between the origin of knowledge (the *making* and *doing*) and its designated *consumer* (us as cultural learners, producers and, in turn, perpetual consumers of what we re-learn and re-produce) has altered (and continuously invalidates) any rules for a common ground. The democratic origin of accountability is overtaken by the market value of the product—by which indeed, the product is standardised and regulated.

Somehow Gramsci fails to comment on one important aspect of Taylorism (although this may well be implicit in his critique): that Taylorism has also managed a state of affairs by which production becomes so far removed from the original point of manufacture that any criticism of the epistemological estrangement (originally borne out of Taylorist production) becomes redundant. The redundancy of the critique of Taylorism emerges from a state of affairs where the distance between the origin and the consequent consumption of human labour becomes so remote that any contradiction in the process is instantly overtaken by a wholly different state of affairs. Basically it is 'too late' for any critique to be effective. Any reversal is simply absurd.[13] This means that at the point of consumption we are already facing a *post-Taylorist* condition, and it is this condition that we need to wrestle with when it comes to the critique of standardised knowledge.

To better explore this dilemma I refer to the discussion of language and formation as developed in Gramsci's distinction between *lingua* and *linguaggio*. While (i) *lingua* is a 'verbal expression, snap-shots of which could be taken in a certain time and place from grammar'; (ii) *linguaggio* is 'a sum total of images and modes of expression that re-enter the grammar' (Gramsci, Q6, 1975b, p. 26).

Externalised from its grammatical origin *lingua* highlights the creativity of formative struggle. *Lingua* is a state of affairs where standardised measure is resisted by the autonomy of the individual. This autonomy emerges from the playful and paradoxical character of *lingua*. Yet because of its playful premise, *lingua* is also open to its being instrumentalized into a defined process and foreclosed experience. As a cultural-pedagogical (i.e. a formative-hegemonic) instrument, *lingua* remains within the confines of a post-Taylorist condition, and is thereby subsumed in the amnesia of a form of knowledge that is predisposed to immediate—and therefore *uncritical*—consumption. This is because the post-Taylorist condition (not unlike its post-modernist counterpart) mortgages knowledge to an *already-consumed* state (camouflaged as *relevant* to a market of consumers) and cannot accept language as *lingua*.[14]

This *lacuna* partly originates from the tautological character of its technical premise. Its exclusive argument rests on a technical level, where knowledge is curtailed by positivist positions on use and morality; and where the diverse nature of knowledge as articulated by the arts, the sciences, literature, mathematics (... etc.), is diffused by the priorities of consumption on the formalised grounds of learning and culture. Neverthe-less once the playfulness of *lingua* is *known*, knowledge stands a good chance of being recognised in its paradoxical formations. Once the paradox of *lingua* is 'liberated', it becomes possible to think of a situation where the sum-total of images and modes of expression would re-renter the grammar of *linguaggio* in the form of a cultural and pedagogical recollection of our historical and knowable *aporiei*. This would shift the arena of knowledge and would have an effect on the economics by which knowledge has been rendered irrelevant in its post-Taylorist condition. This state of affairs is evident in how within our epistemological imaginary, objective and subjective forms of inquiry are never recognised in the specificity of individual forms of knowledge, but in their use-value.

What is now historically urgent is how *lingua* could be ultimately 'liberated'. This remains a difficult task especially when the post-Taylorist condition precludes any form of 'reversal'. At this point one could only assume that as a playful (or should we say aporetic) narrative, *lingua* remains within the grasp of a future science. Like the noumenon for Kant an aporetic *lingua* remains, at this point in history, an object of 'relative ignorance' for which a formative aesthetic may need to be found, or indeed, articulated.

Closing Remarks

In view of the above, I would like to sum up this essay as follows:

- Gramsci's work on *formation* cannot be reduced to a question of hegemony and education, and cannot be taken from a viewpoint that is often taken for granted to be a kind of valuation of popular culture, or as cue to Liberal intellectual proclivity towards some soft-edged form of consensual change as an alternative to radical politics.
- By heralding original approaches to the detail of philosophical argument (such as the notions of catharsis, noumena and phenomena) in a context that remains sentient of the historical urgencies that define human knowledge, Gramsci's philosophical posi-

tion prompts the notion of formative struggle as that which underlines the context for praxis and thereby signals the hopeful reclamation of human criticality. In view of the irreversibility of history this is conditional on the possibility of a formative aesthetic that enables the speculation of an aporetic *lingua* that makes further paradoxical relations possible—as understood (and, or assumed) in 'relative ignorance'.

- The personal sphere and its need to claim endurance and moral autonomy, remains fundamental to the notion and practice of struggle (and its consequent *formative* narratives). This is seen not only in Gramsci's actual personal testimony of struggle, but is further evidenced by the approach that he takes on the philosophical discourse through avenues like struggle (as a universal concept) and catharsis (as the endorsement individuality in *re-cognition* of the dialectical relationship between particular and universal).

- Post-Taylorism is a condition that signals the impossibility of socio-economic, cultural, pedagogical (read: formative) or political reversal. Yet, while we become more conscious of this, we also develop a deeper sense of the aesthetic character of formation. This affords us with answers that are in no way solutions but, because adept to struggle and are characteristically 'aesthetical', would afford us with an understanding of the logic of irreversibility in major areas like politics, culture and (perhaps more markedly), the process of learning and education. We thus remain mindful of the fact that the logic of irreversibility provides the condition for an aporetic *lingua* and a consequently *active* (and, under certain conditions) (trans)formative aesthetic.

In conclusion one hopes that this essay begins to discuss how from Gramsci's work one could infer that a formative aesthetic is both possible and necessary. While it is made possible by what appear to be the hopeless conditions of historical irreversibility; it becomes necessary because by its aesthetic constructs it affords us the discursive means by which we could make sense of (and see beyond) the conditions thrown at us by a post-Taylorist state of affairs. This also makes it possible for women and men, individuals and social groups, insiders and outsiders, citizens and foreigners, the emancipated and the marginalised (... etc.) to recognise the irreversible nature of such a state of affairs. This recognition signals the historical urgency by which necessity becomes contingent on finding other ways of moving beyond this *stasis*—this time, without retorting to the failed recipes of political irenism, whether progressive or reactionary. Indeed Gramsci's work anticipates, and urges us to avoid, what Lyotard and Thébaud later saw as a condition where 'the prescriptive is derived from the descriptive' (Lyotard &Thébaud, 1994, pp. 23ff).

Notes

1. Unless otherwise noted, all English versions of cited original Italian sources are my translations.
2. While normally one would assume that *gnoseology* must stand for *epistemology*, there remains a distinction between these two strands of philosophy. Perhaps these distinctions are more visible in the Italian philosophical tradition than in Anglophone counterparts.

   I make mention of this distinction because in their translation of this passage, Hoare and Nowell Smith translate *gnoseologico* as epistemological (Gramsci, 1978, p. 365). While one does recognise that the term gnoseology as currently used in English may be misleading, the distinction used in Italian between *gnoseologia* and *epistemologia* is lost in the English translation. Indeed the Greek distinction between *gnosis* (a notion of *knowledge* which is more akin to *consciousness*) and *episteme* (*knowledge* as approximating the word *science*) is equally lost in our modern translation and use of the terms—which is where the distinction between the two disciplines seems to have been equally blurred. Here I choose to highlight this distinction for the purpose of the argument that follows on catharsis.

3. Here I follow the numbering that appears in the Gramsci Institute's edition of Gramsci's *Quaderni*, published by Einaudi Editori (in 4 volumes). This remains the authoritative edition as it reproduces the exact sequence that Gramsci used in his notebooks. Editions like the Gramsci Institute's Riuniti edition of the *Quaderni* (in 6 volumes) which I use here, have grouped Gramsci's notebooks according to themes, while still indicating their original notebook number in the table of contents.

4. Here I refer to Pirandello's novel *Il Fu Mattia Pascal* (1971b), considered to be one of his major works.

5. In his *Prolegomena To Any Future Metaphysics That Can Qualify As A Science* Kant makes a succinct argument for *phenomena* and *noumena*: 'Since the oldest days of philosophy inquirers into pure reason have conceived, besides the things of sense, or appearances (phenomena), which make up the sensible world, certain creations of the understanding, called noumena, which should constitute an intelligible world. And as appearance and illusion were by those men identified [...], actuality was only conceded to the creations of thought. [...] Our critical deduction by no means excludes things of that sort (noumena), but rather limits the principles of the Aesthetic (the science of the sensibility) to this, that they shall not extend to all things, as everything would then be turned into mere appearance, but that they shall only hold good of objects of possible experience. Hereby then objects of the understanding are granted, but with the inculcation of this rule which admits of no exception: "that we neither know nor can know anything at all definite of these pure objects of the understanding, because our pure concepts of the understanding as well as our pure intuition extend to nothing but objects of possible experience, consequently to mere things of sense, and as soon as we leave this sphere these concepts retain no meaning whatsoever" ' (Kant, 1990, §32, pp. 75–76).

6. For a reading of Croce from a pragmatist standpoint see Richard Shusterman's essay 'Croce on Interpretation: Deconstruction and pragmatism' (1988). This essay may be considered 'seminal' in the context of Croce's reappraisal in Anglophone scholarship, where the attention to Crocean scholarship is, to say the least, inconsistent.

7. For my contribution to an analysis of Gramsci and Lukàcs's 'new presentations' *vis-à-vis* Marxist thought see Baldacchino, 1996, pp. 56ff.

8. On Lyotard's discussion of Marxian certainty see his essay 'Pierre Souyri: Le Marxisme qui n'a pas fini' translated and published in English as 'A Memorial of Marxism: For Pierre Souyri'. (Lyotard, 1988)

9. See for example Gramsci's moral fibre, as testified by his personal testimony of his imprisonment in the following excerpt from a letter that he wrote to his mother from prison: 'We need to be patient, and my patience comes in tons, in carriagefuls, in housefuls. (Do you remember what Carlo used to say when he was little, after finishing a delicious pudding? "I want a hundred housefuls". My patience comes in *kentu domus e prus*). [...]

    Corrias, corriazu, do you remember? I am sure we will all meet again, together with our children, grandchildren, and perhaps—who knows?—our great-grandchildren. We'll have a grand supper with *kulurzones* and *pardulas*, and *zippulas* and *pippias de zuccuru*, and *figu sigada* (not those made with dried-figs by our famous aunt Maria di Tadasuni). Do you think Delio would like *pirichittos* and *pippias de zuccuru*? I think so, and he'll say that he wants a hundred housefuls' (Gramsci, 1971, pp. 32–33).

    The Sardinian terms used by Gramsci roughly translate as follows (Here I follow the Italian translation of these terms by Paolo Spriano, in Gramsci, 1971, p. 34n.): *kentu domus e prus*: a hundred housefuls and more; *Corrias, corriazu*: a play of words implying that the Corrias (his mother's family-name) are a resistant lot—they have *courage* (*corriazu*); *kulurzones*: Sardinian cheese ravioli; *pardulas, zippulas*: typical Sardinian puddings; *pippias de zuccuru* and *figu sigada*: various Sardinian sweets in doll-form.

10. As a term and concept, *Bildung* is central to the discussion of culture in Hegel's *Phenomenology of Spirit* (1977, pp. 294ff). I discuss *Bildung* with regards to the notion of 'anamnetic exchange' in *Easels of Utopia* (Baldacchino, 1998, pp. 115ff). Also note the meaning of *formativo* and *formazione* which, for want of better words, I translate as 'formative' and 'formation'. Like *Bildung*, formation indicates both an entity and the process that denotes the entity.

11. By 'mimetic knowledge' I am assuming a form of reported knowledge that has been laundered and selected on the grounds of the same fallacy of accountable measure that is often required of these institutions as means of democratic justification or meritocratic legitimacy.

12. Here I use the word 'ground' with great caution, as I would contend after Vattimo that the notion and function of a *ground* is always subject to the hermeneutic horizons that give it credence. For my discussion of ground and its relationship to art see my essays 'Between Illusions: Art's argument for "weak" reality' (Baldacchino, 2005a) and 'Hope in Groundlessness: Art's denial as pedagogy' (Baldacchino, 2005b).

13. I have made a related case for the impossibility of reversal elsewhere, arguing that: 'Because the dialectic by which capital has alienated labor was seen by the Left as a quantitative hegemonic mechanism, the tautological nature of capital was wrongly assumed as a reversible process whose identitarian mechanism could re-emancipate living labor with its original potentiality. Here lies the trap of the dialectical tautology of capital: the assumption of hegemonic alienation and the equal hope that it could be unravelled by its own rules is itself further fuel to the productive subjectification of labour by its own object—capital' (Baldacchino, 2002, pp. 142–3).

14. To better illustrate this, one must revisit the long-standing polemic between meritocratic *achievement* and democratic *justice* in education. The problem with this ongoing argument could never be solved. This is because it is based on the false premise that balances meritocracy against the equal weight of democracy. More so, the premise is false because the contrast between a standardised form of knowledge and an open-ended notion of knowledge does not exist while learning remains trapped in the limits of technical practice. This is because the School per se prevents aporetic knowledge—in fact it is there to 'mend' any paradox. For my critique of meritocracy in education see my *Education Beyond Education* (Baldacchino, 2008).

References

Aristotle (1987) *Poetics*, R. Janko, trans. (Indianapolis, IN, Hackett).

Baldacchino, J. (1996) *Post-Marxist Marxism: Questioning the answer* (Aldershot, Avebury).

Baldacchino, J. (1998) *Easels of Utopia: Arts fact returned* (Aldershot, Ashgate).

Baldacchino, J. (2002) On 'a Dog Chasing its Tail': Gramscis challenge to the sociology of knowledge, in: C. Borg, J. Buttigieg & P. Mayo (eds), *Gramsci and Education* (Lanham, MD, Rowman & Littlefield Publishers), pp. 142–3.

Baldacchino, J. (2005a) Between Illusions: Arts argument for 'weak' reality, in: A. T. Tymieniecka (ed.), *Human Creation Between Reality and Illusion, Analecta Husserliana*, vol. 87 (Dordrecht, Springer), pp. 157–168.

Baldacchino, J. (2005b) Hope in Groundlessness: Arts denial as pedagogy, *Journal of Maltese Educational Research*, 3: 1. Available at: http://www.educ.um.edu.mt/jmer/).

Baldacchino, J. (2008) *Education Beyond Education: Self and the imaginary in Maxine Greene's philosophy* (New York, Peter Lang).

Baldacchino, J. (forthcoming, 2009/10) *Makings of the Sea: Journey, doubt and nostalgia. On Mediterranean aesthetics*. Volume 1 (Piscataway, NJ, Gorgias Press).

Croce, B. (1945) Il concetto della filosofia come storicismo assoluto, *Il carattere della filosofia moderna* (Bari, Laterza).

Croce, B. (2001) *Materialismo Storico ed Economia Marxistica* (Napoli, Bibliopolis).

Gramsci, A. (1971) *Lettere dal Carcere*, Paulo Spriano (ed.) (Torino, Einaudi).

Gramsci, A. (1975a) *Il Materialismo Storico e la Filosofia di Benedetto Croce* (Torino, Editori Riuniti).

Gramsci, A. (1975b) *Letteratura e Vita Nazionale* (Torino, Editori Riuniti).

Gramsci, A. (1975c) *Note sul Machiavelli sulla politica e sullo stato Moderno* (Torino, Editori Riuniti).

Gramsci, A. (1978) *Selections from Prison Notebooks*, Q. Hoare, G. Nowell Smith, ed. & trans. (London, Lawrence and Wishart).

Hegel, G.W. (1977) *Phenomenology of Spirit*, A.V. Miller, trans. (Oxford, Oxford University Press).

Kant, I. (1988) *Logic*, R. S. Hartmann & W. Schwarts, trans. (New York, Dover).

Kant, I. (1990) *Prolegomena To Any Future Metaphysics That Can Qualify As A Science*, P. Carus, trans. (La Salle, IL, Open Court).

Labriola, A. (1971) *La Concezione Materialistica Della Storia*. (Bari, Laterza).

Laclau, E. & Mouffe, C. (1985) *Hegemony and Socialist Strategy: Towards a radical democratic politics* (London, Verso).

Lyotard, J.-F. (1988) *Peregrinations: Law, Form, Event*, C. Lindsay, trans. (New York, Columbia University Press).

Lyotard, J.-F. (1989) Answering the Question: 'What is Postmodernism?', in *The Postmodern Condition: A report on knowledge* (Manchester, Manchester University Press).

Lyotard, J-F. & Thébaud, J. L. (1994) *Just Gaming*, W. Godzich, trans. (Minneapolis, MN, University of Minnesota Press).

Negri, A. (1991) *Marx Beyond Marx. Lessons on the Grundrisse* (London, Pluto Press).

Pirandello, L. (1971a) *Uno, nessuno e centomila* (Milano, Oscar Mondadori).

Pirandello, L. (1971b) *Il Fu Mattia Pascal* in *Tutti i Romanzi* (Milano, Arnoldo Mondadori).

Shusterman, R. (1988) Croce on Interpretation: Deconstruction and pragmatism, *New Literary History*, 20: 1, pp. 199–216.

Vattimo, G. (1995) *Oltre lInterpretazione* (Bari, Laterza).

Vattimo, G. (1999) *La Fine della Modernità* (Milano, Garzanti).

4
Beyond Discourse? Using Deleuze and Guattari's schizoanalysis to explore affective assemblages, heterosexually striated space and lines of flight online and at school

Jessica Ringrose

Introduction

In the call for papers for this special edition on the Power In/Of Language, it is noted that 'strategies and tactics of domination are often discursive—hidden beneath every-day language' and discursive tactics work to position the self and other. This is a common understanding in postmodern/poststructural educational theory that typically borrows from Foucault, to posit theories of 'discursive positionings' (e.g. Davies & Harre, 1990). New momentum in social thought is shifting focus from language/discourse to affect in what has been called the 'affective turn' (Clough & Halley, 2007). This turn underscores the importance of affect and embodiment in thinking about issues of power, and possibilities for understanding social and subjective change (Blackman *et al.*, 2007). Psychoanalysis has been increasingly drawn on in educational research to explore the subjective and psychical meanings of educational processes, such as the unconscious, the irrational, internal resistance, defensiveness, and anxi-eties, as well as possibilities for reparative thinking in teaching and learning (Britzman, 1998). What some have called 'poststructural psychoanalysis' (Walkerdine *et al.*, 2001) and 'psycho-social' research (Holloway & Jefferson, 2000) has led to new analytic tools exploring how the subject negotiates discursive positionings, around masculinity and femininity for instance, in psychically complex ways, in various forms of empirical data (Frosh *et al.*, 2003).

Judith Butler's work has also been drawn on extensively in education to elaborate the psychical costs of subjectification via discourse and language, particularly in relation to gender/sexuality and dominant norms. Educational researchers elaborate theories of (dis)identification and recognition in relation to femininity and masculinity (Gonick, 2003) and also melancholic attachment to gender subjectification (Davies *et al.*, 2001). Uses of Judith Butler's work in empirical research on discursive subjectification (Davies, 2006) have explored social regulation and possibilities of change through discursive re-signification; for instance, in the classic example of the social re-signification of the

The Power In/Of Language, First Edition. Edited by David R. Cole and Linda J. Graham.
Chapters © 2012 The Authors. Book compilation © 2012 Philosophy of Education Society of Australasia.
Published 2012 by Blackwell Publishing Ltd.

injurious norm 'queer' (Hey, 2006). In these formulations the possibilities for 'resistance' remain tied, however, to theories of 'discursive agency' (Youdell, 2006). Subjectivization occurs through the 'almighty symbolic', and with both psychoanalytic and discursive accounts we are met with the ongoing problem of how the symbolic and/or discursive order might change? It has been suggested that an underlying structuralism can lead to discursive and/or symbolic determinism, hampering our understandings of the complexity of both subjective/social constraint and movement (McNay, 2000)

In this paper I draw on Deleuze and Guattari's philosophy, which has offered significant theoretical resources for thinking beyond impasses of discursive determinism, through theories of affect. Researchers in the social sciences have used conceptual tools from Deleuze and Guattari to conduct and analyze empirical research, calling their philosophy a form of 'transcendental empiricism' because it offers strategies for mapping both modalities of social/subjective 'capture' through notions like territorialization or striated space, for example, but also the possibilities of transformation and becoming, through notions like 'lines' of flight' (Hickey-Moody & Malins, 2006). Deleuze and Guattari draw on a micro-sociological tradition (i.e. that of Gabriel Tarde, see Tamboukou, 2009) and geographical concepts (Bonta & Protevi, 2004) elaborating a 'geo-philosophy'—new vocabulary that enables the mapping of the complex and contradictory nature of social transformation and recuperation in education and beyond (Kaufman & Heller, 1998; Peters, 2004).

Deleuze and Guattari called their method 'schizoanalysis' (in early writing) to capture contradictory, schizoid conditions that typically surround us in conditions of 'late capitalist modernity' (Braidotti, 2006a), but which we are demanded to erase through calls to inhabit unambiguous 'unitary' subjectivity. As I will outline in greater detail below, schizoanalysis is a method of mapping complex embodied, relational, spatial, affective energies and the 'chaotic multiplicities that organize global capitalism' (Hickey-Moody & Malins, 2006, p. 14). I point out how and when Deleuze and Guattari's concepts extend and elaborate discursive and psychoanalytic interpretations of data. I am particularly indebted to their critiques of psychoanalytic notions of oedipal organized desire as *individual, interior spaces* constituted through lack, since this interpretation stops us from also seeing and understanding desire's positive motion and multiplicitous flows in *the social* (Braidotti, 2006b).[1] In *Anti-Oedipus* (1984), Deleuze and Guattari both heavily critique and build upon psychoanalytic notions of desire. They argue capitalism does constitute desire by exploiting the gap between desire and lack. But they also insist bodies *exceed* this lack and we need to focus on how desire moves in the social. Deleuze and Guattari discuss bodies as 'desiring machines' or 'assemblages' suggesting desire flows through and between (human and non-human) machines/assemblages/bodies in complex ways.

Here I use Deleuze and Guattari's schizoanalytic method to map how desire flows and power operates in the relationships between school and online assemblages and bodies. I explore these dynamics by drawing on interviews and online data from a study of 23 young people (10 boys and 13 girls, aged 14–16) attending two UK schools: New Mills High School[2] is in London in an area of economic hardship, Thornbury High School is a top performing school in a rural area with a socio-economically mixed population.[3] The research centered mainly on exploring the participants' engagement with the Social

Networking Site (SNS) Bebo, a site used in the UK predominantly by the 13- to 24-year-old age group (Smithers, 2008). I map how online space on SNSs is hetero-sexually striated, which operates as a mode of capture and territorialization of energy. I argue SNSs create new intensified gendered and sexualized identities and affective and bodily relations between young people at school. In particular I explore a case study of a white working class girl, Louise, who lashes out against injurious norms (i.e. being discursively positioned as a 'fat slag' online) with physical violence and is pathologized in the school assemblage. I explore the social conditions as schizoid, and consider the power of language and discourse to subjugate. But I also show how Deleuze and Guattari offer 'an alternative vocabulary' for conceptualizing desire beyond the limitations of structural discourse analysis (Gilbert, 2004, p. 7). I ask: what can Louise's body do? And by mapping complex micro shifts in affective relations I illustrate how Louise re-stages her online identity in complex, potentially resistant ways.

Researching Online and School Space: Affective Assemblages and Lines of Flight

According to Ian Buchanan:

> If we were to follow Deleuze's watchword, that philosophy has the concepts it deserves according to how well it formulates its problems, then we would not start from the idea that the Internet might be a body without organs or looks like a rhizome or indeed any other pre-existing point of view. Instead we would try to see how the Internet works and develop our concepts from there. (Buchanan, 2007, p. 1)

Deleuzian logics of becoming have been used to make utopian arguments about online space as panacea of flight, freedom from the corporeal body, and limitless space for constructing new identity and 'cybersubjectivity' that feeds into 'the new age fantasies of cosmic redemption via technology' (Braidotti, 2006a, p. 4). Capitalist growth does mobilize space for communication and connection online, but it also reterritoralizes or 'axiomatizes' desire, re-ordering flows through capitalist relations that exploit the con-nection between desire and lack (Holland, 1998, p. 68). Research on what the internet actually 'does' reveals virtual space to be highly stratified (hierarchicized) through commodified, corporate packaging and advertising that marketizes online spaces from search engines to social networking sites, organizing desire according to lack which commodities can fix, fill and perfect (Kenway & Bullen, 2008). Online space is also 'plugged into' offline space in a continual flow of energies that constitute the virtual/ 'real', and therefore online engagement is no way free from the social norms of the users and user communities; for instance, peer groups at school.

Thus, contrary to utopian analysis of online websites or profiles as spaces for new unencumbered 'safe' 'self-expression' for young people (Stern, 2007, p. 160), my work explores how online engagements on SNSs mediate and can intensify peer hierarchies and power dynamics at school. Recent research exploring how young people use online space, has revealed that SNSs are often used to solidify existing peer networks to a much higher degree than facilitating new 'outside school' contacts (boyd, 2008; Livingstone,

2007). But the relationship between school communities and online communities of SNSs has not been well theorized or researched so far (Selwyn, 2008).

In what follows, I use Deleuze and Guattari's theories to conceptualize both the school community and social networking communities as 'machinic assemblages'—complex social configurations through which energy flows (Malins, 2004). Assemblages are a way to think about social entities as 'wholes whose properties emerge from the interactions between the parts' (De Landa, in Tamboukou, 2009, p. 9). Assemblages are 'character-ized by relations of exteriority ... [that] imply that a component part of the assemblage may be detached from it and plugged into a different assemblage in which its interactions are different (*ibid.*, p. 10). Through assemblage theory, the body is also a 'machinic assemblage', which interacts with and has various capacities to affect other bodies and other scales of assemblages: 'A body's function or potential or "meaning" becomes entirely dependent on which other bodies or machines it forms an assemblage with' (Malins, 2004, p. 85).

Deleuze and Guattari also insist assemblages and bodies also need to be evaluated according to their *affective capacities*—that is their ability to affect and be affected by one another (Coleman, 2008). As Deleuze and Guattari insist:

> ... we know nothing of a body until we know what it can do, in other words, what its affects are, how they can or cannot enter into composition with other affects, with the affects of another body, either to destroy that body or be destroyed by it, either to exchange actions and passions with it or to join with it in composing a more powerful body. (Deleuze & Guattari, 1987, p. 284)

Moreover, they argue that 'affect is not a personal feeling, nor is it a characteristic, it is the *effectuation of a power*' (*ibid.*, p. 265, my italics). We see a shift from an ontology of being and fixity to an ontology of 'effectuation' and affective process in constant motion. Massumi's introduction to *A Thousand Plateaus* also talks about affect as 'an ability to affect and be affected ... a pre-personal *intensity* ... implying an augmentation or dimi-nution of that body's capacity to act' (in Gilbert, 2004, p. 3, my italics). The 'affective' dimension thus presents a way of analyzing power relations within and between bodies and assemblages, and mapping 'flows of energy' and desire (Cole, this issue), which are differentiated from the normative patterns or discourses of individual 'emotion', which may mask complex libidinal flows and relations. What social scientists can do with this shift is to think about bodily capacities to affect and be affected (at various scales and intensities) and map these (Coleman, 2008).

I will therefore use the idea of affective capacities together with the idea of assemblages to conceptualize the schools under study as 'affective assemblages'—that is 'multiplici-tous' 'social entities' constituted through interactions among the various parts, with various affective capacities. Social Networking Sites are also affective assemblages which interact in variable ways with specific communities of users, in this case a school based community or assemblage. Crucially, however, we need to map 'what affects ... assem-blages produce and what flows of desire they cut off (its components and affects)' in specific relational contexts (Malins, 2004, p. 85). Indeed, the 'relations of exteriority' of 'multiscaled' assemblages (Tamboukou, 2009) are never simply open to a free flow of energy or desire, but cut through with relations of power. According to Bonta and Protevi

(2004, p. 10), Deleuze and Guattari's work allows for the 'investigation of "bodies politic" material systems of "assemblages" ' that 'can be analyzed in political terms … along an ethical axis (the life-affirming or life destroying character of the assemblage)'. Thus we have to analyze what the affective capacities of assemblages are in political and ethical terms—are they 'life affirming' or 'destroying'? As Deleuze and Guattari (1987, p. 444) ask: 'Do assemblages have affinity with the state or with the nomadic war machine?'

Deleuze and Guattari also develop the notions of striated and smooth space to analyze the ease or constrictions of flows of energy in the social: 'striated spaces are hierarchical, rule-intensive, strictly bounded and confining, whereas smooth spaces are open dynamic and allow for transformation to occur' (Tamboukou, 2008, p. 360). I argue that both online and school space is shaped through commodified gendered and sexualized norms and idealizations (discourses), which 'striate' the space. I explicitly build upon a discursive analysis, here, by exploring the effects of the discourses circulating in social networking and school assemblages, and how they operate to shape the affective capacities of bodies. I am interested in the *relationships between online and school assemblages*, which I argue can intensify power hierarchies. As suggested by Massumi's (1987) readings of Deleuze and Guattari, intensification is a modality of affective experience and sociospaciality that helps us understand how particles and energies flow, their directionality, and the building up of energies through specific time/space events. For the young people in my research, the internet including instant messaging and social networking sites appears to intensify existing gendered and sexualized affective relations, in ways that harden striations of social space and social hierarchies at school, through potentially life and desire destroying forms of molar (normalized) ideals and discourses of gendered and sexualized identity.

According to Tamboukou (2008, p. 360), however, 'we constantly move between deterritorialization—freeing ourselves from the restrictions and boundaries of controlled, striated spaces—and reterritorialization—repositioning ourselves within new regimes of striated spaces'. The notion of territorialization describes when energy is captured and striated in specific space/time contexts. De-territorialization is when energy might escape or momentarily move outside normative strata, and re-territorialization describes processes of recuperation of those ruptures 'Lines of flight' are de-territorializations or proliferations and excess that do not stop 'but branches out and produces multiple series and rhizomic connections' (Deleuze & Guattari, 1987, p. 15). Lines of flight are 'becomings', 'tiny connections' and 'movements' which are operative at the minute or molecular level, and which need to be mapped (Beddoes, 1996).

Lines of flight are not magical escapes, however. Judith Butler (2004) extends a critique of Deleuze's philosophy as imbued with manic desires to flee existing matrixes of power, saying 'I feared that he was proposing a manic defense against negativity' (Butler, 2004, p. 198). This is an important concern about possible uses of Deleuze and Guattari to obscure the relevance of language (the power of the discursive and symbolic order) by suggesting any break from the system is liberating. But Deleuze and Guattari are actually quite clear some lines of flight are totally destructive as when they describe drug addiction, for instance: 'the creative line, or line of flight immediately turns into a line of death and abolition' (1987, p. 314).[4] They are also explicit about the need to map whether lines of flight are *destructive or productive (or both)* and to consider what they *enable or affect* in specific space/time configurations. I trace this complexity in my case study of Louise.

Heterosexually Striated and Commodified Visual Space on Bebo

Bebo is the social networking site used predominantly by 14–18 year olds in the UK. It is a commercial product, a brand which has been marketed and taken up by a specifically teen target audience. Bebo is a complex affective assemblage, with pages or profiles operating as component multiplicitous parts that plug into the online community. These interacting online assemblages are structured through commercial cultural artifacts used to represent online identity and which operate to organize and channel affect. For example, Bebo Profiles typically contain links to: favourite songs, videos, TV shows, movies, advertisements, football teams, cars and sports brands. The possibility of expression and movement in this space is therefore constrained through striations that cohere around commercialized norms of consumption and physical embodied ideals, which are gender specific, as I explore. These emerge on the social networking sites through repeated visual templates including the circulation of 'skins' and applications.

'Skins' are the design background that covers the generic site. These are typically downloaded off other sites or googled on the internet and updated regularly. Skins are backgrounds that already exist or can be modified with specialized technical skills, so they are not authored in the same way as text or blogs on SNSs are. They exist as commodities themselves that circulate in the SNS assemblage. Young people trade them, or even pay someone to make specialized skins through their Bebo connections.

An autumn 2008 UK search revealed Louis Vuitton skin to be the number one Bebo skin. Other top skins showcase the singers Kelis, Alicia Keys, the boxer Ricky Hatton and the footballer Michael Owen. A popular skin at New Mills High, picture a male in Adidas shoes that have presumably caused a woman in stiletto heels to drop her knickers. Another popular Adidas skin features 6 women clad only in volleyball socks, shoes and bikini thongs, in a huddle with their naked butts turned to the camera. There are also 'playboy' (Marie, 16, New Mills) and 'dirty playboy' skins used by girls. Daniella's (14, Thornbury) skin featured a picture of a naked Marilyn Monroe in bed, while the Bebo skin used by Sam (15, Thornbury) the boy Daniella was dating showed a scantily-clad woman who is posing in platform heels beside a Ford GT exotic sports car (price approx. £100,000). Pamela's (16, New Mills) skin reads 'hold me in your arms and tell me that I'm your baby girl'.

Applications, such as interactive quizzes on SNSs also reinforce the sexually commodified striated space. On Bebo, some of these include: 'Celebrity look-a-likes', 'Are you sexy, flirty or a slut?',[5] 'What type of lingerie are you?' and 'What sexual fantasy are you?' Quiz results tell you which Hollywood star you most resemble, while others produce pictures of girls in g-strings, or as pole dancers or in 'sexy' cheerleading/ schoolgirl outfits.

As I have suggested elsewhere (Ringrose, forthcoming), these dominant skins and applications channel young people's energies into seeking to emulate the symbolic conditions for performing idealized forms of teen masculinity and femininity, in ways that relate to wider dominant discourses of heterosexualized and heteronormative sex and romance (Nayak & Kehily, 2008; Youdell, 2006). Where schizoanalysis moves us on from a discursive tracing of these discourses, is by offering tools to map how complex normative strata organized through capitalist (commodified) and oedipal formations operate to dam up desire and channel affective capacities. In the cases briefly discussed here, the Bebo skins represent masculinity as predatory, epitomized through the purchase of consumer goods (i.e. cars and shoes) with which to gain access to a sexually commodified female body. Femininity is epitomized by performing the position of sexually desirable 'baby girl'; passive and ready to service the phallus.

Online striations can have direct affective affects on the performance of femininity and masculinity at school. Daniella (14, Thornbury) describes the ongoing production of ideal femininity:

> ... popular boys in this school, you don't see them going out with girls that they would probably see as ugly ... puts a lot of pressure on girls to make themselves look pretty, to make themselves just look perfect to that one boy that they really want, because otherwise if they don't try, or make an effort, they're not going to want to go out ...

My research indicates that the ongoing production of this 'perfect' femininity at school may be intensified by the constraints around the visual production of identity online. The display photo is the first thing one sees when looking at friends or doing a search through Bebo, and there are also archives of photos you can access and tag on profiles. 'Perfect' visual display is crucial, particularly for girls, and a great deal of discussion focused on how to do 'hair and make up' for photos, how a picture could be taken with greatest visual effect, but also how much cleavage one should display to look good but not 'slutty'. Almost all the girls' Bebo sites we looked at contained altered or 'airbrushed' photographs that were stylized through applications, shadowing and/or highlighting. Daniella (14, Thornbury) from the above quote pasted flashing icons around her exposed cleavage to draw attention to her breasts in photos displayed on her Bebo profile. The intensity of celebrity culture online and images of the 'perfect' body online bore heavily on girls, who related pressures to display the self in 'bikinis' or 'bras and knickers' and fears of people ridiculing them if they showed imperfections, such as Daniella who 'hates' her legs, or Marie (16, New Mills) who 'hates' her stomach.[6] Evaluative comments about how good or bad someone looks in a photograph and its relationship to reality abounded. Interviewees reported comments like 'you're well fit', 'nice pic', 'good looking', 'Hello Sexy', but there was also the danger of 'rude comments' like 'well ugly', 'slag', 'slut' or even of Bebo profiles being 'hacked' into and profile photos being manipulated to look 'horrible' (Heather, 16, New Mills). Louise whom reported airbrushing to make herself to 'look better', suggested others might say she was 'fat and ugly'. She mostly hid her body, taking only face and neck shots, explaining: 'I don't expect comments like oh you look really sexy or fit in this picture'. She was also subject to online abuse, and allegedly targeted as 'fat slag' as I discuss in much greater detail below.

A Deleuzian analysis suggests the sites territorialize affective capacities of bodies. Commodified, capitalist cultures 'axiomatize' (Hickey-Moody & Malins, 2006) flows of desire exploiting the gap 'between lack and desire' (i.e. the desire for larger, more prominent breasts). Energy flows toward fulfilling conditions of lack to be desirably feminine—'sexy', thin, full-breasted (etc.) for girls—and a sexually predatory masculin-ized consumption of the feminine body for boys. These discursive formations stratify the online space and organize bodies and affect, absorbing considerable time and energy. As Beller (1998, p. 92) suggests in a Deleuzian analysis of the visual, 'vision has become a form of work ... [with] technologies ... mining the body of the productive value of its time, occupying it on location'. Online striations may intensify lack[7] experienced in 'real' relationships as I explore below.

Affective Striations of Friendship, 'Luv' and Conflict

These visual striations of normative gendered/sexualized identity in the SNS assemblage shape the organization of friend/sexual/romantic attachments. The SNSs template orga-nizes how you display your attachments. Top friends' lists and categories you fill in, such as 'relationship status' and 'other half' (for romantic attachments), are templates that organize the display and flow of affect, shaping a new 'libidinal economy' channeled through new 'configurations of bodies, technology and matter' (Clough, 2007, p. 2).[8] While many boys and girls subvert the 'other half' category by filling in their closest friend of the same sex, it is more highly coveted to be able to display your romantic attachment, and even a friend 'other half' relies upon a negotiated agreement to choose one another.

While SNSs assemblages do hold the promise of new affiliations and contacts in 'cyberspace', my analysis, like others, suggests applications and templates on SNSs quantify relationships (Hodgkinson, 2008). With some friend lists on SNSs in the 1000s there is a radical transformation in what 'friend' signifies. The quantification of friendship on SNSs has significant affective effects like intensified competition for friends and 'hits' on one's site (Papacharissi, 2009). Louise's site, for instance, listed over 350 friends, but many of their comments left on her Bebo site revealed they did not know her and wondered why and how she had added them. In discussion she offered an elaborate story of accidentally adding 'friends'. Marie (16, New Mills) related a story where her younger sister hacked into her site and 'stole' her friends list causing an ongoing rift in their relationship.

'Friends' also exchange numerous items, which have value in this social space, such as virtual gifts and applications like 'kiss me', where you send people a set of lips. 'Share the luv' is a unique application to Bebo which is signalled at the top of every profile. In 2007, near Valentine's Day, the application was introduced which allowed each user to 'share the luv' with one user per day. The 'luv' appears on profiles as a small red heart, and there is a counter which shows how many people have 'shared the luv' with that user. Students at both schools discussed how it was becoming 'a competition to see who can get more' (Heather, 16, New Mills), 'who can get the most 'luvs' ' (Daniella, 14, Thornbury) (Willett & Ringrose, 2008).

Ambiguity and fluidity in social relationships are replaced by hardened affective rules and numbers through the SNS templates. Popularity through friendship and romantic attachment is to either be displayed or not, presenting a whole new set of affective conditions for young people to negotiate. As in danah boyd's study of SNSs (2008) we see in Louise's interview that there were conflicts around displays of friendships on Bebo:

L: You've got to be careful who you pick because if you pick certain people, other people will get upset that you haven't picked them ... It can cause a lot of arguments actually.

J: You have to choose your top friends?

L: Yeah, well, it's like on that one ... it's weird because they want them to be your first. But then why aren't you their first? You want me to be my first? Why am I your third or second? It's what I don't understand.

J: So how do you negotiate that?

L: You just don't do it back. I just let them go round doing it to everyone else and it's like, why should I do it back? You want me to be my first? Why, why am I your third or second?

J: So you don't, so you don't have one where you're the first and she's the first?

L: No ... It's choosing really because, when you're sitting there choosing you have to think about, of, if I don't choose this person what argument can it cause? ... will it cause an argument, will it, will it?

Problems of hierarchies in orders of friends, being neglected, overlooked, chosen behind others, and actually *not being chosen as anyone's 'top friend'* are all apparent in Louise's description of Bebo. Through a Deleuzoguattarian (Bonta & Proveti, 2004) analysis we can see how the online affective assemblage of Bebo directly interacts with and affects the school community causing frustration and arguments. The SNSs striates affective possibilities. Capture and performance in this 'libidinal economy' create new difficulties, as was also evident in Louise's negotiation of romantic ties on Bebo:

J: Are you 'dating' someone now or ...?

L: I'm not, I do like someone but at the moment things are just a bit complicated with school and I'd rather leave it until out of school.

J: Does he, do you talk to him on-line?

L: Yeah, he's one of my closest mates.

J: And how does that help or how does that affect it?

L: He, it doesn't really affect it because he knows how I feel and he feels the same but he understands that I want to wait until I leave so I can *get all* my studies out of the way. So, it's like that.

J: OK. So how often do you talk to him?

L: Every day. [online]

J: And does he go to the school?

L: No ... he's left school ... but he's only 17.

J: And when you see him in real life, are you guys like kissing or ... ?

L: No, we don't do that. We leave that for our private self, like if it's just me and him one night going out somewhere.

J: OK.

L: But if we're going out with a group of friends, we may give each other the odd hug but then we'd do it to everyone else as well so no one else would get suspicious if we don't want people to know.

J: You don't want people to know.

L: At the moment no, not until we are or not. So it's like that.

J: And do you feel OK with that?

L: Yeah. I do feel OK with that but it's whether the fact that I don't know whether he doesn't want people to know maybe he might be embarrassed and doesn't want to tell me. But I don't think he would be. I think he just wants to keep it private for now in case like, he doesn't want me going round saying to everyone oh, we might be going out but then we might not be. So that's why we want to leave it.

Bebo paradoxically offers Louise a chance to stay in touch with her 'closest mate' who has left school. The medium also constructs a space to publicly document a romantic attachment, but this does not happen. Despite Louise's protestations that they have mutually decided to keep their relationship 'private' and it is because of her studies, Louise goes on to describe being worried he might be 'embarrassed' by her. This relates in important ways to how the visual culture of Bebo commodifies affect and relationships, and potentially intensifies the gap between desire and lack. Visual displays of an attractive, desirable self, and quantifiable measures of popularity—having friends, being top friends, and being 'in relationship'—shape displays of affection online and at school. Louise must negotiate hierarchical affective categories like the 'other half' and 'relationship status' online, and this channeling of affect and desire leads to intensified risks of rejection, and life destroying anxieties in her everyday life. This is also particularly apparent in Louise's discussion of negotiating conflicts on MSN (Microsoft instant messaging), which affects her ability to 'face' school:

J: If you have an argument [online] what do you do?

L: I'd say, well why did you say that ... and then ... the other person would say, well you said this and I'd be like, no, I didn't, you said that, trying to blame it on me ... It's very difficult when it's with MSN and then you have to approach them the next day. Very, very difficult.

J: Do you think it causes stress at all?

L: Mm. Does. A lot of stress ... 'Cause ... it's like when you're laying there sleeping, you're thinking I can't believe I just had that conversation. Such a stupid argument and now I've got to face it tomorrow at school.

J: Mm.

> L: And you sit there and you think about it and then you wake up the next day and you're still thinking about it. It's like ... I don't want to go anywhere.

The difficulty negotiating relationships online leads to stress, inability to sleep and not wanting to go 'anywhere'. There is also an intensification of affect—the building energies and conflict in the online assemblages. Indeed, in Louise's case, various modes of rejection and vulnerability in the online assemblages lead directly to physical violence at school:

> J: Ok. I was interested when you brought up your fight with Marie ... could you tell me what happened again?
>
> L: I was talking to one of my other mates on MSN ...
>
> J: Mm.
>
> L: ... as well as Marie, and my other mate said to me, oh, Marie has called you a fat slag and she doesn't want nothing to do with you no more and she said you go round with everyone, you try and get with everyone's exes and everything like that. So I said to her on MSN, have you been saying stuff about me? She says 'No ... I've got to go now because it's my time to come off but if you're still on later on I'll talk to you then'. I looked back on she wasn't on. So I waited for her outside the school the next day and I'd been so angry 'cause more people had been coming ... telling me what she's been saying. And the more people that come and tell me against one person kind of gets me thinking that well, she's obviously been saying it.
>
> J: Mm.
>
> L: So I asked her and she said, no, no, no, no, I haven't said nothing. I promise you I haven't said anything. I said well you must have because I've had about 5 or 6 people coming to me saying you've been calling me a fat slag and everything. She goes 'why would I say that?' I don't' know, why would you? And she said, 'At the end of the day, you know, you're one of my best friends. Why would I want to do that?' And I ended up hitting her, 'cause I got so stressed because everyone was telling me why I was trying to talk to her. She's been saying this she's been saying that, ra, ra, ra, ra. All in one ear.
>
> J: All around you, at the time?
>
> L: Yeah. I got so stressed I hit her and I regret, regret it to this day that I hit one of my best friends ... So horrible.

To analyze the situation described by Louise in Deleuzoguattarian terms means to underscore the affective relations channeled through the online assemblages (both Bebo and MSN) which lead to her apparently being targeted as a 'fat slag'. As we've seen, on the Bebo assemblage, Louise has had to negotiate being no-one's top friend and having no proclaimed romantic attachments online. She is vulnerable to attack and the rumor she's been called a 'fat slag' is generated through these connected links in the online and school assemblages.[9] The 'injurious' 'performative' force (Butler,

2004) of 'fat slag'—to incorporate Butlerian, discursive terms—relates entirely to the visual culture of idealized feminine display that is intensified online. While Marie uses a playboy bunny skin and even constructs photos of herself as a playboy bunny, Louise is judged 'fat', meaning she violates the rules of being 'fit' (slim) and 'sexy' manifest in the visual striations of online and school spaces. 'Slag'[10] relates to the 'heterosexualized rules' around affective relations with boys—Marie says she's 'going round with everyone and trying to get with other girls' exes, whom are off-limits. It is possible to interpret that Louise's 'fatness' makes her abject—to use Kristeva's psychoanalytic notion (Ringrose & Walkerdine, 2008)—which can be brought together with a Deleuzian analysis to suggest she is subjectified in a 'mode of capture' that territorializes her as 'fat slag'. This at least temporarily bars her from the legitimacy of desire and intimacy with boys in the striations of the assemblage. Louise is constituted through the gap between desire and lack: she's no one's top friend; her romantic status is ambiguous; her body is condemned. As Deleuze and Guattari (1984, p. 29) suggest: 'desire does not express a molar lack within the subject; rather, the molar organization deprives desire of its objective being'. Through the molar (their term for macro and normative) organization of desire in this assemblage, Louise is constituted as lacking and subject to life destroying attack and she in turn lashes out with violence—a destructive line of flight.

The relations in the online assemblages directly affect the relations in the school assemblage. Similar to other examples I have analyzed in prior work on girls' aggression and conflict (see Ringrose 2008a, b; Ringrose & Renold, 2009) the school staff respond to Louise's bursting out of violence through behavioural interventions at school that diagnose her as deviant because she violates conditions of normative, passively aggressive femininity. Verbal cruelty, on the other hand, is 'normative' for girls and thus overlooked (Ringrose, 2006; Ringrose & Renold, 2009). This is evident in Louise's description of how the school addressed the conflict:

J: Can you tell me a little bit more about ... how you dealt with that experience?

L: Well, I didn't really deal with it. Sally went to Miss Thomas, one of our teachers, and told her about it. Miss Thomas pulled me out of a lesson and we had to deal with it like that. Me and Marie were sitting there crying in front of each other. Marie was explaining to me that, look, I'd never do that, I promise you I'd never ever, ever say anything about you, I'd never want to hurt you. And I said to her well, I've got about 7 or 8 people coming to me saying that you said this and they're all saying it to me while I'm trying to talk to you, kind of gets me thinking and Miss Thomas said, 'well you didn't need to lash out and hit her'.

J: Mm.

L: And I said, Miss, but I got so stressed, it was so hard not to.

J: Mm.

L: We had to deal with it like that.

J: Has there been any reaction about that? Any different perception of you about being hard or tough or do you think?

L: No, no. Nothing's changed really. People know that I haven't an anger problem when I get angry I can hit people like that but doesn't really change, because if people know what I'm like they should be able to accept me for it.

J: Mm, Mm. Just, so you, do, do you feel that you have an anger problem?

L: When I have a really bad argument, yeah. When it's just like some, he said, she said, it's like that one time, I lashed out but I've never ever done it again.

J: Mm. Yeah. It's hard. [Laughs]

L: Very.

In this excerpt we can see that the teacher's intervention territorializes Louise's physical attack pathologizing it, while the alleged verbal attack online is largely ignored. The symbolic, signifying violence of the norms around appearance and behavior are not in question. The external conditions of being called fat and a slag are dismissed and internal reasons in Louise's psyche and background are drawn upon as Louise considers whether or not she has an 'anger problem'. What Deleuze and Guattari call the 'dualism machine' exerts a binary between Marie as victim and Louise as aggressor, as is further evident in Marie's interview:

Marie: Miss Thomas sat us both down and made Louise apologise to me and explain why she hit me and that. And Louise said sorry and that she was never going to do it again and that. She, she promised me that she would never, that she would listen to me from now on and would never go like that.

Without regressing into an 'evidence-based' debate over whether Marie did or did not call Louise a 'fat slag', what is significant is that the school intervention is organized around disciplining Louise. The apology intervention has the character of 'order words' (see Cole, this issue), which 'take on board power and life and circulate around institutions ... like the routing of electricity'. The official story circulating in the affective assemblage of the school is that Louise has anger problems. As I have explored at length in previous work, UK schools remain largely trapped in psychological models of intervention that pathologize the bully, leaving the complex social conditions surrounding conflicts like 'cyberbullying' unexamined (Ringrose, 2008a; Ringrose & Renold, 2009; see also Kofoed, 2009). This clamping down of affective relations and imperatives to get along no matter what, completely ignores the complexity of relations between the online and school based peer relations.

Deleuze and Guattari, like Foucault, however, ask us to look closer at what is constituted as pathological. Their method of schizoanalysis turns madness on its head, insisting we consider the schizoid social conditions constitutive of madness (Braidotti, 2006b)—for instance, the contradiction between being called injurious names, yet feminine imperatives to not act out, particularly as a 'girl' at school. Rather than address these contradictions, Louise and Marie are encouraged to acquiesce to the striations of the school space organized around victim/bully binaries. They vow to 'get along' and that 'things are fine' in both group and individual interviews. Indeed, immediately after the conflict Louise's SNS declares Marie as her 'other half'. Louise also manages the events through recourse to pathological blaming of her own personality, having 'anger problems', and writes on her SNS 'to all my friends': 'some bad things have happened to me leaving me with brain damage mentally' as a rationale for 'what happens' (her behaviour). In this case Louise's SNS is used as a space to construct an explanatory narrative, but bio-medical discourses of mental illness are drawn on to legitimize her de facto madness—her classification into 'damaged', violent, pathological girl.

What Can a Body Do?

A Deleuzoguattarian framework also, however, moves beyond discursive determinism, suggesting the injurious subjectification of 'fat slag' and diagnosis of 'anger problems' are not fixed. It also moves beyond psychoanalytic (Lacanian) readings of lack: Louise is not only limited through or defined by her lack of the right femininity. A Deleuzoguattarian approach encourages us to consider the multiples ways energy is being channelled and to ask: *What can a body do?* (Hickey-Moody & Malins, 2006). *What are a body's affective capacities?*

In this case Louise's body has exceeded the discursive force of subjectification through her physical affective response—Louise reacted to the rumour of the online attack through a burst of violence against Marie at school. I am interested in conceptualizing Louise's violent rage as a line of flight, which holds the possibility of multiple becomings viewed through the logic of immanence. This is *not* a legitimization of violence—violence is the destructive side of the line of flight. As explicitly argued by Deleuze and Guattari lines of flight can be destructive, productive or both. But we have to *follow them* and map their affects (Tamboukou, 2008).

Alongside the destruction of the violence, it appears Louise's rage is also life affirming. Immanent affective flows, which break out of and rupture the normative strata of the school affective assemblage, are evident on Louise's Bebo site, which provides a virtual space to talk back to the injurious comments and difficult conditions of the school assemblage. On her site, Louise posted this blog:

> Them things that i effin hate would have to be them spitefull bitches and bastards when they say stuff and then they shit stir and then there two faced about it and then they backstab you ... i cannot believe why some people would be such pains in the effin asses u get me let me know in message if you have ever had this as i have been through this alot so i have alot of advice to give towards all you ppl.[11]

During one of our interviews, Louise suggested this comment related specifically to the incident with Marie. Her site offered space to continue the energy of refusal mobilized in her embodied response to the injurious capture of her as 'fat slag'. This blog space is a line of flight, rhizomatically connected to her earlier affective, violent response. The SNS provides a crucial space for Louise to disrupt the feeling rules and order-words at the school that insist she remain friends with Marie. She has an opportunity to point to the hypocrisy of betrayal and verbal attack. She mobilizes cultural resources like gangsta-rap style discourse to channel her rage. Her rage thus 'escapes' or flees the 'capture and closure' (Massumi, 1987, p. 285) of the strata of the school assemblage, finding new outlets via the online assemblage. It is possible to interpret her rage as sustaining her, as she suggests in the interview about her SNS blog:

> Louise: It relates back to the Marie thing. I hate people that are spiteful and stab you in the back and that are, are two-faced. You don't know whether this person has said it but you can get out of it by saying I don't want to know ... And just being, and walking away. Walk, being myself.

It is the online space as assemblage that enables her to express her rage, and offers the virtual space to 'walk away', although this is not possible at school. Through her SNS she appeals to others and takes up the position of knowing—'I have a lot of advice to give'. Her SNS as assemblage aligns with the 'war machine' which refuses to sit still and passively accept either the normative affective striations around being desirable or feminine, or the cruelty of disciplinary binaries enacted at school.

Using schizoanalysis to advance this argument deviates considerably from Freudian psychoanalysis which might interpret her rage as feminine psychosis, or a Kleinian approach, which would pathologize her 'splitting' and urge the pinnacle of growth to be 'reparation' (Holloway & Jefferson, 2000). So Louise would gain psychological health through refusing to project and split Marie into a 'spiteful bitch'. As we've seen, the school assemblage is invested in both a pathologizing narrative about Louise and repara-tive 'solution' that these two should make amends and get along. But Deleuze and Guattari critique these pathologizing and reparative imperatives, arguing 'psychoanalysis has no feeling for unnatural participations, nor for the assemblages a child can mount in order to solve a problem from which all exits are barred him [SIC]: a plan(e) not a fantasy'[12] (Deleuze & Guattari, 1987, p. 286). I find this statement important so we understand Louise's online assemblage as a strategy of survival, as a 'plane of immanence'—action and becoming; what Deleuze and Guattari might also call a 'war machine' through which she can hold on to rage and potentially connect and com-municate with others.

Deleuze and Guattari's framework also asks us to search for evidence of what a body can continue to do through time/space, and online research enabled me to map Louise's SNS over time. Significantly, at the time the conflict was happening Louise created a new Bebo SNS,[13] leaving the old one untouched, as perhaps an archive of these events and her anger. When I last visited Louise's new site seven months after the interviews, after Louise had finished high school, it confirmed her SNS as an assemblage that was both recuperative but also disruptive of the striations that ordered the school assemblage. Louise is not stuck, she is in motion. She has erased Marie from her site and friend list. She has not repaired. She has cut and 'walked away' online. Only one picture buried in her photo-log of her and Marie with other girls in the school-yard remained. Loosened from her relations with the striated space of the school affective assemblage, within the now potentially 'smoother', 'transformative' (Tamboukou, 2008) space of her new SNS, it is possible to speculate Louise could free herself from this difficult attachment.

Louise had also fulfilled the terms of recognition of performing being 'luved' and desirable online as her user photo is of herself and the boy she had been 'privately' intimate with, lying down and embracing for the camera. Relationship status is 'in relationship' with Jay, who is now her 'other half'. This is all solidified with the purple tagline that reads 'I love my baby boy ... I love you so much'.

Employing Deleuze and Guattari's micro-sociological mapping helps in understanding how this representation is both recuperative *and* disruptive. While Louise's SNS profile conforms to the commodified affective templates of declaring 'luv' online, these emotional declarations at once fit with the norms of recognition of heterosexualized desirability demanded through the online assemblage, and yet defy the visual striations of feminine appearance that order both the online SNS and school assemblages. Louise's body still does not seem to fit into the terms of 'slim, sexy' desirability, yet she declares her desire and love when it has been denied or constituted as mad by the molar organization of the affective community at school. No longer plugged into the school affective assemblage has perhaps freed up the feeling rules around displaying and performing affective ties.

Conclusions

My analysis works both with and against Deleuze and Guattari, since on the one hand they condemn desire and life energy continually channelled and blocked through 'the great molar powers of family (oedipalization), career (capitalism) and conjugality (heterosexual marriage)' (Deleuze & Guattari, 1987, p. 257); yet on the other they suggest it is futile to search for revolutionary or total change, given how social rupturing operates through a process of constant 'deterritorialization and reterritorialization' (*ibid.*, p. 62). Louise does not flee heterosexual relations in some revolutionary line of escape outside the social and discursive. She does, however, reconfigure her identity as desirable and desiring of others through shifts in 'relations of exteriority' between online and school affective assemblages. No longer plugged into the life destroying assemblage of the school community appears to free up some of the closed conditions of possibility around feminine desire.

To bring this analysis into dialogue with a discursive and Butlerian frame, the very specific borders of the heterosexual norms and rules around visually desirable femininity configured through this specific school assemblage are stretched or 'ruptured' by Louise (Renold & Ringrose, 2008). This is not a grand theory of discursive 're-signification'(Butler, 2004) of 'fat slag', but rather a mapping of complex lines of flight that move away from her earlier constitution through lack and pathology. Louise's move from 'fat slag' to desirable and 'desiring machine' shows change over time visible by illuminating 'tiny connections' and 'movements' in the 'theatre of representation' (Beddoes, 1996).

This discussion has attempted to build on educational theories and methodologies of discourse analysis, via the important conceptual tools offered by Deleuze and Guattari's philosophy. They offer a 'new vocabulary for designating ... experience' outside the limitations of discursive determinism and structural paradigms (Gilbert, 2004, p. 12). Their concepts enable a mapping of the striations and channelling of affective relations, but also suggest the possibility of lines of flight. Deleuze and Guattari's philosophy of immanence also suggests the research process itself is a space-time where bodies and forces intersect creating new possibilities for thinking and doing. As Hickey-Moody and Malins (2006, p. 18) argue 'Deleuze's philosophy makes socio-political empiricism an imperative, because the assemblages that social researchers and practitioners form with the world necessarily have implications for bodies and their capacities.' And as Deleuze proclaims: 'If you believe in the world you precipitate events, however inconspicuous, that elude control, you engender new space-times, however small their surface or volume' (Deleuze & Negri, 1990, p. 176)

In this paper, Deleuze and Guattari's schizoanalysis has allowed me to 'experiment' with theoretical tools to 'capture' the 'non-linear' play of 'affect' (Clough, 2007, p. 2) in my research findings. It allowed me to map complex movement in Louise's online self-assemblages and the 'relations of exteriority' between school and online affective assemblages. Ultimately this allowed for greater researcher reflexivity, since by mapping Louise's representations over time we can see that the conditions of possibility around feminine display are not as fixed as some parts of my (more discursive) analysis implied. One of Louise's SNSs sustained rage against injurious norms ('fat slag'), while another SNSs enabled space for the re-staging of desire, identity and bodily performance that was life-affirming, however much it adhered to heterosexualized norms of recognition. It is crucial to account for these complex 'desire-flows' when we find them (Hickey-Moody & Malins, 2006). Indeed, it is in attempting to map immanence, both re-territorialization and transformative movement and 'becoming' in the social, that we put Deleuze and Guattari's 'transcendental empiricism' into motion (*ibid.*)

Acknowledgements

I would like to thank Maria Tamboukou, Deborah Youdell, Emma Renold and the guest editors of this special edition for their helpful comments, discussions and support while writing this paper.

Notes

1. Deleuze and Guattari are particularly useful for critiquing and thinking against the psycho-analytic oedipal formulation of feminine desire as constituted through castration and lack of the phallus (Grosz, 1994; Renold & Ringrose, 2008).
2. All names used to describe the research are pseudonyms.
3. The research used interviewing methodology as well as analysis of young people's SNSs. For a fuller description of the methodology and research sites please see Ringrose, forthcoming.
4. Butler's indictment of Deleuze and Guattari's framework as 'manic' is, however, pathologizing. For a more complex analysis of the relationship between Butler and Deleuze and Guattari that elaborates both disjunctions and resonances between their theoretical projects please see Hickey-Moody & Rasmussen, 2008 and Renold & Ringrose, 2008.
5. For a more extensive analysis of SNSs hypersexualized and 'pornified' quiz applications see Ringrose, forthcoming.
6. Visual striations around ideal masculinity were also evident. Girls discussed boy's also posing topless to show off a 'six pack' like David Beckham. As Marie suggests: 'I think they're doing it just to impress all the other girls 'cause most girls like the six-packs, like muscle men and that, so ...' In my analysis, the striations around the commodified masculine body act in similar but less intensified ways to channel affective possibilities for boys, with more identity options open to them (Ringrose, forthcoming).
7. While air-brushing might allow teen girls to modify their appearance and redress their 'lack' online, the embodied 'real' of school relationships, the complex relations of exteriority

between the online assemblage and the school assemblage, create disjunctures in performing identity at school. You could not airbrush 'to make yourself look better' in the school hallway.

8. Deleuze and Guattari's consistent attention to the interface and relations between organic and non-organic or non-human life are significant for thinking about how social networking sites are 'non-human actors' channelling affect (Kofoed, 2009).

9. Although beyond the scope of this paper, the speeds and temporalities of being targeted on the internet is also something Deleuze and Guattari would urge us to map in great detail as affective relations young people have to manage on a daily basis. Kofoed (2009) using a Deleuzian frame to theorize 'cyberbullying', suggests the 'non-simultaneity' of relations online leads to intensifying conflict. In this case Marie does not respond that night to Louise's questions leading to intensifying affect, which simmers until the next day when physical violence explodes at school.

10. An online dictionary of UK slang defines slag as: *Noun.* 1. A prostitute or promiscuous woman ... Derog. 2. A contemptible person. Derog. *Verb* To put down, verbally. Meaning the same as 'slag off'.

11. The wording of this blog has been altered slightly to protect Louise's anonymity.

12. Deleuze and Guattari insist here we view assemblages as operating on a 'plane' of action, not conceive of them as fantasies that we can either dismiss or read through psychoanalytic interpretations as simply expressions of interior desire based solely on lack. Fantasy, however, as a category, can be re-thought outside the Freudian and Lacanian frame as a modality of action and flight itself (Ringrose & Renold, 2008).

13. Many participants reported having two Bebo profiles. Young people talked about losing passwords and creating new profiles and people thinking they are 'different people'. This suggests the multiplicity and immanence of online engagement, where one identity assemblage can be left to construct a new SNS profile that plugs into the wider SNS assemblage in different ways. Other explanations for multiple SNSs profiles might be to avoid being 'spied on' by parents, teachers, or researchers (see also Boyd, 2008).

References

Beddoes, D. J. (1996) Breeding Demons: A critical enquiry into the relationship between Kant and Deleuze with specific reference to women. Unpublished PhD thesis. Available at: http://www.cinestatic.com/trans-mat/Beddoes/BD6s4.htm (accessed 12 November 2006).

Beller, J. (1998) Cinema, Perception and Space, in: E. Kaufman & K. J. Heller (eds), *Deleuze & Guattari: New mappings in politics, philosophy, and culture* (Minneapolis, MN, University of Minnesota Press).

Blackman, L., Cromby, J. Hook, D. Papadopoulos. D. & Walkerdine, V. (2007) 'Creating Subjectivities', *Subjectivity*, 22:1, pp. 1–27.

Bonta, M. & Protevi, J. (2004) *Deleuze and Geophilosophy: A Guide and Glossary* (Edinburgh, Edinburgh University Press).

Boyd, D. M. (2008). Why Youth (Heart) Social Network Sites: The role of networked publics in teenage social life, in: D. Buckingham (ed.), *Youth, Identity, and Digital Media* (Cambridge, MA, MIT Press), pp. 119–142.

Braidotti, R. (2006a) Affirming the Affirmative: On nomadic affectivity, *Rhizomes*, 11/12.

Braidotti, R. (2006b) *Transpositions: On nomadic ethics* (New York, Polity Press).

Britzman, D. P. (1998) *Lost Subjects, Contested Objects: Toward a psychoanalytic inquiry of learning* (Albany, NY, SUNY Press).

Buchanan, I. (2007) Deleuze and the Internet, *Australian Humanities Review*, 43. Available at: http://www.australianhumanitiesreview.org/archive/Issue-December-2007/Buchanan.html

Butler, J. (2004) *Undoing Gender* (New York, Routledge).

Clough, P. T. (2007) Introduction, in: P. T. Clough & J. Halley (eds), *The Affective Turn: Theorizing the social* (Durham, NC, Duke University Press).

Clough, P. T. & Halley, J. (2007) *The Affective Turn: Theorizing the social* (Durham, NC, Duke University Press).

Cole, D. R. (this issue) The Actions of Affect in Deleuze—Others using language and the language we make, *Educational Philosophy and Theory: Special Issue–The Power In/Of Language*.

Coleman, B. (2008) The Becoming of Bodies, *Feminist Media Studies*, 8:2, pp. 163–179.

Davies, B. (2006) Subjectification: The relevance of Butler's analysis for education, *British Journal of Sociology of Education*, 27:4, pp. 425–438.

Davies, B., Dormer, S., Gannon, S., Laws, C. & Rocco, S. (2001) Becoming Schoolgirls: The ambivalent project of subjectification, *Gender and Education*, 13, pp. 167–182.

Davies, B. & Harre, R. (1990) Positioning: The discursive production of selves, *Journal for the Theory of Social Behaviour*, 20:1, pp. 43–63.

Deleuze, G. & Guattari, F. (1984/2004) *Anti-Oedipus: Capitalism and schizophrenia* (London, Continuum).

Deleuze, G. & Guattari, F. (1987/2004) *A Thousand Plateaus: Capitalism and schizophrenia*, B. Massumi, ed. and trans. (London, Continuum).

Deleuze, G. & Negri, A. (1990) Control and Becoming, in G. Deleuze, *Negotiations* [Pourparlers], M. Joughin trans. Available at: http://www.generation-online.org/p/fpdeleuze3.htm

Frosh, S., Phoenix, A. & Pattman, R. (2003) Taking a Stand: Using psychoanalysis to explore the positioning of subjects in discourse, *British Journal of Social Psychology*, 42, pp. 39–53.

Gilbert, J. (2004) Signifying Nothing: 'Culture', 'discourse', and the sociality of affect, *Culture Machine*, 6. Available at: http://www.culturemachine.net/index.php/cm/article/viewArticle/8/7

Gonick, M. (2003) *Between Femininities: Ambivalence, identity and the education of girls* (Albany, NY, SUNY Press).

Grosz, E. (1994) *Volatile Bodies: Toward a corporeal feminism* (Bloomington, IN, Indiana University Press).

Hey, V. (2006) The Politics of Performative Resignification: Translating Judith Butler's theoretical discourse and its potential for a sociology of education, *British Journal of Sociology of Education*, 27:4, pp. 439–457.

Hickey-Moody, A. & Malins, P. (2006) *Deleuzian Encounters: Studies in contemporary social issues* (London, Palgrave).

Hickey-Moody, A.C. & Rasmussen, M. L. (2008) 'n-Between Deleuze & Butler, in: C. Nigianni (ed.), *Deleuze and Queer Studies* (Edinburgh, Edinburgh University Press).

Hodgkinson, T. (2008) With friends like these ... , *The Guardian*, 14 January. Available at: http://www.guardian.co.uk/technology/2008/jan/14/facebook (accessed 23 January 2008).

Holland, E.W. (1998) From Schizophrenia to Social Control, in: E. Kaufman & K. J. Heller (eds), *Deleuze & Guattari: New mappings in politics, philosophy, and culture* (Minneapolis, MN, University of Minnesota Press).

Holloway, W. & Jefferson, T. (2000) *Doing Qualitative Research Differently: Free association, narrative and the interview method* (Thousand Oaks, CA, Sage Publications).

Kaufman, E. & Heller, K. J. (1998) *Deleuze & Guattari: New mappings in politics, philosophy, and culture* (Minneapolis, MN, University of Minnesota Press).

Kenway, J. & Bullen E. (2008) The Global Cultural Economy and the Young Cyberflaneur: A pedagogy for global citizenship, in: N. Dolby & F. Rizvi (eds), *Youth Moves, Identities and Education in Global Perspective* (London, Routledge).

Kofoed, J. (2009) Emotional Evaluations in Activities Recognized as Cyberbullying. Unpublished paper.

Livingstone, S. (2007) Taking Risky Opportunities In Youthful Content Creation: Teenagers' use of social networking sites for intimacy, privacy and self-expression. Paper presented to the 'Poke 1.0—Facebook Social Research Symposium', University of London, 15th November 2007.

Malins, P. (2004) Machinic Assemblages: Deleuze, Guattari and an ethico-aesthetics of drug use, *Janus Head*, 7:1, pp. 84–104.

Massumi, B. (1987) Notes on the Translation and Acknowledgements, in: G. Deleuze & F. Guattari, *A Thousand Plateaus* (Minneapolis, MN, University of Minnesota Press).

McNay, L. (2000) *Gender and Agency: Reconfiguring the subject in feminist and social theory* (Malden, MA, Polity Press).

Nayak, A. & Kehily, M. J. (2008) *Gender, Youth and Culture: Young masculinities and femininities* (Basingstoke, Palgrave Macmillan).

Papacharissi, Z. (2009) The Virtual Geographies of Social Networks: A comparative analysis of Facebook, LinkedIn and ASmallWorld, *New Media and Society*, 11:1&2, pp. 199–220.

Peters, M. A. (2004) Editorial: Geophilosophy, education and the pedagogy of the concept, *Educational Philosophy and Theory, Special Issue: Deleuze and Education*, 36:3, pp. 217–226.

Renold, E. & Ringrose, J. (2008) Regulation and Rupture: Mapping tween and teenage girls' 'resistance' to the heterosexual matrix, *Feminist Theory*, 9:3, pp. 335–360.

Ringrose, J. (2006) A New Universal Mean Girl: Examining the discursive construction and social regulation of a new feminine pathology, *Feminism and Psychology*, 16:4, pp. 405–424.

Ringrose, J. (2008a) 'Just be Friends': Exposing the limits of educational bully discourses for understanding teen girls' heterosexualized friendships and conflicts, *British Journal of Sociology of Education*, 29:5, pp. 509–522.

Ringrose, J. (2008b) 'Every Time She Bends Over She Pulls Up Her Thong': Teen girls negotiating discourses of competitive, heterosexualized aggression, *Girlhood Studies: An Interdisciplinary Journal*, 1:1, pp. 33–59.

Ringrose, J. (forthcoming) Are you Sexy, Flirty or a Slut? Teen girls navigating sexualization and pornification on social networking sites, in: R. Gill & C. Scharff (eds), *New Femininities: Postfeminism, neoliberalism and identity* (London, Palgrave).

Ringrose, J. & Renold, R. (2008) *Fantasy, Regulation and Rupture: Girls' negotiating heteronormative femininity and heterosexualized violences, AERA New York*. Panel: Girl Studies and Education.

Ringrose, J. & Renold, E. (2009) Normative Cruelties and Gender Deviants: The performative effects of bully discourses for girls and boys in school, *British Educational Research Journal*, 35:5, pp. 1–24.

Ringrose, J. & Walkerdine, V. (2008) Regulating the Abject: The TV make-over as site of neo-liberal reinvention toward bourgeois femininity, *Feminist Media Studies*, 8:3, pp. 227–246.

Selwyn, N. (2008) Online Social Networks—Friend or Foe? Teachers TV program. Available at: http://www.teachers.tv/video/24687 (accessed 15 July 2008).

Smithers, R. (2008) Bebo Named as Best Social Networking Site in Survey, *The Guardian*, 4 January.

Stern, S. (2007) Adolescent Girls' Expression on Web Home Pages: Spirited, somber, and self-conscious sites, in: S. Weber & S. Dixon (eds), *Growing Up Online: young people and digital technologies* (Basingstoke, Palgrave).

Tamboukou, M. (2008) Machinic Assemblages: Women, art education and space, *Discourse* 29:3, pp. 359–375.

Tamboukou, M. (2009) Education for Art: Narratives of becoming an artist, paper presented at GEA Conference, 25–27 March, Institute of Education, London.

Walkerdine, V., Lucey, H., & Melody, J. (2001) *Growing Up Girl: Psychosocial explorations of gender and class* (Basingstoke, Palgrave).

Willett, R. & Ringrose, J. (2008) 'Sharing the luv': Consumers, identity and social networking sites, Child and Teen Consumption Conference, 24–25 April 2008, Trondheim, Norway

Youdell, D. (2006) Subjectivation and Performative Politics—Butler Thinking Althusser and Foucault: intelligibility, agency and the raced-nationed-religioned subjects of education, *British Journal of Sociology of Education*, 27:4, pp. 511–528.

5

Will They Ever Speak with Authority? Race, post-coloniality and the symbolic violence of language

Awad Ibrahim

> [O]ne can *testify* only to the unbelievable. To what can, at any rate, only be believed; to what appeals only to belief and hence to the given word ... [here] when we ask others to take our word for it, we are already in the order of what is merely believable. (Derrida, 1996, p. 20)

Indeed the hardest thing, especially in post-coloniality, is to testify to the unbelievable, that which is symbolic in nature and which is felt but hard to 'talk' or 'speak' about. We are always almost there, but it eludes language. As soon as we 'speak' it, as we are dealing with emotionality, it slips away. But we must speak it. When we do, however, we are constantly told: 'That's just unbelievable!'. We are left therefore wondering: is this an exclamation, a questioning or a reminder? Yet, this article dares to ask: Having fully mastered the colonial language, can post-colonial subjects ever speak with authority? Put otherwise, at what point do we own the language we speak? By way of an answer, the article tells the story of a group of French-speaking refugee and immigrant continental African youth who are attending an urban Franco-Ontarian high school in southwestern Ontario, Canada. They arrive at French-language schools with a highly-valued variety of French, *le français parisien* or Parisian French. As Monica Heller (2006) showed, the linguistic variety of French spoken in Ontario is both devalued and unauthorized in schools. However, Heller explains, most teachers in Franco-Ontarian schools speak this 'devalued' variety of French. Hence, I am arguing, we enter a 'linguistic war', where the struggle is no longer about language *per se*, but about power.[1] And in the context of this article, it is about race and language ownership. Because of race and legal status, I will show, this highly symbolic capital that African youth bring with them to Franco-Ontarian schools seems to become an unauthorized norm, a liability, a burden rather than an event to celebrate. Continental African students are treated, classified and streamed in either lower grades or in general levels, where their chances for advanced or university studies are limited. 'It was *unbelievable* how they spoke', one teacher exclaimed, expressing what Ben Rampton (1995), within the British context, calls *deceptive fluency*. For those who believe in this notion of deceptive fluency in Britain, Rampton explains, even though they may sound British and are born in Britain, South Asians cannot be native speakers of English. Therefore, the notion goes, their fluency or British accent is deceptive.[2] For

The Power In/Of Language, First Edition. Edited by David R. Cole and Linda J. Graham.
Chapters © 2012 The Authors. Book compilation © 2012 Philosophy of Education Society of Australasia.
Published 2012 by Blackwell Publishing Ltd.

Jacques Derrida (1996), this is an exemplary moment of 'performative contradiction,' an antinomy if you like, one where he would have declared: 'Yes, I only have one language, yet it is not mine' (p. 2).

Then, Who Owns Language?

Strongly worded, but Derrida (1996) is worth quoting at length here; after all he is my referent in intersecting authority-language-and-symbolic power. For Derrida, language is and has always been in the plural, and any claim especially by 'the master' to its possession can only be that: a claim.[3] In fact, 'the master himself' [sic], Derrida declares, is no longer:

> [C]ontrary to what one is often most tempted to believe, the master is nothing. Because the master does not possess exclusively, and naturally, what he calls his language, because, whatever he wants or does, he cannot maintain any relations of property or identity that are natural, national, congenital, or ontological, with it ... [And] because language is not his natural possession, he can, thanks to that very fact, pretend historically, through the rape of a cultural usurpation, which means always essentially colonial, to appropriate it in order to impose it as 'his own'. (p. 13)

As we shall see, one has to be very careful in using the language of coloniality within the Franco-Ontarian context where I conducted my research. The discourse of coloniality does not lend itself easily here and the situation is tenuous if not confusing at best. Without entering the debate on the term's orthography or definition,[4] I will use interchangeably the two orthographies (postcolonial and post-colonial) more in the subaltern sense. When subalterns speak, said Spivak (1999), they are not heard. They are subaltern not because of total social immobility or for inherent reasons; they are subaltern because they are spoken for, they are authored and already talked about. Hence their silence is made possible if not expected. Spivak (1999) tells her own story as an Indian woman who is not heard (not even by other women) until recently: 'Here is a woman who tried to be decisive *in extremis*. She " spoke", but women did not, do not, "hear" her. Thus she can be defined as a "subaltern"—a person without lines of social mobility' (p. 28).

So picture this: It is Canada—an officially French-English bilingual country, and one of the most prominent countries worldwide in implementing bilingualism and multiculturalism. The study's population is French-language speakers in Ontario, an English-language speaking province that is situated next to Québec. Québec is the only French-language speaking province besides New Brunswick, which is the only bilingual province in Canada.[5] As we know, the so-called *français canadien* or Canadian French is older than Canada itself as a nation, goes back to 15th century France, and has unique lexical, morphological, syntactic and phonetic characteristics (Heller, 2006, 1994; Mougeon & Beniak, 1989). Ontario has the highest French-language speaking population outside Québec (StatCan.gc.ca, 2008). They are known as *Franco-ontariens* or Franco-Ontarians, comprising anywhere between 4.3-to-5% of Ontario's population, and concentrated primarily in Eastern Ontario, especially Ottawa (the national capital).

Franco-Ontarians are exceptionally savvy in using the apparatus of the State and in social and political mobilization. They pride themselves on this mobilization ability and refer to themselves as *francophones de souche* (old or 'original' French) to distinguish themselves from other francophones (e.g. Arabic speakers, Haitians or West Africans). Thanks to activism and the Canadian Charter of Rights and Freedom, which guarantees a sprominent a place for the French language as it does English in Canada, Ontario has 12 French-language school boards (both public and Catholic), a number of community colleges and four universities that offer programs in French and the University of Ottawa as fully bilingual, attracting a sizeable number of Ontario's francophone population.

Francophone de souche is as much a linguistic, historical and cultural reference, as it is a racial one. It is a term commonly used for White Europeans who speak French and are part of the earlier settlers in Canada. They speak varieties of French that are similar to Québec French, but still quite distinct. Some of the distinct linguistic features of Franco-Ontarian French (FOF) include, among many others: 1) simplification (e.g. third-person plural that is cited as first-person singular: *ils veulent* [they want] turned into *ils veut* [they wants]); 2) the use of *sontaient*, a non-standard variant of *étaient* [were], the standard third person plural imperfect form of the verb *être* [to be]; 3) the common use of the possessive *à* in lieu of *de* (e.g. *la voiture à mon père* [my father's car]; the 'standard' use is: *la voiture de mon père*).[6] It is significantly important to note that these are mostly non-standard features which, as we shall see, create a very peculiar situation. On the one hand, internally, it creates a Franco-Ontarian linguistic community with its bond and intra-community recognition but, on the other, it becomes a simultaneous mechanism, a technology of exclusion.

To explain, those who speak standard French, oddly enough, would feel either excluded or highly valued. The 'lack,' as Édouard Glissant (1981) would have put it, is a better description for those who feel excluded. Postcolonial subjects, Glissant (1981) explains in *Le discours antillais*, are constantly identified and reminded by their lack of language possession. Here, language is locked in as a possession of a nation, a culture and a group of people. It *belongs* to 'them,' and identity (Franco-Ontarianness in this context) is no longer regarded as a being-of-the-entity [*l'être de l'étant*], a being-that-is-always-to-become (Derrida, 1996; Ibrahim, 2004, 2008), but as a *fait accompli*, an ontology whose essence and features are already known and non-changing. It may be a hyphen-identity in this context—Franco *and* Ontarian—but it is still purely 'French'.[7]

This is precisely why the real or imagined Frenchness is highly valued symbolic capital (Bourdieu, 1991). But for it to function as such, Frenchness has to have the 'right ingredients' in linguistic, cultural and racial terms. French, it seems, is a convoluted term referring mostly to White Europeans *belonging* to or *citizens* of France. The rest, as Derrida (1996) put it, is the 'Francophones *belonging*, as we strangely say, to several nations, cultures, and states' (p. 10; original emphasis). They are hyphened: Franco-Maghrebian, Franco-Antillais, Franco-Senegalese, etc.[8] Because of this hyphen, or maybe thanks to it, they go through moments of mourning, where they speak a language—masterfully indeed—which they are told is not theirs. The source of that work of mourning (Todd, 2003) is in the psychic tension where, in many post-colonial moments, French is the only language they speak or they master it more than their mother tongues. Derrida (1996, p. 1) again:

—Picture this, imagine someone who would cultivate the French language.
What is called the French language.
Someone whom the French language would cultivate.
And who [as post-colonial subject] would be, moreover, a subject of French
culture, as we say.
Now suppose, for example, that one day this subject of French culture were to
tell you in good French:
'I only have one language; it is not mine.'

Such 'exclusions,' Derrida continues, come to leave their marks on colonial, but as well
on post-colonial subjects, and their identity formation. They create a 'disorder of
identity', and are best captured in Paulo Freire's *Pedagogy of the Oppressed* (2000). Here,
despite her/his presumed superiority, the so-called possessor of language, the oppressor
in Freire's language, enters the work of mourning as much as the oppressed. That is,
oppression and exclusion affect to a large extent the oppressed as they do the oppressor.
Derrida pushes us further by, on the one hand, framing the work of mourning around
language and, on the other, questioning the essence of language possession:

> But who exactly possesses it [language]? And whom does it possess? Is lan-
> guage in possession, ever a possessing or possessed possession? Possessed or
> possessing in exclusive possession, like a piece of personal property? What of
> this being-at-home [*être-chez-soi*] in language toward which we never cease
> returning? (Derrida, 1996, p. 17)

Season of Migration to Canada

In *Season of Migration to the North*, Tayyib Salih (1991) tells the story of Mustafa Sa'eed.
Sa'eed is a post-colonial subject originally from the Sudan who finds himself in Britain.
He goes through identity translation and re-configuration whereby he ends up in a
Third-Space, a split-subject between two cultures, languages and ways of being
(Ibrahim, 2008). This is the case with my research subjects. In 2007, I conducted a
small-scale research study in an urban Franco-Ontarian high school in southwestern
Ontario, Canada. This research was a follow up to an earlier study conducted between
January and June 1996 (Ibrahim, in press).

Both in 1996 and 2007, the research is a critical ethnography[9] and looks at the lives
of a group of continental Francophone African youth and the formation of their social
identity. Besides their gendered and racialized experience, their youth and refugee
status was vital in their, what I termed elsewhere, *moments of identification* (Ibrahim,
2008): where and how they were interpolated in the mirror of their society (cf. Althusser, 1971; Bhabha, 1994). Put otherwise, once in North America, I showed, these
youth were faced with a social imaginary in which they were already Blacks. This social
imaginary was directly implicated in how and with whom they identified, which in turn
influenced what they linguistically and culturally learned and how they learned it. What
they learned, as I showed elsewhere (Ibrahim, 1999), is Black English as a Second
Language (BESL), which they accessed in and through Black popular culture. They

learned by taking up and repositing the Rap linguistic and musical genre and, in different ways, acquiring and rearticulating the Hip-Hop cultural identity (Ibrahim, 1999, 2004, 2009).

Here the research participants are a group of continental Francophone African youth who find themselves in a small French-language high school in southwestern Ontario, with a school population of approximately 400 students from various ethnic, racial, cultural, religious, and linguistic backgrounds, which I will refer to as Marie-Victorin or MV [all names in this article are pseudonyms]. Besides French, English, Arabic, Somali, and Farsi were also spoken at the school. This group of continental Francophone African youth varied, first, in their length of stay in Canada (from 1–2 to 5–6 years); second, in their legal status (some were immigrants, but the majority were refugees) and, third, in their gender, class, age, linguistic, and national background. They came from places as diverse as Democratic Republic of Congo (formerly Zaïre), Djibouti, Gabon, Senegal, Somalia, South Africa, and Togo. With no exception, all of the African students in MV were at least trilingual, speaking French, English and an African language, a mother tongue. Given their postcolonial educational history, significantly, most African youths in fact come to Franco-Ontarian schools already possessing the highly valued symbolic capital: *le français parisien* (Parisian French, also known as *français standard* or *français international*).

Ethnography and Hospitality

> [I]s there anything worse, said Nietzsche, than to find oneself facing a German when one was expecting a Greek? (Deleuze & Guattari, 1994, p. 109)

As a critical ethnographic research project, I spent over six months in 1996 and three months in 2007 engaged in the research: I attended classes, talked to students, and observed curricular and extracurricular activities two or three times per week. I audio-and-videotaped classes and natural conversations, visited their houses, played basketball (a game dominated by African students) and became the basketball team coach, and was invited for picnics. In short, I literally lived with the students, and because of previous involvement before 1996 in another project in the same school for almost two years, at the time of this research I was well acquainted with MV and its population, especially its African students, with whom I was able to develop a good communicative relationship. What is more, my background as a continental African myself also helped me to decipher their narratives and experiences. Clearly, we shared a *safe space* of comfort that allowed us to open up, speak and engage freely.[10]

Of this growing continental francophone African population in Franco-Ontarian schools (Ibrahim, in press), I ended up choosing ten boys and six girls for extensive ethnographic observation inside and outside the classroom and inside and outside the school and interviewed all sixteen. Of the ten boys, six were Somali speakers (from Somalia and Djibouti), one was Ethiopian, two were Senegalese, and one was from Togo. Their ages ranged from sixteen to twenty years. The six girls were all Somali speakers (also from Somalia and Djibouti), aged from fourteen to eighteen years. Interviews were conducted either in French or English and French interviews were translated into English. Here, language was a crucial part of this comfort zone, this safe space.

This space was built against the backdrop of, first, total absence of diversity in the teaching, personnel or administration staff except for one teacher of Haitian descent and, second, the traumatic psychic experience of exclusion, discrimination and symbolic violence that students have experienced (see Ibrahim, 2009). Before the 1990s, MV had not experienced such a mass of diversity, especially the continental African presence. Teachers therefore had no experiential knowledge on how to interact with African youth in either comfortable or informed ways. Intentionally or not, students made it clear that there was a serious race-relation problem in the school.[11] This problem is manifested in three different ways:

1) *The host as hostage*: Here, one is hosted, but conditionally. In Jacques Derrida's (2000) language there are two forms or formulae of/for hospitality: conditional and unconditional (see Ibrahim, 2005 for full discussion). In the former, one is hosted, but under certain conditions, restrictions, choices and possibilities. Omer (M, 19, Ethiopia),[12] who came to Canada by himself when he was 15 years old, exemplifies this situation. Omer was living in a shelter at the time of the interview, yet enthusiastically he was longing and planning to go to Laurentian University. Following an Althusserian (1971) language, Omer conceives this conditional hospitality as interpellation: 'Hello there! You are Black you can't do anything. Muslims, you can do nothing. This is what astonishing to me. It is already seen [what Blacks and Muslims can or cannot do]' (individual interview, French). As Gayatri Spivak explained above, here the subalterns are already 'talked' about, authored and hence their silence is either made or expected.

2) *Undemocratic decisions*: This is when students *feel* they are not consulted on matters related to their lives. These decisions, then, are perceived as discriminatory, insensitive, if not plain racist. For instance, because all school teachers and personnel are White and Christian (except for one Jewish teacher), when the school decided that the midday Muslim prayer was no longer permissable, the decision was read in multiple ways, including as racism. Aziza (F, 18, Somalia) described it thus:

> So now there is this new rule. They met, the personnel of the school that is, they met. They agreed, like we were nothing at all. They said 'Oh, who cares!' you see. We have to just tell them not leave the class, because our class is more important than their pray... So, there wasn't, I am sure, there wasn't even one teacher who objected to that. They all agreed. (group interview, French)

Although students continued their protest, they found themselves submitting to the school decision after a few days. Their protest, they explained to me afterwards, was an expressed desire to participate in the democratic process of decision making. To soften the situation, the school brought in a Moroccan teacher from James High School, the other French-language high school in the city, who explained to students that midday prayer did not have a specific hour but an extended period of time from 12-noon to 3 p.m.

What is problematic here, however, besides the undemocratic decision taken by the school, is the way in which this Moroccan teacher was brought into the school. This outside teacher was brought in to reinterpret the students' experience of this decision for them in a way that reinforced the White and non-Muslim teachers assessment of this decision. This is akin to the common occurrence with a White person who tells a Black person: 'My Black friend told me that I am not racist, so [although they may have made a racist comment] what you are telling me [that I am racist] is wrong'. This is what George Dei *et al.* (2000) call 'everyday racism', which is hard to talk about and deal with (as we shall see below).

3) *The minute and the trivial*: This is the third and final way of racialization where *non-appartenance*, non-belonging or rejection is seen as an accumulative memory of small details, but when put together they tend to leave students with a clear message that they are not trusted, wanted or that they are deviant. Listen to Aziza again where she explains that even their names become a burden. The teacher's repetition of how African students' names should be pronounced has become a marker that sets them apart:

> I am going to give you an example. A female teacher always gives the absent sheet [*la feuille d'absence*], always to White students. Moreover, teachers are going to know the names when they know them, for a teacher always knows the names of all the students in class. He is going to know more the names of the White students than the names of African students. 'What's your name again? Bûralé? How do you want to me to pronounce that, Bûrralé, Boralé?' You see things like that. It's a bit, it gives, it gives you pain here [pointing to her chest]. This is like, these things are small small, but they can be big, which can also be something catastrophic you see. And you, you have to live with this every-day, you see. (group interview, French)

Musa (M, 19, Djibouti) expands on Aziza's example. One day he was absent the first period. Because some African students live on their own, they confront adult life earlier: they pay their own bills, cook their own food, work odd jobs, etc. In many cases, in short, they need ears to listen to them or a helping hand. They aren't getting that at the school. Musa is worth quoting at length:

> The other day, I was absent the first period. I came to school in the second period. And that day, I didn't even see her [the principal]. I came the following day and I told her 'yesterday, I was absent.' 'All day? You were absent because you had problems.' I had problems with *Hydro*, [city name] *Hydro*. I told her that I was going there; if not, they were going to cut off electricity ... She said 'no no, that doesn't concern me. That is your problem. If you have to solve that, you should do it during your holiday time.' But holiday times, they are closed. Saturday and Sunday, *Hydro* is not open. So, I have to go, I told her, I have to miss a class in order to go there and solve my problems. She didn't even listen, she said 'you were absent all day.' 'But Madame, how do you want me to [solve it?], and I was only absent the first period.' I didn't even finish, she said 'no no, you were absent all day for *Hydro*, to solve this *Hydro* problem.' I told her 'Madame, try to **listen**, try to **hear** me.' And I told her that I was only absent the first period. 'Ah,' she said, 'you were only absent the first period, I am sorry. Then, I give a paper to [the secretary] this time, but don't be late.'

But that is me, I told her straight: 'That is your problem, you don't try to listen to the African students. You only scream. That is your problem, and you have to change this character.' I told her, straight up, I told her that. (group interview, French, emphasis added)

These examples are offered here as a demonstration for what Winant (2004) calls *racialization* or *racialized experiences*. They are insidious, convoluted, hard-to-pin-down, but psychically and painfully felt. As well, they are best captured as symbolic violence (Bourdieu, 1991).[13] The beauty (and I recognize the irony of the term) of symbolic violence in this case is that it works through slippage; that is, when the doers are confronted or called up to answer to their deeds, they can escape by saying: 'We didn't know; indeed we had the best intentions; we wanted to treat African students like any other students' (see also Graham & Slee, 2008 and their notion of 'benevolent humani-tarianism'). *Intentions matter only in their final effect,* as we know. That is, in socio-psychic terms, how one makes people feel matters as much if not more than one's intentions. Intentional or not, African students in MV have built an experiential memory that is not so pleasant to remember, which is strongly expressed in language.

Race-in(g)-Language: Le *français parisien* Illegitimately Spoken

In MV, it is clear that race (read Blackness in this case) is experienced in at least three different ways, as we saw above, and with variable degrees of emotional intensity. My contention in this section is that language is central to this experience. Given their postcolonial education, by and large, African students arrive at school fluent in, and armed with, the highly valuable symbolic capital: le *français parisien*. Interestingly enough, as is noted many times by Heller *et al.* (1999), the role and the mandate of the French-language schools in Ontario is to introduce students to this variety of French as well as to the variety spoken by middle-class Franco-Ontarians. However, when African students come to school with this capital, there is an astonishment and disbelief on the part of teachers and school counselors. Their language, it seems, is *deceptively fluent*: they cannot be so fluent and speak the language with such mastery! This skepticism stems from the fact that, as Bourdieu (1991) would have said, the 'legitimate' language is spoken by an 'illegitimate' speaker: a refugee who is imagined to be, at least in the dominant media representations, a source of pity and not astonishment and envy. This mistrust of the linguistic capital that African students possess has led to a patronizing attitude that is easily open to a racialized, if not blunt racist reading. Without naming it as such, students were aware of both: the process of racialization and how it illegitimizes their speech. In my group interview with them, female students reflected on this situation thus:

Amani: The teacher could not stop thanking me every time I speak and tells me 'Here, your French, you can, it is different than the others. How that happens, where did you learn that? Are you sure that you are not in the wrong stream [this was a general level course]?'[14] You know, things like that. And then, she was really surprised you know. I told her 'No, I know what I have to know for my level, my my ...' [interrupted]

Aziza: And then she was very impressed when we said that we learn our French in our country. And then things like that, and then she said, 'really, in your country, there is really this system?'

Samira: 'Are there professors who speak French like that? But my God you have *l'accent français!*' But of course we have *l'accent français*, there were teachers that taught us, no? And then this: 'you are coming from Somalia oh, we never heard that in Somalia people speak French with ...' [interrupted]

Aziza: 'Really in Somalia you have this system?' You know, **they don't accept that** (group interview, French, bold added).

In my individual interview with Aziza, she expands on how teachers' disbelief is patronizing and grossly disturbing, especially given its racial connotation:

Aziza: The first day when I wrote my [evaluation] test, of my French level, he [the counselor] was really surprised because I spoke an excellent French. The good and rich French; you know when you live in Africa? He was really surprised, you see. 'You have an excellent French,' you see! Because that is new you see, **an African who speaks a good French**, **much better than they do**. It is a bit [too much? unbelievable?] you see. And also there is a teacher who said to me 'where did you learn your French? Your French is good.' And then I said that I learned there where I came from, in Africa. And then she said, she could not believe you see. You see; she said that all the time. (individual interview, French, bold added).

In spite of their 'good,' 'rich,' and 'excellent' French, continental African students are disproportionately streamed in the general, non-college-bound level. This disproportionate number is noted by the students themselves. Using his ethnographic gaze, Musa (M, 19, Djibouti) observed that, 'the majority of African students who are in Marie-Victorin take general level courses'. Although not all African students are in the general level, it is noteworthy that Musa introduced this observation to the discussion during my focus group interview with the boys without a question from me to this effect. Building on their memory of how schools functioned in Africa, African students were not fully aware of the difference between fundamental, general, and advanced level courses. In Africa, reflected the boys during my group interview with them, all students go to the same class to perform the same academic task:

A male voice: When you come, when you first arrive in the school, you don't know what general, advanced, fundamental courses mean. It is them [counselors and school administration] who give you your courses. You just want to go to school to study. They force you to take general courses [telephone rings]. You don't know what a general course means.

Musa: With general courses you can't go too far. (group interview, French)

On the other hand, not surprising but exceptionally disturbing, most African students are pushed towards sports. In their studies, Dei *et al.* (2000), James & Shadd (2001),

Mensah (2002), Nelson & Nelson (2004), and Yon (2000) have all observed the same phenomenon in Canada. Thinking about their counselor, the boys continue:

Mukhi: But still, there is Monsieur Raymond [a counselor] who even if you took five physical education [courses], he is going to give a sixth.

A male voice: *Yah, I don't know why.*

Mukhi: I don't know why like, to make you waste time or something. (group interview, French)

The girls, on their part, seem to believe that it is the boys who are streamed more in the lower levels; but because of lack of statistical information, I can neither confirm nor overrule this observation. Nonetheless, I made the same ethnographic observation. Boys' presence in general level is substantially higher than the girls'; close to 90% boys as opposed to less than 10% girls. When asked why, the girls hypothesized that that has to do with the exclusivity the boys make between sports and academic performance. Always according to the girls, becoming a successful athlete for the boys is seen in opposition to doing well academically. When one is doing one's homework successfully, one is seen as a 'nerd', a term connected to what Ogbu and Fordham (1986) call 'acting white'. The girls have seen these boys 'back-home' where they were 'first class' students. Something has happened that caused them to see academics in opposition to athleticism.

Awad: I have noticed that at the school, especially there is a very very strong majority [of the African students] who are present in the general level.

Asma: That I know why. You know why?

Awad: Why?

Asma: The majority are the boys. The majority are the boys, they want *basketball. Dream Team*, I love the *basketball* [a girl talking], Yes, wait.

Ossi: Yah, what does that mean?

Awad: Yes, yes, what does that mean?

Asma: They really want, they really could, I know these boys. They are really good. I remember in my country, they were really intelligent students.

Aziza: First class.

Asma: Yes, they know, they know. They know their academics, they know how to do this, how to do that. The problem is that if I start doing my homework, and I am a boy, this means I am a nerd. (group interview, French)

The gendered answer was exceptionally interesting here. When I asked the boys the same questions of why they dichotomize academics and athleticism, on the one hand, and why they are disproportionately in general, non-university-bound level courses, there was an unanimous response around their racialized experience, school counseling, or being refugees and living on their own as the reasons for their streaming and sense of alienation. Mukhi (M, 18. Djibouti) sums thus: 'Si tu allais faire un sondage, ça vient souvent de l'orientation ou des personnels' ['If you conduct a survey, the reason stems either from counseling or school personnel']. Taking the role of the African elder, Musa (M, 19, Djibouti) expressed the African students' agony concerning living on their own, working through the immigration papers and dealing with their social workers: 'The African students, they have a lot of problems. Here, the Canadians don't have problems, they have their parents, there is that. We, we have problems. You, you are late, she [the principal] sends you home. You go home for three or four days. We, we can't afford that because there is the immigration that calls us: "you have to come to see me today". You have to sign your check, things like that. There is back and forth. So, you have to go to the immigration, you have to go to, your, how do you call it, social worker?' (group interview, French)

Expanding on Mukhi's notion of school personnel and their role on student streaming in the general level, Musa continued his contention and elderly role: 'But the majority of the African students who are at Marie-Victorin, every time I see them, they take general level courses. I don't know why. "Why are you taking a general level course?" [explaining how he talks to other younger students] "It's Madame Robert [the principal] who gave it to me". "But, *gee* Madame Robert, [let her] go to hell, and take an advanced level course", I said' (group interview, French). In my field notes dated 5 February, 1996, I wrote, 'Musa came up to me requesting if I can offer an English-language tutoring course because he thinks that African students have problems with English'. What is significant in all of this is the fact that, first, unselfishly Musa is looking after other younger African students and, second, Musa's hopes are high that students can do much better. He knows they can do much better.

Consequently: Making Linkages and Conclusions

> Consequently, anyone should be able to declare under oath: I have only one language and it is not mine; my 'own' language is, for me, a language that cannot be assimilated. My language, the only one I hear myself speak and agree to speak, is the language of the other. (Derrida, 1996, p. 25)

At this point, I am sure my 'gentle reader' (as W. E. Du Bois would have called you), may be wondering if the connection was made between race, language, postcoloniality and authority of speaking. I certainly hope so. I have to admit though, tersely and speculatively, the paper is meant to be food for thought which sometimes is more provocative than a French three-course meal. My intent was to show how, given students' racialized bodily experience, students' speech was illegitimized despite its highly symbolic value. This is what I am referring to as 'symbolic violence'. This is closer to Foucault's (1979) notion of punishment, where the flesh is replaced with psychic experience. That is to say, one is left questioning not only one's speech and language but even one's subjectivity (not to say humanity). Derrida (1996) again—talking about himself as an Algerian-Jew who has nothing else but French to 'speak': 'In what language does one write memoirs when there has been no authorized [language]? How does one utter a worthwhile "I recall" when it is necessary to invent both one's language and one's "I"?' (p. 31).

African students, it seems, are left with the same question: Can we ever speak with authority? They are to invent both their language and their subjectivity. Here students were conscious of what is involved in this (re)invention, this *linguistic return*, where one spells one's own name and names oneself. It involves:

1) A full mastery of the rules of the game, what Bourdieu (1991) would call the 'market of exchange'. In any market, Bourdieu explains, there are currencies or capitals that are needed, there are rules on how to exchange these capitals, and he emphasized that the players along with the rules determine the value of capital. Hassan (M, 17, Djibouti) was fully aware of his role in the school as a 'market of exchange' and the capitals he possesses:

Hassan: So, there are all these structures and differences that you have to play with [*jouer avec*]. Such include the fact that you have to have the competency of playing with others, you have to know how to play with others. (individual interview, French)

Clearly, we do not all enter the game the same way, nor with the same capital. Nonetheless, 'gaming the system' or knowing how to play the game (i.e. system) is essential for Hassan.

2) Once aware of exclusion and discrimination, or knowing how the system works and how it excludes people, one is under the ethical responsibility to 'out' it, to talk about, and to turn it around to one's own benefit. To do so, however, one can work within the 'system,' from the inside. Hassan articulates it thus:

Hassan: To begin with, there are all these stereotypes about Black people. There is discrimination and all that, OK! The only way to combat discrimination is outing [or publicizing] discrimination. Why do we have all this [discrimination]? We have to play their games to our own benefit. We don't have to do the impossible you know. (individual interview, French)

Since one is working with the system, the 'game' if you like, one does not look for alternative markets and identities—as did the boys when they chose basketball as opposed to volleyball and Hip-Hop as opposed to dominant identities. Instead, one chooses to affirm one's identity from within the particular *authorized, legitimized* and *dominant* market and identity. Yet, Hassan is mindful of the fact that, in the case of Blackness, there are no guarantees even when one possesses the market's required credentials and capitals. That is why, he adds in the same interview, 'if you come in [for an interview] with a tie, or with a suit, with your PhD, they are *probably* going to accept you more than before'. By 'they,' one may argue, Hassan is referring to the power bloc, those who have a larger control of the market, and who set themselves as the norm, the yardstick against which all is measured. Given their benefit from the dominant structure, 'they' have little incentive and lucrative investment in imagining others differently, especially Black people, and in decentering themselves. For to do so is to question one's own power and in some cases give all or some of it up.[15]

3) As educators, finally, and especially as anti-racism workers, we need to deconstruct the social structure of domination, discrimination and negation. Otherwise, some are damned to struggle all their lives and find themselves in the periphery of power with

little or no resources and capitals. Thanks to these hegemonic structures, Black/African youth, by and large, find themselves putting in twice the effort to reach an average position (at least as defined by rules of the market). They carry the burden of 'proving' themselves, which means in some cases, they have to dichotomize, on the one hand, the school and the schooling process and, on the other, their personal desires, history, language and culture:

Hassan: But, I can prove it, I can do whatever I want to, dress[16] however I want to, have whatever I want to, and be myself. You do what you have to do, you have 100% in your classes, and you are well-liked by everyone. It is really deceiving, it is really deceiving that despite all of these, we have to prove what we have to everyone, or who we are, and the others don't. (individual interview, French)

One way to do so, Hassan contends, is to 'flip the script' as Hip-Hoppers love to say. That is, in place of failure one emphasizes pedagogies of hope, possibility and success; and talks about the unsaid, the absent, and the silenced:

Hassan: And the only way to do it [prove ourselves to others?] is not to conform or buy into stereotypical data like: 'Oh 50% of African youth had failed, they can't do it.' What has to happen is to show them that 50% had passed, not only to show them the 50% that failed. But they only see the part that failed, they don't look for the part that passed. We have to show them the part that passed, that's what we have to do; and this is one of my objectives: to do more in this regard, to leave a dream ... (individual interview, French)

To materialize this dream Hassan is placing the onus squarely on himself. He is not *Waiting for Godot*, as Samuel Beckett would have put it, to do something about the social situation he sees around him. He is willing to 'sacrifice' and take up that burden and he knows the price he has to pay. As the old African saying goes: if the spirit is high, the body can only feel its height/weight. That is to say, the body does not have too many choices when there is a will, since we are guided by our will not our bodies.

Hassan: I am sacrificing enormous amount of time. I have been in a chain of commit-tees for example, so there are always prices to pay. He who wants something, he is going to pay prices. You want something, you have to pay for it. You may have to prove something, your strength or whatever. Personally, I know I sacrificed: I missed evenings and there is my mother, anxious [*debordée*]. 'You come really late at night. Why do you stay after school, occupied with so much work?' she says, you see! (individual interview, French)

Hassan's spirit of sacrifice, personal responsibility, and vision are vital in the struggle against exclusion and discrimination. However, the institutional and systematic nature of racialization, discrimination and exclusion motivate us to think not only how discrimi-nation takes place, but also, significantly, how it tends to reproduce privilege, especially White privilege (Graham & Slee, 2008). As Peggy McIntosh (1998) argues, for the longest time we tend to think about discrimination and racism and their effects on the victim. We need, she contends, to think about discrimination and racism as technologies of power that end up reproducing privileges, ways of thinking, being and speaking. To conclude, Hassan's mother is absolutely right in asking, 'Why do you personally, my son, sacrifice so much?' What both Hassan and his mother need to ask as well is: 'Why do we as African and Black people have to prove who we are and what we have to anyone?' In an Obama-era, this latter question seems more than ever urgent since the silenced are yet to speak, and to speak with authority. They love but their love is yet to be heard as a creative margin for a radical pedagogy of hope, love and desire.

Notes

1. To clarify, there are two varieties of French that are talked about here: *français de France* and *français canadien.* I refer to the former as *'français parisien'* (Parisian French) and the latter as *'français de souche'* (original or old French; a term used both in Quebec and Ontario to refer to 'original' French settlers and their language). In the Franco-Ontarian context, the Parisian French is highly valued whereas *français de souche,* the variety spoken by most Franco-Ontarian schoolteachers, is both marginalized and discouraged. For further discussion, see the section in this article titled: 'Then, Who Owns Language?' For now, however, one may argue that we are dealing with 'racialized class conflict' where classism and racism are expressed through linguicism, that is, in the variety spoken and valued. Interestingly enough, Franco-Ontarian teachers speak *français de souche,* which they in turn devalued. This is a phenomenon of cognitive dissidence, if not a schizophronic moment; one where one devalues what one speaks. However, when continental African youth arrived to the school with their *français international* (which I am provocatively calling *français parisien*), as we shall see, they are told: 'That's just unbelievable!'

2. Linda Graham and Roger Slee (2008) show a similar process taking place in Australia, where White Australians do not seem to fall under the umbrella of *deceptive fluency;* only the Other, it seems, are placed outside what they call 'ghostly center' (p. 284). In his book, *White by Law,* Ian Haney-Lopez (2006) addresses a similar notion which he calls 'rule of common knowledge'. Emerging in the 1930s-50s in the United States, the *rule of common knowledge* was used to preclude people of Asian descent from immigrating to the US, who were forced to argue in the courts that they were either 'White' or 'of African descent'. All the cases heard took the former tack, Haney-Lopez explains, partly because it was during Jim Crow segregation. In attempting to argue that Asians were White (a color, not a geographic or biological origin), those who called skilled anthropologists to testify on their behalf lost their bid to immigrate because the courts applied what was called the rule of common knowledge, in stating that, even if you are scientifically White, we all know that you are not what common knowledge tells us is White, so for that reason you can not come into the country. Clearly, the so-called truth of Western science is subverted in the service of racist perception. To finish, I owe much of this text and the notion of the rule of common knowledge to one of the reviewers of this article.

3. In reality, 'language' is and has always been plural. For Derrida (1996), the French language, for example, always had (and still has) multiple speakers, accents and daily expressions. However, it was standardized as it was written, thus attempting to eliminate its multiplicity. This standardization, Derrida argues, is part of a colonial project, where even people within France who spoke a variety of French were brought into the project of the Republic, which is assumed to have one language, one accent and one voice.

4. See Mishra, 2005 for a comprehensive recent discussion of the term 'post-colonial'.

5. Quebec, as some might know, is a monolingual French-only province; and New Brunswick is the only bilingual French-English province. The rest of Canada is English-language speaking. This may be confusing to some since Canada is a bilingual country. Here, when Canada declares itself a bilingual country, this is usually in reference to the languages used by the federal government in its formal functioning. It does not mean that every province or every Canadian is bilingual. On its part, however, the federal government spends a substantial amount of money to make Canadians bilingual or at least functional in both official languages. For the purpose of this

paper, two things are noteworthy: 1) more French speakers become bilingual (which puts them at a greater advantage when it comes to federal government jobs) and 2) for Franco-Ontarians, given the omnipresence of English in Ontario, this endangers the French language because by the second or third generation they become English-dominant speakers. That is, they tend to speak and be more functional in English than French and therefore their French-language schooling is marginalised if not put off in favor of the English language.

6. The detailed analysis and discussion of these features by Mougeon and Beniak (1991) has been my reference in this area.

7. For Franco-Ontarians, the French language (not to say France itself) is still their highly prized symbolic capital. Even though they may speak it little and in many cases, not at all, that identity (along with its language) is by and large *the* claimed identity. Put simply, though Franco-Ontarians are largely 'hyphened' and fluent in French and English, they will still claim French as their determining identity and language.

8. When it comes to Franco-Ontarians, notions of coloniality, postcoloniality and oppression are exceptionally complicated. Franco-Ontarians are a French-speaking minority in Ontario. They struggle as much as any minority does, and historically has been prevented from teaching their language or opening French-language schools (Heller, 2006). Yet, presently they have unearned privileges that others have to struggle either for or against: Whiteness, language, (institutionalized) power, school and social institutions, and above all the protection of the state. Because of these privileges, the population of my research (continental francophone Africans) finds itself a minority within a minority. Put simply, Franco-Ontarians do feel that their language variety is not as valued as *le français parisien* or *français de France*, but they ally themselves with this privileged symbolic capital by naming themselves: *Français de souche* [original or old French], hence creating complex situation where the oppressed or dispossessed can be an oppressor or a possessor, where the very notion of oppression and exclusion is no longer a unidimensional idea.

9. For Simon and Dippo (1986, p. 195), *critical ethnographic research* is a set of activities situated within a project that seeks and works its way towards social transformation. This project is political as well as pedagogical, and who the researcher is and what his or her racial, gender, and class embodiments are necessarily govern the research questions and findings. The project, then, according to Simon and Dippo, is 'an activity determined both by real and present conditions, *and* certain conditions still to come which it is trying to bring into being' (p. 196). The assumption underpinning my project was based on the assertion that Canadian society is 'inequitably structured and dominated by a hegemonic culture that suppresses a consideration and understanding of why things are the way they are and what must be done for things to be otherwise' (p. 196).

10. Sandra Harding (1987) showed that the claim to objectivity in research has taxed both the research process as well as the research outcome. She thus called for a subjective notion of research, where the researcher and the questions she asks are always subjective; that is, they mean something to the researcher. We end up reading the data we collect through a specific lens. This researcher therefore has always declared himself an organic part of his research. Though there was quite a considerable overlap between the mid-1990s and 2007 findings, for the sake of clarity, the focus for this paper will be on the 1990s findings.

11. To deal with issues of race and racism is to enter the chilling space of discomfort. Not to affect the student-teacher relationship, I decided not to speak with the teachers. But, elsewhere (Ibrahim, in press) I juxtaposed student narratives by talking to the only Black teacher at the school, who ended up leaving the school after a short time there. He expanded and confirmed student stories of racialization and exclusion. He had plenty of stories himself. It is worth noting here that, when I am referring to teachers' 'experiential knowledge' (or the lack thereof), I am invoking both the need for further multicultural sensitivity, especially within teacher education programs, and real life experience. Based on my teaching experience in French-language teacher education programs, I believe real life experience would be my choice in creating a higher level of multi/cultural/lingual awareness.

12. Each student pseudonym is followed by their gender, age and country of origin. I will also indicate whether the interview is individual or group or in French or English.

13. Violence is, by definition, violent, no matter the shape or form. In Bourdieu's (1991) language, however, 'symbolic violence' is no less violence or violent. It is 'symbolic' only in that it works at the psychic and intangible level. It is conceived in relation (not in opposition) to material and bodily violence. The two forms of violence, for Bourdieu, are complementary, go hand in hand, and can/do converge one into the other. (See also his notion of 'symbolic' and 'material' capital.)

14. In Ontario, there are two streams: general and academic. The former leads students either to vocation schools or community colleges, whereas the latter leads to university studies. Despite their language mastery, most African students find themselves in general level, as we shall see, which itself becomes part of their experience with the process of racialization.

15. Using Derrida's notion of 'play', Graham and Slee (2008) offer an interesting analysis on how the center/margin work. One of their main arguments is that, 'there *is no* centre but instead an *absence* of centre for which infinite substitutions are made, for there is no natural essence, origin or "invariable presence" ... , supporting a legitimate claim to centre' (p. 284). We thus end up creating, what Graham and Slee call, discursive 'ghostly centers'; ones where there is a 'substitution of sign, substituting presence (i.e. singularity/normality/whiteness/ablebodiedness and so on) for absence (multiplicity/diversity)' (p. 284). Here, the authors add, 'privilege and position at centre is dependent upon the subjection and marginalisation of the Other,' and the 'maintenance of positions of power through discursive dividing practices as rhetorical strategies ... that (re)secure domination and privilege results in the reinstatement of the politic of the powerful' (p. 284). I am also mindful that Hassan may have left a sense of the classic 'internalized racism', which goes something like this: If I can just be good enough, you will see I am like you, so embrace me! Hassan was too self-conscious and troubled this notion elsewhere (see Ibrahim, 2009).

16. Most of the time, Hassan had on elegant yet baggy clothes, bordering on Hip-Hop and dominant/ 'regular' clothes. Hassan was one of the most popular and elegant students at the school. He was the student Council President for two years and one of the most articulate students at the school. He was invited many times to school board meetings to address African youth concerns.

References

Althusser, L. (1971) *Lenin and Philosophy* (London, New Left Books).

Bhabha, H. (1994) *The Location of Culture* (London & New York, Routledge).

Bourdieu, P. (1991) *Language and Symbolic Power* (Cambridge, MA, Harvard University Press).

Dei, G., James, I., Karumanchery, L., James-Wilson, S. & Zine, J. (2000) *Removing the Margins: The challenges and possibilities of inclusive schooling* (Toronto, Canadian Scholars' Press).

Deleuze, G. & Guattari, F. (1994) *What is Philosophy?* (London, Verso).

Derrida, J. (1996) *Monolingualism of the Other, or, The Prosthesis of Origin* (Stanford, CA, Stanford University Press).

Derrida, J. (2000) *Of Hospitality* (Stanford, CA, Stanford University Press).

Foucault, M. (1979) *Discipline and Punish: The birth of the prison* (New York, Vintage Books).

Freire, P. (2000) *Pedagogy of the Oppressed* (New York, Continuum).

Glissant, E. (1981) *Le discours antillais* (Paris, Seuil).

Graham, L. & Slee, R. (2008) An Illusory Interiority: Interrogating the discourse/s of inclusion, *Educational Philosophy and Theory*, 40:2, pp. 277–294.

Haney-Lopez, I. (2006) *White by Law: The legal construction of race* (New York, New York University Press).

Harding, S. (1987) Is There a Feminist Method?, in: S. Harding (ed.), *Feminism and Methodology* (Bloomington, IN, Indiana University Press), pp. 1–14.

Heller, M. (1994) *Crosswords: Language, education and ethnicity in French Ontario* (Berlin and New York, Mouton de Gruyter).

Heller, M. (2006) *Linguistic Minorities and Modernity: A sociolinguistic ethnography* (London, Continuum).

Heller, M. (with the collaboration of Campbell, M., Dalley, P. & Patrick, D.) (1999) *Linguistic Minorities and Modernity: A sociolinguistic ethnography* (London & New York, Longman).

Ibrahim, A. (1999) Becoming Black: Rap and hip hop, race, gender, identity, and the politics of ESL learning, *TESOL Quarterly*, 33:3, pp. 349–369.

Ibrahim, A. (2004) One is not Born Black: Becoming and the phenomenon(ology) of race, *Philosophical Studies in Education*, 35, pp. 89–97.

Ibrahim, A. (2005) The Question of the Question is the Foreigner: Towards an economy of hospitality, *Journal of Curriculum Theorizing*, 21:2, pp. 149–162.

Ibrahim, A. (2008) The New *Flâneur*: Subaltern cultural studies, African youth in Canada, and the semiology of in-betweenness, *Cultural Studies*, 22:2, pp. 234–253.

Ibrahim, A. (2009) Operating Under Erasure: Race/language/identity, in: A. Ryuko & A. Lin (eds), *Race, Language and Identity* (London & New York, Routledge), pp. 176–194.

Ibrahim, A. (in press) '*Hey, Whassup Homeboy?' Becoming Black: Hip-hop culture and language, race, performativity, and the politics of identity in high school* (Toronto, University of Toronto Press).

James, C. & Shadd, A. (2001) *Talking about Identity: Encounters in race, ethnicity, and language* (Toronto, Between the Lines).

McIntosh, P. (1998) White Privilege: Unpacking the invisible knapsack, in: P. Rothenberg (ed.), *Race, Class, and Gender in the United States* (New York, St. Martin's Press), pp. 165–169.

Mensah, J. (2002) *Black Canadians: History, experiences, social conditions* (Halifax, Fernwood).

Mishra, V. (2005) What was Postcolonialism, *New Literary History*, 36:3, pp. 102–119.

Mougeon, R. & Beniak, E. (1989) *Le Français Canadien Parlé Hors Québec: Aperçu Sociolinguistique* (Québec, Presses de l'Université Laval).

Mougeon, R. & Beniak, E. (1991) *Linguistic Consequences of Language Contact and Restriction: The case of French in Ontario, Canada* (Oxford, Oxford University Press).

Nelson, C. & Nelson, C. (Eds.) (2004) *Racism Eh? A critical inter-disciplinary anthology on race in the Canadian context* (Toronto, Captus University Press).

Ogbu, J. & Fordham, S. (1986) Black Students' School Success: Coping with the 'burden of acting white', *The Urban Review*, 18:3, pp. 98–116.

Rampton, B. (1995) *Crossing: Language and ethnicity among adolescents* (London & New York, Longman).

Salih, T. (1991) *Season of Migration to the North* (Nairobi, Heinemann).

Simon, R. I. & Dippo, D. (1986) On Critical Ethnography Work, *Anthropology & Education Quarterly*, 17, pp. 195–202.

Spivak, G. (1999) *A Critique of Postcolonial Reason: Toward a history of the vanishing present* (Cambridge, MA, Harvard University Press).

StatCan.gc.ca (2008) Statistics Canada Website.

Todd, S. (2003) *Learning from the Other: Levinas, psychoanalysis, and ethical possibilities in education* (Albany, NY, State University of New York Press).

Winant, H. (2004) *The New Politics of Race: Globalism, difference, justice* (Minneapolis, MN, University of Minnesota Press).

Yon, D. (2000) *Elusive Culture: Schooling, race, and identity in global times* (Albany, NY, State University of New York Press).

6

Romantic Agrarianism and Movement Education in the United States: Examining the discursive politics of learning disability science

SCOT DANFORTH

The current American system of special education began in 1975 with the passage of Public Law 94–142, the Education for Handicapped Children Act, requiring that all school districts in the United States provide an education for children with disabilities. Among other provisions, this created a categorical system of qualification for educational services, including what has become the disability category with the highest prevalence, learning disability.

Not long after the enactment of P.L. 94–142, researchers started to notice that students with learning disabilities in the public schools tended to come from upper middle class economic backgrounds. Gelb and Mizokawa (1986) analyzed the relationships between a range of social demographic variables and the special education categories of mental retardation and learning disability. In direct contrast to mental retardation, they found that 'LD was positively associated with income and educational cost, and negatively associated with poverty and public aid' (Gelb & Mizokawa, 1986, p. 551). Similarly, Sleeter's (1986, p. 50) analysis of the research concluded that 'the literature offers additional evidence that students in LD classes were overwhelmingly white and middle class during the category's first 10 years.' Today it is commonly understood that the learning disability label is primarily 'reserved for middle-class children' in the American public schools (Loewenstein, 2004, p. 286; e.g. Osmond, 1995).

But the complexity of the relationship between learning disability, social class, and race goes beyond this common notion. Complicating the widely-accepted conflation of learning disability with middle class, white students is recent evidence of the disproportionate representation of African-Americans in the category. Parrish (2002) found that while African-Americans were most dramatically overrepresented in the categories of emotional disturbance and mental retardation, a lesser degree of racial disproportionally existed in the learning disability classification. In Connor's (2008) analysis of the special education experiences of adolescents in the New York public schools, race, class, and LD status were deeply entangled fonts of political meaning leading to frequent stigmatization and exclusion from general education classrooms. While it has become a common truism

The Power In/Of Language, First Edition. Edited by David R. Cole and Linda J. Graham.
Chapters © 2012 The Authors. Book compilation © 2012 Philosophy of Education Society of Australasia.
Published 2012 by Blackwell Publishing Ltd.

among American special educators that the learning disability construct primarily pertains to upper middle class students, this analysis will reveal directly contrary historical roots. The discourse of learning disability science that gained public prominence in the 1960s and 1970s as an explanation for a specific constellation of behavioral and learning issues was fully steeped in a rhetoric of the educational defects of lower or working class children. This article will explore the deficit-based characterizations of lower social class families, children, and neighborhoods in the history of the scientific discourse that built the learning disability construct, illuminating an often overlooked discursive connection between lower class status and learning disability.

The learning disability construct that came to serve as the basis for a public school category was not built by public school personnel or even educational researchers studying the American schools. It originated in the research of psychologists and neurologists who had little or no public school experience, who worked chiefly in institutions for children with mental retardation and small psycho-educational clinics providing treatments for childhood learning and behavioral difficulties. By the time it was appropriated into federal education legislation in the late 1960s and early 1970s, the learning disability construct crafted over many decades by psychologists and physicians included a strong theory of the relationship between social class and learning problems. Stated briefly, the foundational researchers who crafted a discourse of learning disability in an attempt to explain a range of learning and behavioral problems of childhood incorporated specific understandings about lower class families, neighborhoods, and lifestyles within that construct. What became commonly known as an upper middle class phenomenon in the public schools after 1975, to the contrary, originated as a psychological construct that bound together learning difficulties, lower social class, and urban family living (Danforth, 2009; Sleeter, 1986).

The educational literature examining the role of social class in the history of the science of learning disabilities construct is very thin. The only deep analysis has been provided by James Carrier (1986), notably a researcher working outside of the United States. Carrier (1986, p. 46) described the 1960s rise of learning disability theory and cultural deprivation theory as 'parallel' and ostensibly unrelated research developments that became 'intertwined'. Cultural deprivation theory posited a wide range of factors, including poor health, inadequate housing, unemployment, 'broken' families, childrearing practices, crime, and lower class cultural styles of behavior and language, as causes for low educational achievement among children living in urban poverty. This complex of lower class insults upon the minds of young children led to:

> ... a cyclical relationship with inadequate cognitive development. Deprivation hinders the mental development of the individual, who becomes inadequate and perpetuates the deprived environs, so that when the inadequate person raises a family, the cycle begins anew. (Carrier, 1986, p. 47)

Cultural deprivation theory offered what appeared to be a total explanation for what was understood at the time as a familial cycle of economic poverty.

Researchers in the new field of learning disabilities in the 1960s and early 1970s appropriated a discourse of cultural deprivation into their analyses of learning problems based in cognition and neurology (Ford, 1971; Hallahan, 1970; Hallahan & Cruickshank, 1973). This discourse created a dynamic interplay between social and physical environs and mental character and capability. Defects in the home environment were described as imprinting disorders within the neuropsychology of developing children. One study concluded that 'poverty creates a milieu for the development of childhood learning disorders' (Kappelmann, Kaplan & Ganter, 1969, p. 267). Epidemiologists repeatedly asserted that neurological defects such as minimal brain dysfunction occurred with higher frequency among low income children (Alley, Solomons & Opitz, 1971; Amante, Margules, Hartmann, Storey & Weeber, 1970; Tarnopol, 1970). This supported the general conclusion that the 'socio-cultural inadequacies of the urban ghetto present an environment [that is] formidable and pathologic' (Kappelmann, Kaplan & Ganter, 1969, p. 262).

Special education researcher Daniel Hallahan described low income children as behaviorally indistinguishable from children with hyperactivity and learning disabilities. He theorized that 'the distracting nature of the disadvantaged child's disordered environment' (Hallahan, 1970, p. 5) yielded a behavioral symptomatology similar to that of children with brain injuries. Lower class children 'possess very short attention spans and are easily distracted from the task at hand' (Hallahan, 1970, p. 5). They 'have an impulsive rather than a reflective cognitive style' marked by a 'short attention span, distractibility, figure-ground problems, hyperactivity, and motor disinhibition' (Hallahan, 1970, pp. 5–6). These deficit symptoms were caused by 'the culture of poverty', including 'environmental factors such as overcrowding, maternal and paternal deprivation, undifferentiated noise, inferior health and educational services, and maladaptive, if not utterly pathological, patterns of child-rearing' (Hallahan & Cruickshank, 1973, p. 41).

Since the important work of Carrier over two decades ago, little serious historical scholarship has examined the utilization of a discourse of cultural deprivation by the learning disabilities researchers. This historical analysis addresses that lacuna within the educational literature. The purpose of this article is to provide an historical investigation of the discourse of cultural deficit among the foundational researchers in the post-World War Two era who built the empirical and theoretical basis for the learning disability. This article focuses on the interaction of social class, urban living, and neuropsychology in the learning disability discourse among a specific subset of the new American field of learning disabilities of the 1960s and early 1970s— the movement educators.

By the late 1960s, two strands of psychological research, each with different theoretical emphases, had developed the contours and content of the basic learning disability construct. One, led by prominent researchers such as Samuel A. Kirk and Helmer R. Myklebust, framed learning problems as psychological difficulties in the utilization of spoken and written language. That strand, at least in the prominent work of Sam Kirk, actively employed concepts of cultural deprivation steeped in social class politics in framing the learning disabled child (see Danforth, 2009). This paper focuses primarily on the equally important second tradition called movement education (also known as perceptual motor training), a line of learning disability science that emphasized the young child's development of sensory motor and perceptual skills based within the central nervous system. The movement educators understood the neurological system of the brain injured child to be, at the physiological level, misperceiving environmental stimuli and therefore operating ineffectively in the world. Well-known figures such as Raymond Barsch, Marianne Frostig, Newell C. Kephart, and Gerald N. Getman developed clinical programs for the treatment of sensory motor disturbances. They prescribed a carefully-designed regimen of movement activities and perceptual development tasks to prepare the child's neurological apparatus for academic instruction.

This paper examines the extensive writings of leading learning disability researchers Newell Kephart and Marianne Frostig to illuminate how they blended the rhetoric of cultural deprivation with a discourse of scientific neuropsychology. In their articulation, the problem of learning disability was intimately connected to modernity, urban living, and the cultural lifestyles of lower class urban families. This exploration of their research and practical writings offers a focused glimpse into the politics of class, place, and history that operated within the ideological discourse sustaining the science of learning disabilities. My primary focus is the writings of movement educators, a prominent group of researchers who employed physical training techniques designed to enhance child sensorimotor development. Integrated within that approach to neurological treatment was a pastoral discourse that lamented the plight of the lower class child of the modern city.

Movement Education

During the 1960s and 1970s, educators and psychologists across America ran programs of movement education to prevent and treat problems of academic learning. Movement education involved a curriculum of formal physical training designed to develop the child's sensory-motor perception, to improve the child's ability to utilize sensory input (primarily but not exclusively visual) as a neurological prerequisite to standard forms of school learning. Across the United States, preschools, kindergartens, elementary schools, and special schools for struggling learners employed perceptual development screening and training programs. The theoretical accounts and programmatic tools were generated by a prominent group of educational therapists, most notably Kephart, Frostig, Getman, and Barsch, leading to the national popularization of perceptual-motor training for young children (Barsch, 1965; Barsch, 1968; Reinhold, 1975; Walmsley, 1966; Walker, 1975)

For example, at the Longfellow School in Madison, Wisconsin, young children engaged in a program of physical activities that included hopping, jumping rope, walking on rails, rhythmic walking (to a metronome), bouncing on a trampoline, and copying shapes on a chalkboard (Barsch, 1965; 1968). Children with severe reading problems attending the Reading Research Unit in Lexington, Massachusetts spent 'an hour a day on rhythmic-motor exercises to learn to control their bodies in a coordinated way. They (were) taught to skip rope, walk a rail and to bounce a ball to music' (Walmsley, 1966, p. E3). Elementary schools in Chicago Ridge, Illinois, offered first and second graders a sensory-motor development curriculum involving, for instance, walking a wooden balance beam. The program was designed to enhance language development (Walker, 1975, p. S5).

'You must first develop the skills that underlie reading', explained Frances McGlannon, a private school director in Miami, Florida. The perceptual development activities at the McGlannon School included having blindfolded students identify shapes by feeling objects with their hands. At both the McGlannon School and at the Dewitt Reading Clinic in San Rafael, California, motor skills activities involved walking on a balance beam as well as other coordination and balance exercises (Reinhold, 1975, p. 51)

Public schools in Muncie, Indiana, Trumbull, Connecticut, Ramapo, New York, Salisbury, North Carolina, Newton, Massachusetts, and Richardson, Texas put kinder-garten students through an intensive series of tests designed to catch early learning problems. Educators guided the young children through a range of important screening and development activities: walking on stilts, drawing lines between two points on a chalk board, 'walking on balance beams, drawing circles, listening to recorded tones, repeating numbers and words, and drawing pictures of people' (Reinhold, 1975, p. 51). Movement education, as a developmental preparation for academic learning and a curative for learning problems, was a national phenomenon. Focusing explicitly on helping individual children succeed in school, it seemed to be a distinctly apolitical professional discourse of diagnosis and remediation.

Romantic Agrarianism and Neurology

Steady and consistent throughout the writings of Newell Kephart and Marianne Frostig was pathos-filled rhetoric of pastoral longing. Their extensive social theory sounded an alarm of modern, urban-industrial despair and romanticized a rural redemption in the days of old. Historians have captured this tradition in a variety of ways that envisage a range of intellectual and political possibilities. Danbom (1991, p. 1) uses the term 'romantic agrarianism' to describe an intellectual direction 'following the path trod by Thoreau [to] emphasize the moral, emotional, and spiritual benefits agriculture and rural life convey to the individual'. Buell (1995) illuminates a tradition of 'pastoral ideology,' (p. 31) the formidable cultural challenge of crafting and recrafting 'the notion of nature as refuge from complexity' (p. 40).

Leo Marx (1964) articulates a particular American incarnation of 'romantic pastoral-ism' (p. 229) as an effort to craft social stasis within a historical milieu marked by rapid technological change accompanied by a lived experience of uncertainty and liminality. Pastoralism is 'that essential habit of mind,' (Marx, 1992, p. 209) a way of interpreting the world and one's place in it that facilitates extraordinary mobility 'between the imperatives of nature and culture, between the dangers and deprivations of the unde-veloped environment [wild nature] and the excessive constraints of civilization' (Marx, 1992, p. 212). Faced with a vulnerability of self and community in the rapid change of modern life, the pastoral tradition of literature and thought fashioned 'the idea of an ordered and happier past set against the disturbance and disorder of the present' (Williams, 1973, p. 45). It simultaneously offered a hyper-romantic literary vision, an infeasible 'poetry of nostalgia for the unrecoverable', (Rosand, 1992, p. 161) and an eminently practicable prescription for seeking peaceful stability in the midst of an experience of modern alienation.

The romantic agrarian rhetoric of the movement educators employed an array of recurring images that mourned the lost virtues of old time, rural living and vilified an urbanized, modern lifestyle as physically and psychologically unhealthy for children. The pastoral ideal served as an idyllic contrast to urban environments viewed as being noxious and delivering a toxic array of insults—physical, cultural, linguistic, and psychological—to the developing bodies and minds of young people. The causes of learning difficulties and often concurrent socioemotional problems in children were traced to a modern lifestyle cultivated in America's cities.

In the writings of the movement educators, a hyperbolic impression of the American city in moral crisis served as an historical image of the development of 20th century industrial-technological lifestyle. America had undergone an unfortunate shift from the wholesomeness and simplicity of face-to-face small towns to the anxiety and deperson-alization of mechanized metropolises. Country comfort and authenticity had succumbed to a harried modernity in which individuals lost meaningful contact with themselves and their neighbors.

The romantic agrarianism of Kephart and Frostig was motivated by their view that the problematic children they were seeing in their own clinical work—Frostig working in Los Angeles and Kephart in Indiana and Colorado—were individual examples of the dam-aging effects of metropolitan, technological culture. In their clinical writing, the modern, urban lifestyle in the post-World War Two era had caused a host of problems in the learning and behavior of young children. The public schools had little choice but to respond with programs of instruction of prophylactic and curative purpose.

> Studies of urban living show that it is an added unavoidable responsibility of the school to help counteract the destructive effects of urban living and to help children recover from unhappy experiences caused by the unrest, the anxiety, and the adverse conditions of their lives. (Frostig & Maslow, 1970, p. 15)

The extensive neurosensory and movement education curricula developed by Kephart and Frostig were necessary educational efforts to counteract the negative effects of modern life, to 'provide a partial substitute for this loss' (Frostig & Maslow, 1973, p. 83).

Physical Limitation

> Some of the simple yet quite valuable activities of a rural childhood are fast disappearing from the American scene ... Not too many years ago, virtually every child used to balance himself walking on a railroad track or on top of a wooden fence; most of today's children have missed this experience. (Radler & Kephart, 1960, p. 76)

The detrimental nature of city living was construed as an outgrowth of the physical environment itself. The confined physical spaces of pavement, brick, and high-rise steel placed young bodies into unhealthy environmental situations of restrictiveness and danger. To Kephart, the young child learned through experimentation, gradually accu-mulating adaptive behaviors through exploratory interactions of the child with the environment. Required for such learning exploration was an environment that allowed for free and open play. What growing children needed for healthy learning were 'ladders to climb, fences to walk, horses to ride,' (Kephart, 1960, p. 16)—perhaps the common activities of Kephart's childhood in rural Colorado—features of farm life that are nonexistent in the modern, urban setting. His articulation of this childhood need provides an illuminative example of the movement educators' frequent counter-positioning of past and present, rural and urban, preindustrial and postindustrial, safe and dangerous.

> If the children of the past wanted to experiment with locomotion, they climbed on the family horse and he took care of them. The modern automobile is possessed of no such concern for the safety of our children. If children of the past wanted to see what it was like to run as fast as they could, they ran. But the children of today cannot run far in a modern apartment or even a city lot, and they cannot run out of the yard because of traffic. (Kephart, 1960, p. 16)

The romanticized character of a loyal family horse that genuinely cared for young children was an inviting pastoral symbol that allowed Kephart to gloss over the harsher realities and common hazards experienced by rural children interacting with farm animals and agricultural machinery. In contrast to the effusive warmth of the protective pony, urban life was physically restrictive, dangerous, and uncaring. The city didn't care for children.

Frostig similarly described urban living, often through focusing on the unfortunate predicament of the city child, as lacking the necessary opportunities for natural physical play, exploration, and learning. Like Kephart, her point of nostalgic, normative reference was the open rural landscape.

> Space is an important cue for movement; open space invites children to move. The sight of a wet, sandy beach sets them skipping; a grassy slope incites them [children] to slide and roll, to romp, to run. (Frostig & Maslow, 1970, p. 74)

Frostig's naturalistic holism endowed rural geographic features with preternatural capacities supporting healthy child development. She described an essential sympathy between two aspects of nature, the prairies and hillsides of the rural landscape and the natural development of the child. The landscape is a protagonist who 'invites' and 'incites' specific kinds of movement that are a 'necessity for both adequate physical and healthy psychological development' (Frostig & Maslow, 1970, p. 83). Through 'valuable contact with nature,' (Frostig & Maslow, 1970, p. 155) children develop the neurological and physiological abilities necessary for competent academic learning.

In sharp contrast, Frostig wrote that 'crowded urban conditions and modern conveniences often permit little opportunity for children to move about freely' (Frostig & Maslow, 1970, p. 83). The activities and opportunities necessary 'to build up the sensorimotor skills which are required by the more complex activities of reading, writing, and arithmetic' (Kephart, 1960, p. 16) are lacking in urban homes and neighborhoods. 'The urban child is deprived of the natural exercise needed for him to become aware of his body and the relationship of his body to the environment' (Frostig & Maslow, 1973, p. 160).

Central to this expression was the difference between country play and city play, between the kinds of natural movements available to rural children and the kinds of unnatural motor activities engaged in by urban youth. Frostig explained this at length:

> Imagine children playing in the country. For them, the landscape comprises, in effect, the equivalent of a beautifully equipped gymnasium. There are trees to

climb, a slope to roll down, a lawn to run on, a fallen tree for balancing, a ditch to jump over, a branch to swing on, and a rock to throw. Contrast this picture with a city schoolroom ... The children sit for hours, until at last there may be a session of physical education; and even then the children may spend most of that time standing still, waiting their turn for various activities. (Frostig & Maslow, 1973, p. 160)

This concept derived from a Thoreau-inspired understanding of the correct relationship between the physiology of the child and the surrounding physical environment. Nature— the neurophysiological body—collaborated in nurturing empathy with nature in the woods, streams, and fields. Nature within the child clashed in destructive antipathy with the man-made artifice of the metropolis.

Expansion of Constraints

The insidious problem of restriction in urban life involved not only physical limitation but also a series of related emotional, social, cognitive, and linguistic constraints. The movement educators extrapolated a concept of how a limited physical space bound bodily movement and hampered learning growth into an extensive assortment of harmful notions detailing how modern, urban environments yield 'certain deprivations of experience' (Kephart, 1968, p. 13) that stifle the human condition. The problem of restrictiveness that began with the body migrated into multiple aspects of city life and the damaged urban child in numerous ways.

Kephart professed that the external world perceived by the child becomes the basis for the internal operations of ideation and memory. Through learning in the early years, a child develops an ability to integrate the dominant visual input with other sensory data to fabricate a complex spatioenvironmental scheme, a 'space structure' consisting 'of the interrelationships between all the objects in our space world' (Kephart, 1956, p. 14). This space structure, a neurologically based achievement of perception, is the basis for all cognitive activity. Kephart utilized a filing cabinet metaphor involving systems of index-ing and multiple drawers of categorized concepts to expound his version of cognition. The work of storing and retrieving ideas consisted of file work within an internal, mental space developed as an analog to the external, perceptual space of perception. In this way, not only does good perception lead to good cognition. Open and unconfined external space leads to unrestricted and useful internal space.

> The space structure which the child builds through the developmental pro-cesses which we have described determines the universe in which he will live the rest of his life. If his space structure is restricted he will live in a small and restricted universe. If, on the other hand, his space structure is broad and inclusive and permits adequate freedom of operation, he will live in a broad and inclusive universe. (Kephart, 1956, p. 16)

Kephart translated a concept of limitation from objective space to perceived space to cognitive operations of thought and memory. Early childhood experiences in constricted physical environments yield under-differentiated perceptual capacities, deficiencies in the child's spatial understanding of the physical world. Because cognition is essentially an outgrowth of perception, these spatial deficiencies become the basis for inadequate forms of conceptualization and memory. The result is that children raised in confined, urban homes and neighborhoods end up struggling in small and restricted mental universes.

While Kephart's words rarely wandered far from a scientific rhetoric of neurological impairment, Frostig's arguments were more sweeping and ostensibly less systematic. By her account, the 'increasing urbanization of life in the United States' (Frostig, 1955, p. 2) had created an entire generation of American children with 'lags in their development,' including 'the culturally deprived child, the slow-learning child, and the neurologically handicapped child' (Frostig & Maslow, 1970, p. 84). Frostig theorized that a deficiency of proper bodily movement experiences in childhood caused a wide range of learning, social, and emotional difficulties (Frostig, 1976).

Frostig further maintained that children growing up in the cramped physical spaces of modern life suffered from 'an all-pervading anxiety' (Frostig, 1976, p. 194), a generalized psychophysiological ennui. 'The first handicap resulting from lack of movement is a depreciated joy of living' (Frostig & Maslow, 1973, p. 160). What is lost in an environment of physical constraint 'is not only physical but mental and spiritual' (Frostig & Maslow, 1970, p. 38).

In her 1955 doctoral dissertation, she lamented 'the decreasing influence of religion upon the character formation of children' (Frostig, 1955, p. 2). While her later publications did not mention religion, she described an America tumbling down a cultural decline of powerful psychological and moral dimensions. She depicted the modern era as a 'time of anxiety and unrest, or noise and overcrowding in our cities' (Frostig & Maslow, 1973, p. 145), a period when 'our emotional climate is uncomfortable, including the emotional climate in which millions of children grow up' (Frostig & Maslow, 1973, p. 160). While contact with the goodness of the natural earth seemingly delivered proper health and development to the bodies of children, living in the concrete landscape of the cities scarred children with the cultural toxins of modernity.

The defective neurological and emotional health of modern children, in particular urban children, as outlined within the agrarian discourse of Kephart and Frostig, provided evidence of far-reaching and disastrous changes in the quality of home and neighborhood environments. Over many decades, America had gradually traded the beauty, virtue, and freedom of the natural rural setting for blighted urban environments that failed to support the developing organism. Further, American culture had deteriorated with the loss of the rural landscape. In the lives of most children, trees had been replaced by technology and running brooks by household machines. A consciousness closely allied with nature had been supplanted by a mechanized mindset that was inhospitable to nature.

Technological Culture

The agrarianism of the movement educators involved a general state of despair regarding the growth of a technological culture in the United States. Kephart described the growing culture of mechanized thinking and popular machines as harmful to children in three ways. First, since the child is an organism whose learning relies on gradual adaptation to the requirements of the environment, technological modernity was increasing the number and complexity of environmental requirements so rapidly that children simply could not keep up. Agrarian society had set a comfortable tempo of gradual change. Children could keep pace in developing the behavioral responses necessary to operate effectively. But the rate and complexity of change in modern civilization had become overwhelming, and children lagged behind developmentally because the physiology of the organism could not adapt to meet the new cultural demands.

Second, the modern home presented an environment that was not conductive to children's motor experimentation due to the intricacy and frailty of the many mechanized devices. A parent could not allow a young child to play with televisions, telephones, and tape recorders because these machines could easily break and repair would be expensive. Third, many of the mundane tasks of physical manipulation that humans had historically accomplished with their bodies had been reassigned to automated machines. This dramatically reduced the opportunities for fine and gross motor practice, creating a lack of necessary developmental experiences for young children. The physical basis for all learning and higher cognitive development—basic motor skills—was denied to young children in a world populated by machines (Kephart, 1960; Radler & Kephart, 1960).

Frostig added a dose of passion and perhaps desperation to Kephart's critique. She characterized technology as a sinister foe intruding with a vengeance upon the natural world. 'The more people interfere with nature', she expounded later in her career, 'the greater are the difficulties that arise' (Frostig, 1976, p. 178). The invasion of the machine into the agrarian landscape was the source of widespread negative consequences in the learning and well-being of children. This was, at least in part, due to the fact that the machines of modern life took over tasks that once required bodily activity.

> With the growth of automation and the ubiquitous use of mechanical loco-motion, physical effort is disappearing from the lives of most people of all ages, with the result that muscular and circulatory weaknesses are prevalent. (Frostig & Maslow, 1970, p. 17)

The growth of a technological culture in America signaled the demise of developmentally necessary daily activities of physical movement and exertion. Devices of modern convenience—'household machinery' (Frostig & Maslow, 1973, p. 160)—robbed children of opportunities for physical activity, causing motor and perceptual development lag. In the view of the movement educators, youngsters arrived at school physiologically unprepared to handle the curricular demands.

Concomitant with the infringement of a modern technological lifestyle on the maturation of the physiology of the child was the destructive spread of a mechanized consciousness into normative cultural orientations and practices, including schooling. Kephart's comparison between the agrarian horse and the modern automobile highlighted the difference between a living creature that apprehends its rider with recognition and caring and an inanimate instrument that neither knows nor cares about its human operator. It enacts values of efficiency and depersonalization that, to Frostig, were siphoning the essential meaning out of schooling and living. Children raised in an impersonal and cold culture lose the opportunity to discover and express their selves and to become connected to other human beings.

Popular preoccupation with technological objects brought about a corresponding loss of human value and meaning. Frostig lamented that 'the mechanistic outlook and style of living of our age contribute to, if they do not cause, a sense of meaninglessness and chaotic confusion' (Frostig & Maslow, 1970, p. 67). To the movement educators, the rise of mechanistic culture yielded experiences of isolation, powerlessness, and despair. Children underwent a 'loss of self-awareness. This loss is felt as lack of identity, so often bemoaned' (Frostig & Maslow, 1970, p. 19). Suffering from developmental deficits in perceptual and sensorimotor abilities due to a lack of necessary agrarian activities, many children experienced the environment as a series of incomprehensible distortions. The perceptually disordered organism felt lost and ineffective in acting in relation to the environment (Frostig & Maslow, 1970; Frostig, 1976).

The Urban Child

At the center of the movement educator's narrative of cultural decline was the 'the urban child' (Frostig & Maslow, 1973, p. 160), the tragic victim of modernity. The entire discourse of movement education concerning the kinds of environments that support or hinder healthy child development was embodied, in melodramatic and pithy fashion, in the unfortunate personage of the child of the city. The movement educators utilized a shorthand discourse of cultural deprivation terms that greatly hinged on a concept of social class and, less clearly, race: 'experiential deprivation,' (Kephart, 1968, p. 14) 'culturally different or economically deprived child,' (Frostig & Maslow, 1973, p. 29) 'culturally deprived child,' (Ebersole, Kephart & Ebersole, 1968) and 'socioeconomically deprived' (Frostig, 1976, p. 29). The inner city child was defined by the fact that his 'experiences have been restricted' (Frostig & Maslow, 1973, p. 216) in ways that had stunted his neurosensory development and school readiness.

Kephart and Frostig complemented one another in service to the larger portrait of the culturally deprived child of the inner city. Kephart focused primarily on the way that culturally defined, experiential limitations caused neurologically based, developmental lags among deprived children. Frostig explained how this neurological disruption of development played out in a restricted range of linguistic, emotional, and behavioral performances.

Kephart framed a neuropsychological 'hierarchy of readiness skills' (Kephart, 1968, p. 13) that children must develop in a specific sequence. 'The development of one stage is essential to the development of the next' (Kephart, 1968, p. 13). Due to the insufficient provision of necessary life experiences that support development and learning, a child may fail to acquire a given skill at the appropriate level. As that child moves forward to more complex lessons at higher levels of learning, 'subsequent stages become confused and disturbed' (Kephart, 1968, p. 14). The disturbance of the natural development sequence causes learning difficulties at higher, more complex levels due to the skill gap at a foundational level. In this way, a learning disability may be caused by 'inadequate presentations of learning experiences,' (Kephart, 1968, p. 13) environmental deficiencies viewed as characteristic of urban, lower class family life. 'It is for this reason', Kephart asserted, 'that high proportions of learning disorders are being observed in Head Start and similar programs for the culturally deprived' (Kephart, 1968, p. 13). It was mostly a problem of experiential quantity. The home environment of culturally deprived children 'presents learning situations of all types but does not present enough of any of them' (Kephart, 1968, p. 13).

Similarly, Frostig built a discourse of cultural deprivation within a scientific rhetoric of an experientially undernourished neurological system, citing two specific manifestations: a 'restricted language code' (Frostig & Maslow, 1973, p. 212) and an emotional posture of trepidation. The language restriction concept imported the work of British researcher Basil Bernstein (1971) in describing the language of lower class families and youth as simplified and constrained in comparison to the public school's middle class norms.

> Children from a socioeconomically deprived background, whose experiences have been restricted, and whose language contains few precise descriptive and qualifying words are at a disadvantage when they must start to acquire a knowledge of standard English. (Frostig & Maslow, 1973, p. 216)

The result was that 'a large percentage of economically deprived children suffer from learning disabilities' (Frostig & Maslow, 1973, p. 216).

The emotional and behavioral plight of the urban child, in Frostig's description, was even more troubling. Based on her educational therapy work in New York and Los Angeles, she came to view the inner city child as emotionally traumatized by the urban experience. The child was overwhelmed by fear and anxiety.

> He is expected to pay attention to the teacher, but often he finds he cannot because paying attention is difficult when one is puzzled and afraid. He is afraid—afraid of the teacher, afraid that he will make a mistake ... he may become more and more anxious and talk less and less. (Frostig & Maslow, 1973, p. 28)

The child's trepidation was due to punitive parenting styles and the 'prevalence of crumbling family structures,' resulting in the 'loss of love' required for healthy emotional development (Frostig & Maslow, 1973; Frostig, 1976, p. 40).

A brief story from Frostig's experiences with urban youth captures her interpretation of the emotional state of these children.

> We remember working with inner city children who huddled together for security, leaving no room for movement. Only after we had assuaged their anxiety did they dare stand so that each had sufficient space to move without interfering with another child. At a subsequent session, one of the youngsters shouted happily, 'It's easy to find my place now. I just remember where I stood before. That's my place!' The same children were unable to create movement sequences or vary any movement sequence independently. Although they quickly picked up new sequences and rules that were demonstrated in detail by the teacher, these children were unable to decide for themselves what to do. (Frostig & Maslow, 1970, pp. 163–164)

In this passage, the restrictive urban environment translates into a sense of apprehensive emotional constriction among the children. The children huddle and cower, insecure within themselves and their physical environment. When they finally relax enough to perform, they lack a sense of self-directedness. Frostig concluded that the teachers must focus on teaching the children how to be more 'self-reliant' to counteract the deficiencies of culture that had accrued in the damaged neurology of inner city children (Frostig & Maslow, 1973, p. 63).

Perhaps most striking about the social class politics of the movement educators is the fact that these serious empirical scientists—trained psychologists who embraced a research tradition requiring that claims be buttressed by data—produced an extensive romantic agrarian discourse without once referring to supporting data, theory, or research. It is very possible that neither Kephart not Frostig consciously fortified their neuro-psychology with pastoral discourse. Perhaps they simply viewed their many statements about country lifestyles, modern technology, and urban children as objective facts available to any reasonable observer. They were not forwarding scientific hypotheses requiring the formal support of empirical or theoretical sources because these agrarian notions were, from their standpoint, as plain as the nose on one's face. Conscientious scientists need not provide a footnote every time they assume that the earth is round. What reads now as an oppressive political discourse may well have seemed to them to be self-evident facts about a modern society in decline, about a world needing the helpful and effective treatments that psychologists and educators could provide.

Certainly, the entire discourse of urban families, poverty, and learning difficulties framed by Frostig and Kephart was built within an overall professional mission of helping those in need. They viewed themselves as clinical practitioners, not social theorists. Kephart worked for decades with disabled children and their families in his psychoeducational clinics in Indiana and Colorado. Frostig operated her own therapeutic school in Los Angeles dedicated to treating children with learning and behavior difficulties. Their unique brand of romantic agrarianism was crafted not so much as an intentional effort to devise a political theory of educational failure but as conceptual support to a professional practice of clinical treatment. Confronted with children whose learning problems frequently baffled the public schools and many other psychologists and physicians, they viewed themselves as trying to save young people who very much needing saving.

Saving the World

To this day, helping children in dire need is central to the professional mission of American special education. For example, the Arkansas Department of Education operates a website, funded in part by the United States Department of Education, devoted to recruiting new special education teachers. This is not surprising since there is a long-standing shortage of special educators in the United States. What is also not surprising is the way the ethical and political mission of the special educator is described. The site features a short video entitled 'One Child at a Time,' that concludes with the following statement by the narrator:

> We hope this video has provided you with insight into what it takes to be a special educator. There is a real need for special education teachers, but as you can see, it does take a special person. If you feel that you may have interest in

this field, talk to a special educator. Visit a special education classroom. Look into it. You too may want to save the world—one child at a time. (Arkansas Department of Education, http://www.arkansaspartnersineducation.org/)

The notion of saving the world by providing educational intervention for a single child is a foundational ethos within American special education, crafted and embraced by the movement educators of the 1960s. Frostig and Kephart's science of learning disabilities united a social and historical theory of a deteriorated society needing massive repair with a clinical practice of individual healing. They addressed what they understood to be a complex cultural decline that had befallen American over decades through psychological practices of individual diagnosis and treatment.

The logical contradiction of this individualist mantra is readily apparent. However one construes the social and economic problems of American society, it is certain that teachers or psychologists providing treatments for individual educational disorders will not rehabilitate a broken nation. Mass cultural change does not take place through clinical correction of individual defects.

One affordance offered to Kephart and Frostig by their pastoral discourse was the ability to effectively ignore, or perhaps gloss over, this contradiction. The romantic agrarianism of the movement educators served as an ideological means to neatly navigate this inconsistency, allowing them to capture and address a wide range of historical and cultural problems within the defective neuropsychology of an individual child.

Historian David Danbom has insightfully observed that what makes romantic agrarianism so appealing to the American psyche is its 'individualistic ideology, stressing the possibility—even the necessity—of individual solutions to social problems' (Danbom, 1991, p. 10). Numerous critics of American special education have made a similar claim about the categorical system of educational services provided to students with learning disabilities and other diagnosed disorders. A variety of social issues involving the cultural politics of public schooling in America, including poverty, social class hierarchy, and racism, have been habitually translated by the special education system into regimens of diagnosis and treatment for problematic individuals (Brantlinger, 2006; Ferri & Connor, 2006). Danbom directs our attention to the ways that an American ideology of individualism operates within both the pastoral tradition and the foundational science of learning disabilities. The unification of an agrarian social theory with a developmental neuropsychology of childhood disorder in the work of the movement educators only made sense given the American impetus to heal society one defective child at a time.

References

Alley, G. R., Solomons, G. & Opitz, E. (1971) Minimal Cerebral Dysfunction as it Relates to Social Class, *Journal of Learning Disabilities*, 4, pp. 246–250.

Amante, D., Margules, P. H., Hartmann, D. M, Storey, D. B. & Weeber, L. J. (1970) The Epidemiological Distribution of CNS Dysfunction, *Journal of Social Issues*, 26:4, pp. 105–136.

Arkansas Department of Education (nd) *One Child at a Time*. Available at: http://www.arkansaspartnersineducation.org/ (accessed 2 April 2009).

Barsch, R. H. (1965) *A Movigenic Curriculum* (Madison, WI, State Department of Public Instruction).

Barsch, R. H. (1968) *Enriching Perception and Cognition: Techniques for teachers* (Seattle, WA, Special Child Publications).

Bernstein, B. (1971) *Class, Codes, and Control* (London, Routledge and Kegan Paul).

Brantlinger, E. A. (2006) *Who Benefits from Special Education?: Remediating (fixing) other people's children* (Mahwah, NJ, Lawrence Erlbaum).

Buell, L. (1995) *The Environmental Imagination: Thoreau, nature writing, and the formation of American culture* (Cambridge, MA, Harvard University Press).

Carrier, J. (1986) *Learning Disability: Social class and the construction of inequality in American education* (New York, Greenwood Press).

Connor, D. C. (2008) *Urban Narratives: Portraits in progress—life at the intersections of learning disability, race, and social class* (New York, Peter Lang).

Danbom, D. B. (1991) Romantic Agrarianism in Twentieth-Century America, *Agricultural History*, 65:4, pp. 1–12.

Danforth, S. (2009) *The Incomplete Child: An intellectual history of learning disabilities* (New York, Peter Lang).

Ebersole, M., Kephart, N. C. & Ebersole, J. B. (1968) *Steps to Achievement for the Slow Learner* (Columbus, OH, Merrill).

Ferri, B. A. & Connor, D. J. (2006) *Reading Resistance: Discourses of exclusion in desegregation and inclusion debates* (New York, Peter Lang).

Ford, M. P. (1971) New Directions in Special Education, *Journal of School Psychology*, 9:1, pp. 73–83.

Frostig, M. (1955) *Clinical Approaches to Education*. PhD dissertation, University of Southern California.

Frostig, M. (1976) *Education for Dignity* (New York, Grune and Stratton).

Frostig, M. & Maslow, P. (1970) *Movement Education: Theory and practice* (Chicago, Follett Educational).

Frostig, M. and Maslow, P. (1973) *Learning Problems in the Classroom: Prevention and remediation* (New York, Grune and Stratton).

Gelb, S. A. & Mizokawa, D. T. (1986) Special Education and Social Structure: The commonality of 'exceptionality', *American Educational Research Journal*, 23:4, pp. 543–557.

Hallahan, D. P. (1970) Cognitive Styles—Preschool Implications for the Disadvantaged, *Journal of Learning Disabilities*, 3, pp. 5–9.

Hallahan, D. P. & Cruickshank, W. M. (1973) *Psychoeducational Foundations of Learning Disabilities* (Englewood Cliffs, NJ, Prentice Hall).

Kappelmann, M. M., Kaplan, E. & Ganter, R. L. (1969) A Study of Learning Disorders Among Disadvantaged Children, *Journal of Learning Disabilities*, 2, pp. 267.

Kephart, N. C. (1956) *Vision and the Retarded Child* (Duncan, OK, Optometric Extension Program).

Kephart, N. C. (1960) *The Slow Learner in the Classroom* (Columbus, OH, C.E. Merrill Books).

Kephart, N. C. (1968) *Learning Disability: An educational adventure* (West Lafayette, IN, Kappa Delta Pi Press).

Loewenstein, A. F. (2004) My Learning Disability: A (digressive) essay, *College English*, 66:6, pp. 585–602.

Marx, L. (1964) *The Machine in the Garden: Technology and the pastoral ideal in America* (Oxford, Oxford University Press).

Marx, L. (1992) Does Pastoralism Have a Future?, in: J. D. Hunt (ed.), *The Pastoral Landscape* (Hanover, NH, National Gallery of Art).

Osmond, J. (1995) *The Reality of Dyslexia* (Cambridge, MA, Brookline Books).

Parrish, T. (2002) Racial disparities in the identification, funding, and provision of special education, in: D. J. Losen & G. Orfield (eds), *Racial Inequity in Special Education* (Cambridge, MA, Harvard Education Press).

Radler, D. H. & Kephart, N. C. (1960) *Success through Play: How to prepare your child for school achievement—and enjoy it* (New York, Harper and Row).

Reinhold, R. (1975) Educators are Divided on Preschool Screening, *New York Times*, 18 April, p. 51.

Rosand, D. (1992) Pastoral Topoi: On the construction of meaning in landscape, in: J. D. Hunt (ed.), *The Pastoral Landscape* (Hanover, NH, National Gallery of Art).

Sleeter, C. (1986) Learning Disabilities: The social construction of a special education category, *Exceptional Children*, 53:1, pp. 46–54.

Tarnopol, L. (1970) Delinquency and Minimal Brain Dysfunction, *Journal of Learning Disabilities*, 3, pp. 200–207.

Walker, J. (1975) Schools Teach 'Sensory Learning', *Chicago Tribune*, 1 September, S5.

Walmsley, S. (1966) Yob cuts wood with was; Special schools help children conquer language problem called dyslexia, developmental dyslexia: the Major Symptoms Tutorial Program, *Washington Post*, 18 December, E3.

Williams, R. (1973) *The Country and the City* (Oxford, Oxford University Press).

7

Lost in Translation:
The power of language

SANDY FARQUHAR & PETER FITZSIMONS

Introduction

The paper begins by locating language (and thus, translation) within a Foucauldian analysis of power as a strategy to generate and structure the realm of new possibilities. The interpretive play that accompanies linguistic communication is an open-ended and creative process that allows new meanings to proliferate. The paper then provides a brief genealogy of philosophical approaches to translation, tracing the work of Walter Benjamin and Roman Jakobson to suggest that translation is not merely the transposition of meaning from one language to another, promoting the idea that even within the same linguistic community, phenomena and meaning are interpreted differently. To be 'lost' in translation is to accept both the contingency of language and our inability to fully encapsulate otherness within our frame of reference. This ethical dilemma is explored in terms of Ricoeur's notion of linguistic hospitality, recognising that two worlds may not necessarily agree but that they can mutually co-exist. The paper concludes with an exploration of some creative possibilities for us as educators through the medium of translation.

Power and Translation

The power of language lies in its ability to create what is 'real': through image, metaphor and interpretation. The creative use of language is an influential mechanism in its structuring of social possibilities. It is the medium through which reality is communicated and interpreted. Translation is, thus, a mode of power in which language creates possibilities for multiplicity and difference. The phrase 'lost in translation' brings together both openness to new ideas and a willingness to embrace multiplicity. We explore the idea of being 'lost' as a commitment to engaging in a journey, to finding new meanings and trajectories, and to embracing destinations that are tentative and negotiable. We contend that translation is a commitment to openness and continuous reinterpretation, enhancing possibilities in our ethical endeavour as educators.

For Foucault power is not an institution, a structure, or a particular force with which certain people are endowed; it is the name given to a 'complex strategic relation in a given society' (Gordon, 1980, p. 236). The exercise of power is defined as the way

The Power In/Of Language, First Edition. Edited by David R. Cole and Linda J. Graham.

in which 'certain actions may structure the field of other possible actions' (Foucault, 2001, p. 343). The way we speak establishes what we consider possible. Clearly then, language is a significant factor in the exercise of power. This is so in terms of how we structure possibilities for ourselves and others: how we relate to others while at the same time treating as tentative the social norms mapped out for us. Foucault dreams of a 'new age of curiosity' that might provide a broad contextual framework for 'interrogating ourselves', altering both our relation to truth and our way of behaving, and increasing the possibility for 'movement backward and forward'. This curiosity involves:

> ... the care one takes of what exists and what might exist; a sharpened sense of reality, but one that is never immobilised before it; a readiness to find what surrounds us strange and odd; a certain determination to throw off familiar ways of thought and to look at the same things in a different way; a passion of seizing what is happening now and what is disappearing; a lack of respect for the traditional hierarchies of what is important and fundamental. (Foucault, 1997, p. 325)

In an effort to increase the possibility for movement that Foucault refers to, we seize upon the notion of translation. In this paper, we argue that translation allows for both the inevitable interpretive shift that accompanies any attempt at communication, while at the same time providing for the untranslatable—the surplus meaning (Ricoeur, 1976). Translation constitutes a paradigm for many exchanges—in language, within and among cultures, and between teacher and student. As a metaphor for education, we are interested in translation as communication, as crossing borders, as the creation of new meaning, and further, as human understanding with and in relation to others.

In Search of a Common Language

Translation can hardly solve the problem of meaning if any question remains about the terms that define translation itself. Without a common language, there is no way of knowing whether two parties really understand each other or whether they are in fact talking about the same things, even when they use the same words. We need at least some agreement about the use of basic terms, or at least a willingness to consider various proposals as possibly true and perhaps more plausible than others. What we (then) know is interpreted and tentative at best, 'neither full nor final but fragmentary and temporary' (Graham, 1985, p. 23).

In the Greek tradition, the art of translation/interpretation was incorporated in the notion of *hermeneus* (from *Hermes*, messenger of the gods—literally 'the translator', giving us the basis of today's hermeneutics in philosophy and linguistics, in which essence is downplayed in favour of interpretation). Latin scholars also engaged with the transfer of meaning, using vocabulary such as *traducere, interpres, transferre, translatum*, all of which signify the shifting or transfer from one idiom to another and all of which are

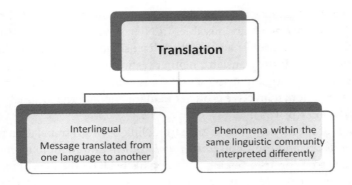

Figure 1

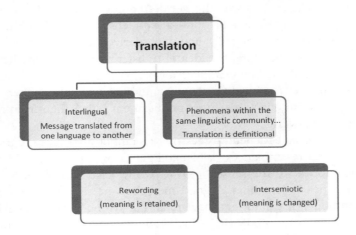

Figure 2

recognisable in today's English derivatives as related to interpretation and transfer of meaning. The task of translation, then, is not new.

Walter Benjamin's short but seminal work *The Task of the Translator* (1999), posits a loose correlation between translated text and originary meaning, distinguishing between two senses of translation: a strict sense in which the message is translated from one language to another; and a loose sense in which phenomena within the same linguistic community are interpreted differently (See Figure 1).

Jakobson (1959) accepts the interlingual function of translation, but differentiates between two versions of translation within the same linguistic community: the first is rewording, and the second is intersemiotic (transmutation) (See Figure 2). In these latter two, translation is definitional, whereas interlingual translation assumes a level of transparency.

From Benjamin and Jakobson, we are left with a dilemma about whether perfect translation is possible or whether translation is a mere approximation to an original. In accepting a level of uncertainty, any text is open to interpretation (subject to some criteria of adequacy in getting things right), yet also prone to error. But rather than think of getting things *right* or *wrong*, we might accept that many kinds of descriptions and many kinds of true statements are possible. In Nietzsche, Derrida and Ricoeur, translation is a creative and interpretive act, in which 'translation is neither an image nor copy' (Derrida, 1985 p. 180). If the translator neither restitutes nor copies an original, Derrida claims, it is because the original lives on and transforms itself. Translation, then, is more than just transformation; it involves growth or enlargement of the original—translation as 'poetic transposition' (p. 189).[1]

Transposition of meaning is clear in the strong link between translation and metaphor. The Greek *metaphora* and the Latin *translatum/transfero* both denote a sense of 'carrying over', 'carrying across', or 'transferring'. Turning his back on the idea of truth as a mirror of reality, Nietzsche casts *all* truth as illusion, as error and as 'worn-out metaphors' (1990c). Since, in a Kantian sense, subject and object are independent of each other, cognition in itself has no contact with the world. In other words, truth cannot be a mirror of reality; a concept is mere abstraction—a 'condensate of multiple metaphors and metonymies' (Kofman, 1993, p. 40) and 'not derived from the essence of things' (Nietzsche, 1990c, §1). Therefore, the idea of transference of meaning between subject and object is better explained by metaphor formation than by the exact replica implied in the *mirroring* model. *Truth* within the metaphor of translation, then, suggests the making of meaning from one's existential predicament rather than from recognition of some 'facts' about the world.

In the *Rule of Metaphor*, Ricoeur argues that metaphor abolishes the *distance between* concepts, makes their resemblances visible, and places things before us in new ways—to make 'discourse appear to the senses' (1977, p. 38). Like Nietzsche, he distinguishes between live and dead metaphors. A good metaphor, he says, tells us something new about reality, although it cannot encapsulate all the symbolic meaning. Metaphors are the 'linguistic surface' of symbols (Ricoeur, 1976, p. 69): the surplus of meaning—that which is residual in the symbol—necessitates ongoing translation, understanding and explanation.

In accepting surplus meaning as part of the process of translation, we adopt the view that translation does not provide a direct copy of the original; it is a transformation involving both addition to and subtraction from the original. Either way, the original meaning is changed—thus, at a superficial level, our commitment to the title of this paper. But there emerges a richer depth to the idea of being lost, if we go beyond the idea of something missing. Synonyms for the word *lost* include *misplaced, off-course, confused, forlorn,* and *deep in thought,* each nuance enhancing the notion of, and highlighting the tentative nature of, translation as an educational metaphor. To be 'lost', then, is to be engaged but uncertain about any final interpretation.

The notion of loss is inherent in the practice of writing *under erasure*, to indicate the inexactness of the use of language in communicating underlying meaning. Rather than just being left out, extraneous meaning is included but signalled as tentative. We also suggest that erasure signals something *more*: the unexpressed or the unattainable. This uncertainty also underpins Richard Rorty's notion of liberal irony. Liberal ironists are those who can live with hope while knowing there is none, those who combine 'commitment with a sense of the contingency of their own commitment' (Rorty, 1989, p. 61).

Perhaps loss is more than just inevitable in the process; it may also be an educational good. Rather than considering loss as a *deficit*, we see a commitment to being lost as an acceptance of *openness*, as possible gain in perspective, or inspiration for new possibilities. The idea that the productive side of loss is gain is an opportunity to 'create for ourselves our own new eyes and ever again new eyes that are even more our own' (Nietzsche, 1974, §143).

The biblical story of Babel recounts the experience of the tribe of the Shems, traditionally considered as their attempt to reach the heavens by building a tower. God interrupted the project, smashing the tower and inflicting on humankind a legacy of incomplete communication. The story of Babel recounts, among other things, 'the origin of the confusion of tongues, the irreducible multiplicity of idioms, the necessary and impossible task of translation, its necessity *as* impossibility' (Derrida, 1985, p. 171). Derrida interprets the Shems' efforts to raise a tower, not just as an attempt to reach all the way to the heavens but also, according to the biblical text, to make a name for themselves through imposing a universal language—their own—on the rest of the world.

> So they want to make a name for themselves—how will they do it? By imposing their tongue on the entire universe on the basis of this sublime edification. Tongue: actually the Hebrew word here is the word that signifies lip. Not tongue but lip. Thus, they want to impose their lip on the entire universe. Had their enterprise succeeded, the universal tongue would have been a particular language imposed by violence, by force, by violent hegemony over the rest of the world. ... This, then, is their project: to make a name for themselves by imposing their lip on the world. (Derrida, 1985, pp. 100–101)

The tower of Babel, then, is not merely about the irreducible multiplicity of tongues; it also signals an incompletion, the impossibility of a totalising system or structure. Ricoeur's understanding of Babel is not that of catastrophe inflicted on humans by a jealous God but, like other commencement myths, a situation of separation—a starting point:

> It is also possible to read this myth ... as a non-judgmental acknowledgement of an original separation ... this is how we are, this is how we exist, scattered and confounded, and called to what? Well ... to translation! There is a post-Babel defined by 'the translators task', to take up again the already mentioned title of Walter Benjamin's famous essay. (Ricoeur, 2006, pp. 18–19)

For Ricoeur, translation is definitely a task, then, not in the sense of a restrictive obligation or a finite job requiring completion, but in the sense of open-ended engagement so that human action can simply continue. Translation is, then, more process than product—a sustained friction between text and culture, an opening up of future possibilities involving continuing dialogue and ongoing explanation and reinterpretation.

Contingency in Translation

Moving away from the idea of an original text with its various translations as merely imperfect representations, we give up the quest for an original essence or pure form.

Nietzsche claims that the point at which a philosopher stops in the quest for truth is merely arbitrary, and does not signal any final or real knowledge: 'Every philosophy also conceals a philosophy; every opinion is also a hiding-place, every word also a mask' (Nietzsche, 1990a, §289). In other words, every translation is merely the next mask in succession, beyond which there are yet more masks. This infinite regress provides a kind of groundlessness, the sense of nostalgia and loss underpinning this paper, reminiscent of Nietzsche's homily to 'we the homeless ones'—those who can bear the icy reality of permanent contingency:

> For their fate is hard, their hopes are uncertain, it is quite a feat to devise some comfort for them—but what avail! We children of the future, how could we be at home in this today! We feel disfavor for all ideals that might lead one to feel at home even in this fragile, broken time of transition; as for its 'realities,' we do not believe that they will last. The ice that still supports people today has become very thin: the wind that brings the thaw is blowing, we ourselves who are homeless constitute a force that breaks open ice and other all too thin 'realities'. (Nietzsche, 1974, §377)

Convictions are, Nietzsche suggests, 'more dangerous enemies of truth than lies' (Nietzsche, 1986, I §483). An insistence on objective certainty masks feelings of weakness, and closes down the possibility of new and different perspectives—of 'seeing the world with more and different eyes' (Nietzsche, 1989, III §12). The world is text; translations are further text; in fact, it's text all the way down.[2]

As an analogy, Connolly (1991) undermines the binary distinction between identity and difference. His notion of identity is not a descriptive label that can be applied to an already existing self entity. Identity formation is a political process that rests on social definitions of difference, with the resulting identity not as an inherent truth about one's being, but a self-reinforcing 'circle of significations'. The contingent and relational nature of the process is emphasised as identity is constantly exceeded, subverted, obstructed, and confounded both by actors who resist roles for which they have been cast and by audiences 'imperfectly colonised by the circle of significations within which the prevailing politics of identity moves' (Connolly, 1991, p. 210). In this analysis, social life is ambiguous and political 'reality' can be challenged as 'conventional categories of insistence'. Connolly draws upon Nietzschean genealogy to interrogate exclusions built into the idea of entrenched identities, to problematise and politicise the forms they have taken, and to 'salute' uncertainty and ambiguity. We can adopt a similar perspective in considering the identity of text—in both its 'original' form and its translation. As with social life, text is ambiguous and open to diverse interpretation. Any particular translation is contingent and relational, subject to the prevailing politics of convention.

Emphasising the need for a relational discourse, Chantal Mouffe advocates a 'radical democracy', acknowledging heterogeneity and leaving room for plurality and conflict. The human subject and its interpretive focus is thus shifting and changing in dialogue with its social surroundings:

> ... we are in fact always multiple and contradictory subjects, inhabitants of a diversity of communities (as many, really, as the social relations in which we

participate and the subject-positions they define), constructed by a variety of discourses and precariously and temporarily sutured at the intersection of those subject-positions. (Mouffe, 1988, p. 44)

Such diversity is necessarily a space of tension and conflict, of mutual recognition of the other, and cannot be reduced to a single translation. Consequently, philosophers of education are turning to 'post' discourses for explanations of diversity. Within the postmodern condition, the artist and the writer are not governed by pre-established rules or judged according to predetermined categories. Rather, they are 'working without rules in order to formulate the rules of what will have been done' (Lyotard, 1984, p. 81). Lyotard suggests it is not our business to supply 'reality', or to provide a totalising unity for irreconcilable language games. The price for such a quest is too high, he warns:

The nineteenth and twentieth centuries have given us as much terror as we can take. We have paid a high enough price for the nostalgia of the whole and the one, for the reconciliation of the concept and the sensible, of the transparent and the communicable experience. (Lyotard, 1984, pp. 81–82)

Nietzsche had a particular admiration for the artist as the creator of new metaphors for life. It was the artist who could affirm (rather than deny) reality and enhance it through a particular representation. The artist's focus on 'appearance' was not an inadequate signifier of some higher unattainable realm, but an engagement with reality as it presents, but 'selected, strengthened, corrected' (Nietzsche, 1990b, 'Reason' in Philosophy §6).

'Appearance' here signifies reality once more, only selected, strengthened, corrected ... The tragic artist is not a pessimist—it is precisely he who affirms all that is questionable and terrible in existence, he is Dionysian. (Nietzsche, 1990b, 'Reason' in Philosophy §6)

American English Professor, Richard Rand applies a similar logic to the art of poetry as a form of translation. Keats' *Ode to Autumn*, he suggests, translates the inarticulate, silent meaningless forms of Autumn into the linguistic sublime (Rand, 1985). Rand goes further though, to argue that Autumn, personified in the ode, is responsible for the various acknowledgements of imagery, characters and events from Keats' earlier poems, and so not only is Keats translating Autumn, the converse is also true: Autumn is translating Keats. In this mutual dependency, it is out of the question to speak of an essential 'original', since origins and identities are undecidable and it is difficult to tell where one leaves off and the other begins. We have, then, a reciprocal relationship between the artist and the work of art—a mutual exchange between creator and creation.

Linguistic Hospitality

Ricoeur illustrates this creative exchange in his threefold theory of mimesis. Integrating metaphor and interpretation, mimesis refers to the art of creating new meaning and understandings. The first part of mimesis refers to the shared understandings of individuals or communities; the second to the reconfiguration of meaning in which metaphor plays the role of re-presenting meaning in new ways; the third refers to the act of readership in which 'the author's intention and the meaning of the text cease to coincide' (Ricoeur, 1977, p. 29).

In translation, he suggests, it is always possible to translate otherwise, without ever hoping to bridge the gap between equivalence and perfect adhesion. Two languages are not the same nor reducible to each other: 'Connotations, contexts and cultural characteristics will always exceed any slide rule of neat equations between tongues' (Ricoeur, 2004, p. xvii). To 'dream of the perfect translation' is to 'wish that translation would gain, gain without losing', to recapture universality, and to attempt 'to abolish the memory of the foreign and maybe the love of one's own language' (*ibid.*, p. 9). We must forgo the possibility of total translation. Notwithstanding the mourning for a *perfect* translation, we can best aim for a *good* translation. Translation, as an encounter to be embraced, is not, then, a quest for perfect meaning. There is a tension between, on the one hand, staying true to the author; and on the other hand, communicating effectively with the reader. For Ricoeur, such tension is not an insurmountable obstacle, but a fragile condition inherent in attempts at communication.

Translation sets out not only intellectual work, but also an ethical problem: to bring the reader to the author, and to bring the author to the reader, at the risk of serving and of betraying two masters. This dilemma emphasises the vigilance the translator must take in constantly checking the otherness of the other while remaining sincere to the work, recognising that authentic relationships exist in tensional spaces. This is to practise what Ricoeur refers to as *linguistic hospitality*: 'the act of inhabiting the word of the Other paralleled by the act of receiving the word of the Other into one's own home, one's own dwelling (Ricoeur, 2006, p. xvi). Linguistic hospitality recognises a small window of opportunity where two worlds may not necessarily agree but can mutually co-exist.

A feature of translation is the ability to distance the subject from the production of the text so that it can be viewed anew and from different perspectives. Appropriation and alienation add a new dimension of agonistic engagement, ensuring that difference is neither overcome nor normalised, but that it remains an important part of human belonging. It is easy (if somewhat conventional) to acknowledge that the translator owes a debt to the author of the original. But Derrida sees the converse as true as well: any author is indebted to an eventual translator. The debt of translation is not only mutual and reciprocal, it is insoluble as neither can possibly repay the other (Graham, 1985). Barthes' assertion of the 'death of the author' refers not to the empirical or literal death of a given author, but to the fact that, in a radical sense, the author is absent from the text.

> We know now that a text is not a line of words releasing a single 'theological' meaning (the 'message' of the Author-God) but a multi-dimensional space in which a variety of writings, none of them original, blend and clash ... but there is one place where this multiplicity is focused and that place is the reader, not, as was hitherto said, the author. The reader is the space on which all the quotations that make up a writing are inscribed without any of them being lost; a text's unity lies not in its origin but in its destination ... the birth of the reader must be at the cost of the death of the Author. (Barthes, 1977, p. 148)

Earlier, we noted the link between translation and metaphor and suggested that neither translation nor metaphor mirror reality, but rather, they actively create new modes and meanings. The metaphorical process required in translation resists our current categorisations of language. Metaphor is the part of language that invites us to interpret and translate. Through metaphor we begin to see reality in terms of potential rather than actuality: it simultaneously shatters and increases our sense of reality: 'with metaphor we experience the metamorphosis of both language and reality' (Ricoeur, 1991, p. 85). To translate, then, is to re-create and to re-state action, requiring a new translation in each passing along of meaning. This new translation is not bound for a final destination, but functions to restore and re-appropriate meaning, to reveal new modes of being and understandings of each other.

In a sense, the translator is caught in a battle between, on the one hand, faithful adherence; and on the other hand, the inevitable interpretive shift that accompanies any attempt at communication. It is, indeed, at the moment of translation that the textual battle comes into its own. Translation is a bridge that creates out of itself the two fields of battle it separates. Heidegger could have been talking about translation when he wrote of the bridge:

> It does not just connect banks that are already there. The banks emerge as banks only as the bridge crosses the stream. The bridge designedly causes them to lie across from each other. One side is set off against the other by the bridge. Nor do the banks stretch along the stream as indifferent border strips of dry land. With the banks, the bridge brings to the stream the one and the other expanse of the landscape lying behind them. It brings stream and bank and land into each other's neighbourhood. (Heidegger, 1997, p. 104)

Conclusion

So, having set out to explore translation as a metaphor for education, we have finished up with the author's voice concealed, the text obscured, and ourselves lost in translation. What is clear, though, is the notion of translation as a complex paradigm for multiple exchanges: in language, within and among cultures, and in the exercise of power. Such complexity problematises any simple social reality.

Language is not just a series of message transfers between sender and receiver. In translation the original becomes larger; it grows rather than reproduces itself, 'like a child ... but with the power to speak on its own' (Derrida, 1985, p. 191), making of the 'child' something other than a reproduction. Translation provides a model that is both relational and creative. In education, a dialogical approach is called for, in which the child is seen not as an individuated subject under the authorial voice of the teacher, but as Zarathustra's child, a powerful spirit able to will its own creation from innocence. Nietzsche's *Zarathustra* describes three stages in the development of the spirit, all of which are important in the overcoming of nihilism. The first stage of development is signified by the camel, aware of the burden imposed by facing up to the challenges of life; second is the lion striking out for freedom by saying no to convention; and finally, the metamorphosis into the child, whose function is, unhampered by tradition, the creation of new values:

> The child is innocence and forgetting, a new beginning, a game, a self-propelled wheel, a first movement, a sacred 'Yes'. For the game of creation, my brothers, a sacred 'Yes' is needed: the spirit now wills his own will, and he who had been lost to the world now conquers his own world. (Nietzsche, 1982, 1, *On the Three Metamorphoses*)

The child is, we might say, lost in translation.

Notes

1. Heidegger (1971) talks in a similar vein about language in *On the Way to Language*.
2. This is an analogy to infinite regression. An anecdote appears in Stephen Hawking's (1996) book *A Brief History of Time*, which starts, 'A well-known scientist (some say it was Bertrand Russell) once gave a public lecture on astronomy. He described how the earth orbits around the sun and how the sun, in turn, orbits around the center of a vast collection of stars called our galaxy. At the end of the lecture, a little old lady at the back of the room got up and said: "What you have told us is rubbish. The world is really a flat plate supported on the back of a giant tortoise." The scientist gave a superior smile before replying, "What is the tortoise standing on?" "You're very clever, young man, very clever," said the old lady. "But it's turtles all the way down!" '.

References

Barthes, R. (1977) The Death of the Author, in: *Image, Music, Text*, S. Heath, trans. (London, Fontana).

Benjamin, W. (1999) The Task of the Translator, H. Zorn, trans, in: H. Arendt (ed.), *Illuminations* (London, Pimlico).

Connolly, W. (1991) *Identity\Difference: Democratic negotiations of political paradox* (Ithaca, NY, Cornell University Press).

Derrida, J. (1985) Des Tours de Babel, in: J. Graham (ed.), *Difference in Translation* (Ithaca, NY, Cornell University Press), pp. 13–30.

Foucault, M. (1997) The Masked Philosopher, in: P. Rabinow (ed.), *Ethics. The essential works 1* (London, Penguin), pp. 321–328.

Foucault, M. (2001) The Subject and Power, in: J. Faubion (ed.), *Power: The essential works 3* (London, Penguin), pp. 326–348.

Gordon, C. (1980) Afterword, in: C. Gordon (ed.), *Power/Knowledge* (Chicago, Harvester), pp. 229–259.

Graham, J. (1985) Introduction, in: J. Graham (ed.), *Difference in Translation* (Ithaca, NY, Cornell University Press), pp. 13–30.

Hawking, S. (1996) *A Brief History of Time*. (New York, Bantam).

Heidegger, M. (1971) *On the Way to Language*, P. Hertz, trans. (New York, Harper & Row).

Heidegger, M. (1997) Building Dwelling Thinking, A. Hofstadter, trans, in: *Rethinking Architecture: A reader in cultural theory* (London, Routledge), pp. 100–125.

Jakobson, R. (1959) On Linguistic Aspects of Translation, in: *On Translation* (Cambridge, MA, Harvard University Press), pp. 232–239.

Kofman, S. (1993) *Nietzsche and Metaphor*, D. Large, trans. (Stanford, CA, Stanford University Press).

Lyotard, J-F. (1984) *The Postmodern Condition: A report on knowledge* (Manchester, Manchester University Press).

Mouffe, C. (1988) Radical Democracy: Modern or postmodern?, in: A. Ross. (ed.), *Universal Abandon? The politics of postmodernism* (Edinburgh, Edinburgh University Press), pp. 31–45.

Nietzsche, F. (1974) *The Gay Science*, W. Kaufmann, trans. (New York, Random House).

Nietzsche, F. (1982) Thus Spoke Zarathustra, *The Portable Nietzsche* (New York, Viking Penguin).

Nietzsche, F. (1986) *Human, All Too Human: A book for free spirits*, R. J. Hollingdale, trans. (Cambridge, Cambridge University Press).

Nietzsche, F. (1989) *On the Genealogy of Morals and Ecce Homo*, W. Kaufmann, trans. (New York, Vintage).

Nietzsche, F. (1990a) *Beyond Good and Evil*, R. Hollingdale, trans. (London, Penguin).

Nietzsche, F. (1990b) *Twilight of the Idols & The Anti-Christ*, R. J. Hollingdale, trans. (London, Penguin).

Nietzsche, F. (1990c) On Truth and Lies in a Nonmoral Sense, in: D. Breazeale (ed.), *Philosophy and Truth: Selections from Nietzsche's notebooks of the early 1870's*. (London, Humanities Paperback Library).

Rand, R. (1985) 'O'er-brimmed', in: J. Graham (ed.), *Difference in Translation* (Ithaca, NY, Cornell University Press), pp. 81–101.

Ricoeur, P. (1976) *Interpretation Theory: Discourse and the surplus of meaning* (Fort Worth, TX, The Texas Christian University Press).

Ricoeur, P. (1977) *The Rule of Metaphor* (Toronto, University of Toronto Press).

Ricoeur, P. (1991) *A Ricoeur Reader: Reflection and Imagination* (New York, Harvester Wheatsheaf).

Ricoeur, P. (2004) *Memory, History and Forgetting* (Chicago, University of Chicago Press).

Ricoeur, P. (2006) *On Translation* (London, Routledge).

Rorty, R. (1989) *Contingency, Irony, and Solidarity* (Cambridge, Cambridge University Press).

8
The Product of Text and 'Other' Statements: Discourse analysis and the critical use of Foucault

LINDA J. GRAHAM

Different Horses for Different Courses ...

Discourse analysis is a flexible term. What one is doing is greatly dependent on the epistemological framework being drawn upon. It appears that many scholars using discourse analysis within a Foucauldian framework have adopted a 'Foucauldian*istic*' reticence to declare method, fearful perhaps of the charge of being prescriptive. There are those again who make references to 'doing' discourse analysis and because they loosely link their analysis to motifs of power and sporadically cite Foucault, there is an assumption that this too is 'Foucauldian' discourse analysis. In any case, it is quite difficult to find coherent descriptions of how one might go about 'Foucauldian' discourse analysis, but perhaps the difficulty in locating concise descriptions is because there is no such thing? In this paper, the reasons why this might be so are discussed whilst the author engages with the awkward tension that arises when one attempts to do poststructural work using Foucault, while at the same time satisfying the conventions of academic writing and scholarship in education research.

Despite there being no model for discourse analysis *qua* Foucault, should one *claim* to be drawing on a Foucauldian framework there is a very real danger of one's work being dismissed as *un*Foucauldian—*if* one doesn't get it right. But how can one get it wrong when there are supposedly no rules to follow? This is an interesting but precarious dilemma that can have an exclusionary effect (see O'Farrell, 2005). Foucauldian theory is perceived as inaccessible and dangerous, which deters some researchers from engaging with this form of analysis, particularly those in more practice-oriented fields. The neoliberal malaise currently affecting universities (Davies, 2005), which privileges so-called 'evidence-based' research methods and causes some to caution against using the 'F' word,[1] only compounds this problem.

As an umbrella term for anything vaguely left of far-right, 'postmodernism' has been the whipping boy of the conservative Right in the Australian 'culture wars' for over the past decade. For example in June 2007, the then Minister of Sport and The Arts, George Brandis MP delivered a sermon to visiting members of the Council of the Humanities, Arts and Social Sciences (CHASS). Brandis attributed the decline in esteem (and

The Power In/Of Language, First Edition. Edited by David R. Cole and Linda J. Graham.
Chapters © 2012 The Authors. Book compilation © 2012 Philosophy of Education Society of Australasia.
Published 2012 by Blackwell Publishing Ltd.

government sponsorship) of the arts, humanities and social sciences to 'academic practitioners who have, in seeking to understand human society, blundered down blind
alleyways and fallen prey to the worship of false gods' (Brandis, 2007, p. 32). He
continued to argue (to an affronted and rapidly diminishing audience) that in order to
'recover their prestige' the humanities need to,

> ... embrace the standards of objective, rigorous scholarship that were once
> among their glories; to accept that critical inquiry is not well served when it is,
> whether admittedly or implicitly, regarded instrumentally, in service of some
> ideology or social philosophy, rather than as an end in itself ... scholarship in
> the mainstream of the humanities has been degraded for the very reason that
> it was dominated by an instrumentalist method, to fit scholarly inquiry into an
> historical paradigm that the events of the late 20th century have utterly
> discredited. (Brandis, 2007, p. 32)

As a key field in the social sciences and the potential 'engine-room of the economy'
(Rudd, 2007), education has received a great deal of attention in the last few years in
Australia. So too has educational research and scholarship, albeit for all the wrong
reasons. Here too postmodernism is to blame for a perceived decline in standards:

> Our thinking processes have been addled by postmodernism, with its insistence
> that nothing is better than anything else ... The circuitous theories of French
> philosophers Michel Foucault, Jacques Derrida and Roland Barthes arrived on
> our shores in the '70s and '80s to be widely misunderstood and misinterpreted.
> Soon they were being applied in even more half-baked form to teacher educa-
> tion and then to teaching in schools. The effect on young brains has been roughly
> the same as what would happen to an assembly line of Rolls-Royces if you
> poured glue into all the door locks ... Two generations of experimented-upon
> young Australians have emerged unable to read, write and think with the skill
> and clarity they should have been able to assume would be theirs ... Too often,
> under the postmodern influence, schooling has turned into a hatchery for baby
> airheads unable to think for themselves or communicate clearly ... Whatever the
> original worth and intention of the movement, postmodernism, with its insis-
> tence that there are no such things as objective truths, knowledge or values, gave
> licence to far too many to take the easy way out. (Gare, 2006, p. 29)

Not surprisingly the corrosive effect of such attacks, together with the vetoing of 'postmod-
ernist' Australian Research Council research grants by Federal Education Minister
Brendon Nelson, have further deterred researchers in education from applying poststructural research methods. The recent growth in the use of mixed-methods and quasi-
experimental design to answer questions more suited to qualitative methods, points towards
an attempt by some to add a measure of 'science-cred' to interpretive research, although this
is not a new phenomenon as anyone familiar with discourse analysis will know.

Analysing 'Rigorously'

A number of years ago, Taylor (2004) provided an analysis of education policy documents using Critical Discourse Analysis.[2] In doing so, she argued that Critical Discourse
Analysis (CDA),

> ... is particularly appropriate for critical policy analysis because it allows a detailed investigation of the relationship of language to other social processes, and of how language *works* within power relations. CDA provides a framework for a *systematic* analysis—researchers can go beyond speculation and demonstrate how policy texts work. (Taylor, 2004, p. 436, emphasis in original)

In Taylor's (2004) discussion, distinction is made between two approaches to discourse analysis. This is principally between CDA, which draws inferences from structural and linguistic features in texts, and discourse analysis said to be informed by the work of Foucault. The difference between the former, which Taylor (2004, p. 435) describes as paying 'close attention to the linguistic features of texts' and the latter, described as 'those which do not', is perhaps more complex than this (see discussion in Wetherall, 2001, pp. 391–393). For a start, there are more than these two approaches to discourse analysis and other epistemological frameworks inform them (Wetherall, Taylor & Yates, 2001). Indeed, the common thread between analyses in the latter group is not Foucault at all. More germane to these approaches is a poststructural sensibility born of a 'theorising that rests upon complexity, uncertainty and doubt and upon a reflexivity about its own production and its claims to knowledge about the social' (Ball, 1995, p. 269).

The difference between CDA[3] and poststructural theoretical approaches (using Foucault, Derrida and Lyotard among others) to discourse analysis may be found in the characteristic eschewing of claims to objectivity and truth by those in the latter tradition; for, as Edwards and Nicoll (2001, p. 105) point out, 'the claim to truth can itself be seen as a powerful rhetorical practice'. Additionally, Humes and Bryce speak to the poststructuralist respect for uncertainty and the influence of key thinkers such as Derrida when they argue that, 'the search for clarity and simplicity of meaning is seen as illusory because there will always be other perspectives from which to interpret the material under review. To seek a definitive account is, thus, a misguided undertaking' (2003, p. 180). As such, discourse analysis informed by Foucauldian or other poststructural theory endeavours to avoid the substitution of one 'truth' for another, recognising that 'there can be no universal truths or absolute ethical positions [and hence] ... belief in social scientific investigation as a detached, historical, utopian, truth-seeking process becomes difficult to sustain' (Wetherall, 2001, p. 384).

Whilst poststructural accounts of meaning in language assert the 'death of the author' (Barthes, 1977b) because the potential for multiple reader interpretation/s has been established (Humes & Bryce, 2003), this does not result in relativism. Nor licence 'to take the easy way out' (Gare, 2006, p. 29). Influenced by the key works of influential thinkers including Barthes (1977b), Lyotard (1984) and Derrida (Derrida, 1967a; 1967b; 1982), as well as the inimitable Foucault, poststructuralists argue that 'the process of analysis is always interpretive, always contingent, always a version or a reading from some theoretical, epistemological or ethical standpoint' (Wetherall, 2001, p. 384). Understanding that meaning is an inherently unstable construct negotiated by and through the 'cultural politics of the sign' (Trifonas, 2000, p. 275), methodologists from this tradition tend to discount the sovereignty of the author, destabilising the treasured relationship between signifier and signified (Peters, 2004; Trifonas, 2000), in the recognition that the reader has ultimate authority over interpretation and therefore meaning—not, in fact, the author.

Researchers drawing on Foucauldian ideas therefore do not speak of their research 'findings'. They tend to use less emphatic language, recognising that truth is contingent upon the subjectivity of the reader and the fickleness of language. They would recognise the futility of trying to mine a policy document for the writer's intention (Graham, 2007b), and would not seek to speak for the subject of analysis (see Graham, 2007a, p. 14). It is for this reason that those using discourse analysis with Foucault shy away from prescribing method, for no matter how standardised the process, the analysis of language by different people will seldom yield the same result. This is not seen as problematic for the aim of poststructural analysis is not to establish a final 'truth' but to question the intelligibility of truth/s we have come to take for granted.

Although not 'scientific' this approach can be a powerful analytical tool, particularly in an applied field such as education. Through the experience such analysis provides, it is possible to come to a different relationship with those truth/s which may enable research-ers to think and see otherwise, to be able to imagine things being other than what they are, and to understand the abstract and concrete links that make them so. Ultimately, the value of poststructural work is intellectual and conceptual. The critical relationship to truth enabled through Foucauldian problematisation does not mean that there is no truth—it means that truth is always contingent and subject to scrutiny. Truth is no longer immutable and this opens the door to powerful possibilities for change. Ultimately, to be able to see truth as a kind of fiction, as something we busily construct around ourselves means that we can come to see 'truth' as something less final; as something we can (re)make 'little by little ... [by] introducing modifications that are able if not to find solutions, at least to change the given terms of the problem' (Foucault, 1994, p. 288).

Despite how poorly understood Foucault's work has been (see O'Farrell, 2005), approaching truth as a 'construction' does not result in relativism. Nor does the admis-sion that truth is contingent leave us peddling mere 'speculation'. Words on a page, utterances, symbols and signs, statements: *these* are the start and end point for the poststructural discourse analyst. If anything this is the most honest and ethical approach to the analysis of language for, as Barthes (1977a, p. 148) points out, 'the unity of a text is not in its origin, it is in its destination'. The acknowledgment of such contingency is a profoundly ethical standpoint and the reluctance to prescribe method reflects, not that 'anything goes,' but the characteristic reticence of those 'doing' discourse analysis within a poststructural framework to make claims to truth through 'scientific', 'objective', 'precise' methodologies. This again is not restricted to Foucauldian work, as Edwards and Nicoll demonstrate this same caution in discussing methodological possibilities in rhetorical analysis:

> The different elements may be combined in a variety of ways to produce different types of analysis that focus on a particular range of practices and issues. *They are not part of a method to be applied, but resources in an interpretive art.* (2001, p. 106, emphasis added)

A distinction between the prescription of scientific method and the development of methodological guidelines should perhaps be emphasized here. The formulation of 'method' has traditionally been attempted to standardize research activity and to assist in the generalization of results. In the human and social sciences particularly, this has been done to lend 'scientific' credibility to fields of study marred by the often-perplexing inconsistency arising from human behaviour (Foucault, 1972). Such an objective, if the insights of the great 'anti-theorists' of postmodernism (Thomas, 1997, p. 80) are to be respected, is an impossible ambition when it comes to the analysis of discourse and language, particularly with respect to a search for original meanings or personal agendas. This does not mean that language cannot be analysed, or that one cannot develop methods to approach this task. It simply means that one has to be clear about objectives, limits and, most importantly, what one is *doing*.

'Doing' Poststructural Discourse Analysis

Discourse analysis consistent with a Foucauldian notion of discourse does not seek to reveal the true meaning by what is said or not said (Foucault, 1972). Instead, when 'doing' discourse analysis within a Foucauldian framework, one looks to statements not so much for what they say but what they *do*; that is, one question's what the constitutive or political effects of saying this instead of that might be? As Foucault (1972, p. 134) argues, 'there is no subtext'. The analyst's job 'does not consist therefore in rediscovering the unsaid whose place [the statement] occupies' (p. 134). Instead, Foucault (ibid.) maintains that 'every*thing* is never said' and that the task is to determine, in all the possible enunciations that could be made on a particular subject, why it is that certain statements emerged to the exclusion of all others and what function they serve.

Such an approach distinguishes itself by interrogating what Foucault (1980a, p. 237) describes as, 'the discourses of true and false ... the correlative formation of domains and objects ... the verifiable, falsifiable discourses that bear on them, and ... the effects in the real to which they are linked'. The objective is to explicate statements that function to place a discursive frame around a particular position; that is, statements which coagulate and form rhetorical constructions that present a particular reading of social texts. Incidentally, this includes all forms of signification: movement, behaviour, performance, gestures, art, symbols, text and so on. Elsewhere (Graham, 2007a), I put an earlier draft of this analytic to work using literary theory to demonstrate *how* the use of particular discursive techniques in the production of meaning present a particular view of the world *and* prepare the ground for the 'practices that derive from them' (Foucault, 1972, p. 139). Building on this work here, I outline three important ideas from Foucault's work—description, recognition and classification—as a guide for how one might approach poststructural discourse analysis using Foucault.

1. Description

In order for an object of discourse to be 'produced', it must first be definable in order to be locatable. Language is the tool through which people communicate ideas, and successful communication between individuals and especially groups of individuals relies on the definition and specification that language allows. In the English language, we have many words that all sound the same: e.g. threw and through; and to, two and too. Placing these words differently can completely alter a sentence and the meaning of the exchange. Therefore, in written communication we depend on the spelling of these different words and the other words used alongside them to guide our understanding of what is being said. In oral communication we rely on context and our ability to comprehend. The more specific our language, the more accurate we can be in conveying and understanding meaning. That specification however, the *words* we use to describe *things*, is the mechanism through which we define and shape what Foucault often referred to as 'objects of discourse'. Thus, the main aim of a Foucauldian approach to discourse analysis is to trace the relationship between words and things: how the words we use to conceptualise and communicate end up producing the very 'things' or objects of which we speak. It is my view based on a reading of Foucault that the foundational starting point of such an analysis would be to define and locate what he calls 'statements'.

Making a statement: Foucault defines the statement as '[t]he atom of discourse' (Foucault, 1972, p. 80) but avoids defining it through any of the models borrowed from grammar, logic or analysis (Foucault, 1972). Instead, Foucault extracts the statement from 'the simple inscription of what is said' (Deleuze, 1988, p. 15) describing it, not as a linguistic unit like the sentence, but as 'a function' (Foucault, 1972, p. 98). The statement as 'function' can be theorised as a discursive junction-box in which words and things intersect and become invested with particular relations of power, resulting in an interpellative event (Althusser, 1971; Butler, 1990) in which one can 'recognize and isolate an act of formulation' (Foucault, 1972, p. 93).

A postcard advertising entertainment for a local council day features three circles that each headline the time and name of two main attractions: The Hooley Dooleys at 11am and Marcia Hines at 2pm. The third circle mentions 'Local and Multicultural Acts'. At first this may not seem problematic. On stage throughout the day were performances by dance groups, numerous bands[4] and performers; however, none of the bands were 'flown in' for the event, which means that all of the bands were essentially 'local'. The use of the word 'local' is interesting in this case because one would assume it was being used to mark geographic identity (See Ibrahim, this issue). Placing the word 'local' alongside 'multicultural' (rather than, say, international) results in what Foucault calls an act of formulation; qualifying the third circle above as a 'statement' appropriate for analysis.

In this example, the signifier 'local' is acting as a euphemism for Anglo-Australian, naturalising the dominant group (see Graham & Slee, 2008). Unfortunately, the signifier 'multicultural' is assuming the use for which it is most often used in Australia: denoting 'other culture', 'non-Australian' or 'the people that live here who aren't Australian' (or aren't white). This statement effectively conjures the cultural/ethnic Other; identities that are obliquely referred to yet 'everyone knows 'who' is being talked about' (Popkewitz & Lindblad, 2000, p. 9). Anglo-Australian culture is not generally being referred to when someone is talking about the 'multicultural'. For example in 2005 during the time of the Cronulla race riots, newsreaders referred to 'carloads of ethnics coming up from Melbourne to join the cause'. In Australia, people not of Anglo-Western European appearance are often referred to as 'ethnics' however, in denying that 'Anglo-European' is itself a form of ethnicity, a cultural Other is produced and stubbornly maintained (Graham & Slee, 2008). This is not simply a matter of media ignorance, as the following excerpt from an interview with an Australian academic will show:

Monash University's Centre for Population and Urban Research head, Bob Birrell, said Melbourne had much lower levels of ethnic concentration than Sydney. Melbourne's northern suburbs had a significant number of immigrants and people of Middle-Eastern descent but its ethnic enclaves were not as big as in Sydney's southwest. 'In Sydney, especially, more affluent **ethnics**, and to a greater rate non-**ethnics**, are moving out of those areas so the concentration grows,' Dr Birrell said. (Masanauskas & Mickelburough, 2005, p. 1, my emphasis)

The effect of such discursive processes have been articulated more fully by McGrath (2008) who draws upon the discursive analytic described here to understand how a set of developmental scales used to program for and assess English language learners in Australian schools works to define 'culturally competent' Australian citizens. McGrath augments this analytic using Foucault's concept of disciplinary power to understand how the national ESL Scales then function to produce and locate 'culturally in/competent' students requiring remediation and cure. She develops a conceptual framework to illustrate how discourses and practices historically embedded in a White Australia consciousness intersect to produce notions of what it means to be 'Australian;' subsequently reaffirming the exclusionary logic set out by the dominant discourse. Such an approach to discourse analysis can lead one back to and through the discursive markers paving the journey from linguistic profiling to ocular and theoretic recognition. This involves tracing the pathways between words and things and the processes of validation involved.

2. Recognition

According to Foucault (1972, p. 100), the statement is a 'special mode of existence' which enables 'groups of signs to exist, and enables rules or forms to become manifest' (Foucault, 1972, p. 99). Thus, in theorising the tactics related to the production of psychiatric 'truth' and the development of a power/knowledge specific to the human sciences, Foucault (1972, p. 86–87) looks,

> ... to describe statements, to describe the enunciative function of which they are the bearers, to analyse the conditions in which this function operates, to cover the different domains that this function presupposes and the way in which those domains are articulated.

In doing so, he notes that 'psychiatric discourse finds a way of limiting its domain, of defining what it is talking about, of giving it the status of an object—and therefore of making it manifest, nameable, and describable' (Foucault, 1972, p. 46). He maintains that the construction of categories and description of disorders (such as the evolving descriptions within the American Psychiatric Association's manual *DSM-IV-TR*) serves to provide the human sciences with a locatable object of scrutiny (Foucault, 1975). However, for an object to be locatable it must first be *recognizable* and that is the 'enunciative function of statements'.

Judith Butler declares that, '[o]ne 'exists' not only by virtue of being recognized, but, in a prior sense, by being *recognizable*' (1997, p. 5, emphasis in original). By this Butler

(p. 2) refers not only to the act of being addressed or hailed, but to the simultaneous effect of a discourse which both 'interpellates and constitutes a subject'. Identities and categories exist prior to the subject, in effect, Butler (1997) argues, we 'become' when interpellated through the prior power of language; that is, when we are described, we can then be 'recognized' and classified. For the discourse analyst using Foucault, the first step in understanding how 'things' have come to be as they are, is to trace the processes involved in their constitution. This involves, as discussed in the previous section, the need to identify statements or articulations within a field of regulation that may function with constitutive effects. In order to understand how 'words' become 'things' in a Foucauldian sense, such an analyst would examine specific bodies of knowledge which, in validating certain statements build a discourse that reaffirms not only that particular perception of phenomena and the way it is described, but also outlines the specific and technical expertise required to deal with it.

3. Classification

Inherent to the medical account of childhood misbehaviour are procedures that outline 'symptoms' of neurological disorder and the processes by which such children can be identified and classified. The cultural description of a child's behaviour as 'impulsive', 'hyperactive', or 'inattentive' builds the case for a medical assessment through which the doctor completes a 14-point checklist compiled using the diagnostic criteria for Attention Deficit Hyperactivity Disorder outlined in the Diagnostic and Statistical Manual for Mental Disorders (DSM-IV), and compliant teachers and parents tick boxes on behavioural scales that indicate whether a child's naughty behaviour is of 'clinical significance'. Professional 'recognition' of particular idiosyncrasies ensures that the child's behaviour is properly classified and therefore, that the child is referred to the appropriate 'expert'. Specialised treatment of the child's disorder may then begin (see Graham, 2007c). The question is: how does one trace the myriad discursive pathways involved?

In discussing Foucault's interest in the statement, Deleuze (1988, p. 8) points to the constitutive properties intrinsic to it by imparting that a 'statement has a "discursive object" which does not derive in any sense from a particular state of things, but stems from the statement itself', for a 'statement always defines itself by establishing a specific link with *something else* that lies on the same level as itself ... almost inevitably, it is something foreign, something outside' (Deleuze, 1988, p. 11, emphasis in original). Through the location and analysis of such statements, it becomes possible to isolate the 'positivity' (Foucault, 1972, p. 214) of a particular power/knowledge. Identifying and following discursive traces leads one back to the knowledge-domain upon which the statement relies for its intelligibility, at the same time revealing other artefacts or statements from that particular discursive formation which together, work to sustain the field from which they originate. In other words, mutually reinforcing discourses construct an associated field which:

> ... is made up of all the formulations whose status the statement in question shares, among which it takes its place without regard to linear order, with which it will fade away, or with which, on the contrary, it will be valued,

> preserved, sacralized, and offered, as a possible object, to a future discourse.
> (Foucault, 1972, p. 110–111)

At this point I wish to return to my earlier discussion of the statement 'Local and Multicultural Acts.' It is only through self-reinforcing discursive processes such as those I outline above, that it becomes possible in a contemporary liberal society with anti-discrimination legislation to discriminate, marginalize and exclude—*and, for this to pass relatively unnoticed*. The validation of statements such as 'Local and Multicultural Acts' through a wider cultural discourse that speaks of ethnicity as something Other, not only produces recognizable and racialised 'ethnics' but ensures their classification and exclusion even more emphatically through what is arguably a contradiction in terms: *non-ethnics*. The term 'non-ethnic' valorizes white Anglo-Australians as members of a natural order; further marginalizing citizens of non-Anglo European descent.[5] In this way, discourse analysis using Foucault can help us to understand how, as Leonardo (in press, this issue) describes, '[r]acial hailing still occurs' and, perhaps more importantly, why 'many of its subjects still turn around when their subjectivity is called upon to answer'. Discourse analysts drawing upon Foucault understand that discourse produces subjects as well as objects and key to understanding people's actions is an appreciation of how discourse shapes their identities, beliefs, actions (see Graham, 2009).

Foucault's theorisation of the constitutive and disciplinary properties of discursive practices within socio-political relations of power is a demonstration of the postmodern concern with how language works to not only produce meaning, *but also particular kinds of objects and subjects upon whom and through which particular relations of power are realised.* Unlike Critical Discourse Analysis or CDA (Fairclough, 2003; van Dijk, 2001), discourse analysis using Foucault focuses less on the micro—the structural/grammatical/linguistic/semiotic features that *make up* the text—and more on the macro (Threadgold, 2003); that is, what is 'made up' by the text itself.

The aim of this form of analysis is to 'try to grasp subjection in its material instance as a constitution of subjects' (Foucault, 1980b, p. 97) through the interrogation of discursive practices that both objectify and subjugate the individual. Objectification acts as a locating device; a mechanism of visibility (Deleuze 1992; Ewald 1992) that formulates how a 'group is seen or known as a problem' (Scheurich 1997, p. 107). Once constituted as an object of a particular sort, individuals can be dispersed into disciplinary spaces within that 'grid of social regularity' (Scheurich, 1997, p. 98) and from there, can become subject to particular discourses and practices that result in what Butler (1997, pp. 358–359) describes as, 'the "on-going" subjugation that is the very operation of interpellation, that (continually repeated) action of discourse by which subjects are formed in subjugation'. In other words through the process of objectification, individuals not only come to occupy *spaces* in the social hierarchy but, through their continual subjugation, come to know and accept their *place*.

Conclusion

Stephen Ball (1995, p. 267) reminds us that 'the point about theory is not that it is simply critical' and that theory in educational research should be 'to engage in struggle, to reveal and undermine what is most invisible and insidious in prevailing practices'. Poststructural discourse analysis that draws on the work of Foucault is well placed to do this. In looking to the function of statements in discourses that work to (re)secure dominant relations of power (Nakayama & Krizek, 1995) and the correlative formation of domains and objects (Deleuze, 1988; Dreyfus & Rabinow, 1982; Foucault, 1972), the poststructural discourse analyst certainly shares the Critical Discourse Analyst's concern as to the 'relationship of language to other social processes, and of how language *works* within power relations' (Taylor, 2004, p. 436). While these two approaches may offer different analyses, this simply confirms the assertion that 'there will always be other perspectives from which to interpret the material under review' (Humes & Bryce, 2003, p. 180) and the kaleidoscopic nature of language and meaning; certainly not that one analyses is any more 'true' than the other.

Notes

1. Here I am referring to the practice where Foucauldian notions are used but reference to Foucault is deliberately stricken from the reference list. It happens, and whilst it is described as 'strategy' it really should be described as self-censorship.
2. I use capitals here to denote CDA because arguably both approaches to discourse analysis are critical.
3. Just to complicate matters, Fairclough himself maintains that CDA is informed by the work of Foucault. The question for scholars then becomes: Is CDA appropriately Foucauldian (and does it want to be?) or is CDA somehow set apart from Foucauldian discourse analysis? And, if so, how and does this negate its resonance with Foucault? Any definitive claim to 'research findings' or similar claim to truth would not sit well with Foucauldian ideas.
4. The significance of the naming of 'local and multicultural acts' first became apparent when watching a band play Brazilian music with *carnivale* dancers. These performers represented 'multicultural acts'.
5. Born in Zimbabwe to Scots/Irish parents and raised in Dublin before emigrating to Australia in the 1980s, this author identifies as Celtic-Australian, not Anglo. However as an immigrant of white European appearance, I have noticed that my nationality is assumed to be 'Australian' whereas this is rarely the case with new Australians of a darker skin tone. This realisation came home powerfully the night Sydney's bid to win the Olympics was announced as successful. One in a group of young men called out 'Bad luck Beijing!' to a man standing close by, who cheerfully replied, 'No worries mate, it's all good'. The exchange stopped the young men in their tracks as this man had a broader Australian accent than they did. It turned out that he was 5th generation Chinese-Australian. His ancestors had come to Australia during the Gold Rush in the 1800s and his claim to 'Australian' heritage turned out to have deeper roots than either myself or any of the young men who had taunted him as a representative of 'Beijing'.

References

Althusser, L. (1971) *Lenin and Philosophy and Other Essays* (New York, New Left Books).

Ball, S. (1995) Intellectuals or Technicians: The urgent role of theory in educational studies. *British Journal of Educational Studies*, 43:3, pp. 255–271.

Barthes, R. (1977a) The Death of the Author, in: *Image—Music—Text* (New York, Hill and Wang), pp. 142–148.

Barthes, R. (1977b) *The Death of the Author*, S. Heath, trans. (New York, Hill).

Brandis, G. (2007) Learning is its Own Reward, *The Australian*, 27 June, p. 32.

Butler, J. (1990) *Gender Trouble: Feminism and the subversion of identity* (New York, Routledge).

Butler, J. (1997) *Excitable Speech: A politics of the performative.* (New York, Routledge).

Davies, B. (2005) The (Im)possibility of Intellectual Work in Neoliberal Regimes, *Discourse: Studies in the Cultural Politics of Education*, 26:1, pp. 1–14.

Deleuze, G. (1988) *Foucault* (Minneapolis, MN, University of Minnesota Press).

Deleuze, G. (1992) What is a Dispositif? in: T. J. Armstrong (ed.), *Michel Foucault: Philosopher* (New York, Harvester Wheatsheaf), pp. 159–168.

Derrida, J. (1967a) Force and Signification, in: *Writing and Difference* (London, Routledge).

Derrida, J. (1967b) Structure, Sign and Play in the Discourse of the Human Sciences, A. Bass, trans, in: *Writing and Difference* (London, Routledge).

Derrida, J. (1982) Différance, A. Bass, trans., in: *Margins of Philosophy* (Hove, The Harvester Press).

Dreyfus, H. L. & Rabinow, P. (eds) (1982) *Michel Foucault: Beyond Structuralism and Hermeneutics.* (London, Harvester Wheatsheaf).

Edwards, R. & Nicoll, K. (2001) Researching the Rhetoric of Lifelong Learning, *Journal of Education Policy*, 16:2, pp. 103–112.

Ewald, F. (1992) A Power Without an Exterior, in: T. J. Armstrong (ed.), *Michel Foucault: Philosopher* (New York, Harvester Wheatsheaf), pp. 169–175.

Fairclough, N. (2003) *Analysing Discourse: Textual analysis for social research* (London, Routledge).

Foucault, M. (1972) *The Archaeology of Knowledge*, A.M. Sheridan Smith, trans. (New York, Pantheon Books).

Foucault, M. (1975) *Abnormal: Lectures at the Collège de France 1974–1975* (London, Verso).

Foucault, M. (1980a) Questions of Method, in: J. D. Faubion (eds), *Michel Foucault: Power* (New York, The New Press), pp. 223–238.

Foucault, M. (1980b) Two Lectures, in: C. Gordon (eds), *Power/Knowledge: Selected interviews & other writings 1972–1977* (New York, Pantheon Books), pp. 78–108.

Foucault, M. (1994) An Interview with Michel Foucault, in: J. D. Faubion (ed.), *Power*, Vol. 3 (New York, The New Press), pp. 239–297.

Gare, S. (2006) Schooled for a Spell of Trouble, *The Weekend Australian*, 11–12 November, p. 29.

Graham, L. (2007a) Speaking of 'disorderly' Objects: A poetics of pedagogical discourse, *Discourse: Studies in the Cultural Politics of Education*, 28:1, pp. 1–20.

Graham, L. J. (2007b) (Re)Visioning the Centre: Education reform and the 'ideal' citizen of the future, *Educational Philosophy and Theory*, 39:2, pp. 197–215.

Graham, L. J. (2007c) Schooling Attention Deficit Hyperactivity Disorders: Educational systems of formation and the 'behaviourally disordered' school child. Unpublished PhD thesis, Queensland University of Technology, Brisbane.

Graham, L. J. (2009) The Cost of Opportunity. Paper presented at the Philosophy in Education Society of Australasia (PESA) Annual Conference, December 3–6 University of Hawaii, Honolulu.

Graham, L. J. & Slee, R. (2008) An Illusory Interiority: Interrogating the discourse/s of inclusion, *Educational Philosophy and Theory*, 40:2, pp. 247–260.

Harwood, V. (2000) Truth, Power and the Self: A Foucaultian analysis of the truth of Conduct Disorder and the construction of young people's mentally disordered subjectivity. Unpublished PhD thesis, University of South Australia, Adelaide.

Humes, W. & Bryce, T. (2003) Post-structuralism and Policy Research in Education, *Journal of Education Policy*, 18:2, pp. 175–187.

Lyotard, J. F. (1984) *The Postmodern Condition: A report on knowledge* (Minneapolis, MN, University of Minnesota Press).

McGrath, T. (2008) *The Role of the National ESL Scales in the Production of Culturally Competent Australian Citizens: A Foucauldian analysis.* Unpublished Honours Thesis. The University of Sydney, Australia.

Masanauskas, J. & Mickelburough, P. (2005) Tolerance Keeps Peace, *The Herald Sun*, 13 December pp. 1, 4.

Meadmore, D., Hatcher, C. & McWilliam, E. (2000) Getting Tense About Genealogy, *Qualitative Studies in Education*, 13:5, pp. 463–476.

Nakayama, T. K. & Krizek, R. L. (1995) Whiteness: A strategic rhetoric, *Quarterly Journal of Speech*, 81, pp. 291–309.

O'Farrell, C. (2005) *Michel Foucault* (London, Sage Publications).

Peters, M. (2004) Lyotard, Marxism and Education: The problem of knowledge capitalism, in: J. D. Marshall (ed.), *Poststructuralism, Philosophy, Pedagogy* (Dordrecht, Kluwer Academic Publishers).

Popkewitz, T. & Lindblad, S. (2000) Educational Governance and Social Inclusion and Exclusion: Some conceptual difficulties and problematics in policy and research, *Discourse: Studies in the Cultural Politics of Education*, 21:1, pp. 5–44.

Rudd, K. (2007) An Education Revolution for Australia's Economic Future: Speech 23 January 2007. Address to the Melbourne Education Research Institute, Melbourne University. Retrieved 10 January 2008, from http://www.alp.org.au/media/0107/spe230.php

Scheurich, J. J. (1997) *Research Method in the Postmodern* (London, Falmer Press).

Tamboukou, M. (1999) Writing Genealogies: An exploration of Foucault's strategies for doing research, *Discourse: Studies in the Cultural Politics of Education*, 20:2, pp. 101–217.

Taylor, S. (2004) Researching Educational Policy and Change in 'New Times': Using critical discourse analysis, *Journal of Education Policy*, 19:4, pp. 433–451.

Thomas, G. (1997) What's the Use of Theory? *Harvard Educational Review*, 67:1, pp. 75–105.

Threadgold, T. (2003) Cultural Studies, Critical Theory and Critical Discourse Analysis: Histories, remembering and futures, *Linguistik Online*, 14:2, pp. 5–37.

Trifonas, P. (2000) Jacques Derrida as a Philosopher of Education, *Educational Philosophy and Theory*, 32:3, pp. 271–281.

van Dijk, T. A. (2001) Multidisciplinary CDA: A plea for diversity, in: R. Wodak & M. Meyer (eds), *Methods of Critical Discourse Analysis*. (London, Sage Publications), pp. 95–120

Wetherall, M. (2001) Debates in Discourse Research, in: M. Wetherall, S. Taylor & S. J. Yates (eds), *Discourse Theory and Practice: A Reader* (London, Sage Publications), pp. 380–399.

Wetherall, M., Taylor, S. & Yates, S. J. (2001) *Discourse Theory and Practice: A Reader* (London, Sage Publications).

9

After the Glow:
Race ambivalence and other
educational prognoses

ZEUS LEONARDO

On 4 November, 2008, the US entered a new era of race relations when the nation elected its first-ever black president, Barack Obama. Whether intellectuals want to brand the event as a new day of post-racial proportions or a new stage for a continuing race politics, or whether it ultimately signifies racial progress or a reconfiguration of white hegemony, *something significant happened*. For some, Obama's election confirmed a prediction that the US was over the racial hump from which it has been running away for centuries, like a dog escaping its own tail. That said, we also hear objections to the idea that Obama is a 'real' African American man, casting aspersions over his authenticity by virtue of the fact that he is mixed-race with white, part of the educated and political elite, among other things. Perhaps ironic and germane to this discussion, doubt about Obama's blackness is also a blow to the one-drop rule that transforms any part-black person fully black in the US, which paradoxically signals a dismantling of the rule of hypodescent, a staple of US racialization. All that said, it is more likely that Obama is a mixed-race black man, and a brilliant politician at that. His mixed-race heritage is a topic he did not eschew during his campaign, embracing the fact that he has a Kenyan father while his mother is white and hails from Kansas. Much has been made of the idea that Obama represents the poster child of 'post-race' identity, indeed the symbol of a new race era.

What was unimaginable not long ago to many US citizens has now become a reality. The deceased rapper, Tupac Shakur, in a track titled 'Changes', once opined that the US was not likely to have a black president. To some, surely this moment is indicative of the US approaching a post-race condition. This would overstate the case in light of the fact that Obama's campaign against Senator Clinton was highly racialized, not to mention the lynch mob mentality of the protestors who stormed the Capitol ostensibly to display their dissatisfaction with Obama's health reform. The irony is not lost when one considers that his health reform would likely help the modest white American protestors. At stake here is precisely whites' long-term interests of racial supremacy even as they are willing to forego short-term benefits by adopting the new health plan. We are tempted to interpret the situation as an expression of white *ressentiment*. Acknowledging white retrenchment in the face of a black man in the White House, Obama's ascendancy also signals another trend in the form of ambivalence with otherwise entrenched notions of race, such as the rule of hypodescent. Whether or not a sea of change is about to happen, these are

The Power In/Of Language, First Edition. Edited by David R. Cole and Linda J. Graham.
Chapters © 2012 The Authors. Book compilation © 2012 Philosophy of Education Society of Australasia.
Published 2012 by Blackwell Publishing Ltd.

interesting times to the intellectual of race relations. The noted ambivalence may represent an opportunity for a discussion on the merits of a post-race analysis rather than the more usual suspicion that it is another limp attempt at color-blindness, a moment which progressive educators can utilize.

With the Obama moment setting the tone, this essay considers the insights of post-race writings within the general field of race theory. It is necessary, at least as it concerns the US, to begin with Obama who has sparked interests in the debates around post-race thinking. To some, it represents *the* signature example of post-race possibilities. First, I introduce the main contours of post-race thinking as a form of aspiration rather than a description of society as it exists. That is, whereas conservative thought uses post-raciality as a *fait accompli*, progressives have the opportunity to consider it as a future goal and in effect wrestles the concept away from its commonsense use. With Omi & Winant (1994), I define race as a contested formation comprised of material and cultural projects along the color line.[1] The task at hand is to ask questions about the possibility of a 'post-racial project'. Second, I analyze the theoretical space of race ambivalence as a source of possible insights when race theory becomes aware and reflective about its own conceptual apparatus. Here, I favor the concept of ambivalence over the usual and helpful construct of racial contradictions because the former allows educators to establish some distance from the naturalness of race, its seeming permanence, which is the first step at making its familiarity appear strange. It does not suggest reconciling contradictions if it means leaving the domain of race unquestioned and conjuring up a non-racist racial formation, something Hirschman (2004) argues is an anachronism. Third, I present post-race thinking as precisely the opportunity that affords educators the space to move race pedagogy into a different direction. It is important to note that color-blindness is the shell of post-race thinking, while its kernel fully endorses racial perpetuity through its denial of race's daily effects as a structuring principle of society. This is hardly post-racial. Finally, I imagine the long-term implications for hope in a post-race society that counters the short-term optimism of whiteness.

Introduction: From Racial to Post-racial Imaginary

Engaging post-race discourse is driven less by the need to pronounce that race is walking out the door, that it is an interpellation that is getting increasingly harder to hear, and more about the future status of race—or better yet, its future standing. Racial hailing still occurs and many of its subjects still turn around when their subjectivity is called upon to answer (Leonardo, 2009a). Race, as Warmington (2009) argues, is still a powerful mediating tool, and 'we live race as if it has meaning and we live within a society in which those raced meaning have innumerable consequences. We live with race as a social fact' (p. 284). As Derrida (1985) notes, although linguistic discrimination is not the only form of racism we can imagine (e.g. labor and wealth disparities), racism *requires* language to do its daily work: no language, no racism. Its meaning is deciphered through language and its enactment requires recruiting language into its logic. While guarding against linguistic idealism or determinism, the racial critic recognizes that racist acts depend on language in order to signify self and other, therefore rationalizing the disparagement of racialized minorities and valorization of whiteness. Although racism involves a whole range of social processes, as I argue later, it never does not involve language, which is always in play. It is not language *qua* language that concerns us, but language as a form of social practice. Subjects do not merely describe the world of race, but actively perform and constitute it through discourse. This establishes the fact that in order to know racism, we must know language intimately. Consistent with this special issue's focus on language and domination, I want to establish the centrality of language in the enactment of race. But I also have another curiosity regarding racism: that is, whether or not the discourse of race, or race language in practice, is itself intimately tied to racism and any hopes of ending racism may have to pose the end of racial signification. Particularly in the US, racialized language is still the dominant public discourse and represents the nation's anxiety with difference. I hope to make this argument clearer below.

The Stubborn Significance of Race and Racism

In terms of a material organization of US society, there is nothing to suggest that race is on the wane when the racial wealth gap (Oliver & Shapiro, 1997) is still a force, yet talks of reparations receive less attention than Paris Hilton's latest exploits. The language of race is still part of everyday life in the US and Obama's case is not an example of transcending race altogether and rather highlights the ambivalent share of it. But suggesting that US society is still organized around the language of skin color says nothing about our preference that it discontinue in this vein. This is the third space of post-race discussion, which exists uncomfortably alongside the first space of race-in-perpetuity and second space of color-blindness. One might suggest that we live in an **era of race ambivalence**. It does not prevent most scholars from engaging the question and study of race; in fact, I argue we must. But it is becoming increasingly difficult to rely on its stability. Brett St. Louis (2002) explains this ambivalence,

> As the intellectual descendants of DuBois we inhabit, for the most part, a scholarly age wise to the scientific myths, spurious rationality and dubious facticity of 'race'. We have long been aware that 'race' has no sustainable bio-logical foundation and, convinced of its socially constructed basis, we instead recognize the *racialization* of different 'groups' that are culturally, socially and historically constituted. We also largely agree that socially recognizable 'races' demonstrate significant degrees of *internal* as well as *external* differentiation. It is clear therefore at least for much of the academy, that the inviolable sanctity of race is under fire, it is under erasure. (pp. 652–653; italics in original)

Race scholars carry on as usual, but we do so with an increasing sense of doubt and doom about the very nature of our topic. It is possible that racial organization has always been under the threat of erasure or obliteration and the latest set of challenges speak to its continuing evolution. The intellectual's livelihood may also be under erasure but something more important than this remains: our search for racial emancipation. When Gilroy (1998) announces that 'race ends here', he points to the conceptual flimsiness of racial organization that may create as many problems as it purports to solve. It leads St. Louis (2002) to propose a nominalist or 'weak' form of race thinking that claims 'race is a contributory, not determining or principal, local existential element within human existence' (p. 670) in order to observe its social materiality without further reifying its fallacious ideality (see also Leonardo, 2005).

Race is not declining as a structuring principle of US society. Moreover, the US is not alone, as demonstrated with experiences from Canada and Australia (Graham, this issue; Ibrahim, this issue). There may be signs for the prognosis of race's decline, as Gilroy (2000) clearly provokes, but they are inconclusive at best and mistaken at worst. This fact notwithstanding, the current moment or 'crisis' presents an opportunity to ask new questions, to search for new understandings. It may be the case that two apparently contradictory trends of color-blindness and racial progress are occurring. Gilroy's argument does not depend primarily on its empirical veracity but its logical conclusions. That is, scholars cannot wish away race but we can recommend its impeachment. Contrary to the declining significance of race, we can make a good case that race relations pulsate as strongly as ever, perhaps even more significantly than previous eras. It is possible that both phenomena are happening simultaneously: race entrenchment and ambivalence. As Mills (1997) asserts, there is neither a transracial class nor gender solidarity and therefore race, at least for the moment, remains axiomatic.

Post-race Thought versus Color-Blindness

A society does not reach a post-race situation by downplaying race and the reality of racial contestation, as in policies that turn a color-blind eye to race and education in a desperate attempt *to make the States united again* (if it ever was). Downplaying race struggle will ensure that it continues at the level of social practice as both race and racism have 'gone underground' (Chesler, Peet & Sevig, 2003, p. 219). Of course, racism may be overt and above ground, and receive insufficient attention as denial becomes the easier route. Suggesting that race does not matter does not necessarily make it so, as Gotanda (1995) clearly shows in his debunking of the apparent color-blindness of the US constitution. Haney Lopez's (2006) study of prerequisite case laws displays in full splendor the awkward way that the courts used both scientific and common sense arguments to legalize the construct of whiteness. In the Thind case, the highest court argued that despite the fact that he has legitimate claims to Caucasian identity by virtue of his geographical ancestry (compatible at the time with Blumenbach's 'scientific' typology of the races), by all commonsense understandings of whiteness, Thind fails to establish his identity as such. He may be Caucasian but he is certainly not white by commonsense law.

This essay's argument goes against the notion that the best way to rid society of racial discrimination is to stop making distinctions based on race, which is more of a slogan than a sign of a genuine engagement of racism (see Lewis, 2003). However, that race matters does not suggest that society should continue existing in a racial form, that race should keep mattering. That is, insofar as the US is racially structured, skin color stratified, and somatically signified does not automatically recommend their perpetuity. So the task is not only to promote anti-racism but also to consider the post-race position, which is to say, the *politics of being anti-race*, or the dispreference for the continuation of a racially organized society. To be clear, this is a race-conscious, as opposed to a race-neutral, proposition. It does not only require acknowledging the fact of race, but also necessitates entering the field of racial contestation in order to end, rather than to perpetuate, it.

The prognostication of race's future asks neither the question of race's current significance nor its real past but more important, its projected destiny. It takes from Nayak's (2006) assertion that 'post-race ideas offer an opportunity to experiment, to re-imagine and to think outside the category of race' (p. 427). To be more precise, post-race ruminations allow educators to recast race, even work against it, as Gilroy suggests, but this move cannot be accomplished with the pretense of thinking *outside* the category of race. As I argue elsewhere (2005, 2009a), in a racialized formation, *race has no outside*. As Graham & Slee (2008) note, following Deleuze, assuming an outside maintains an illusory interiority, thus reproducing the original problems associated with margins and centers (see also Lather, 2003). At this point, in many societies, like the US, there is no way to deal with race from a position outside of race relations. We are caught up in racemaking at every turn and presuming access to its outside comes with dangerous implications, usually complicit with color-blindness. Rather, it suggests the possibility of *undoing race from within rather than from without*, of coming to full disclosure about what race has made of us to which we no longer consent. If race has no outside, is it possible to talk of its *elsewhere*? If color-blindness does not work as policy, is it supportable as a utopic aspiration? Is there a foreseeable end to the language of race? In this sense, the unmaking of race interests the oppressed races more than the master race, the latter arguably more invested in its continuation (see also Ibrahim, this issue). Therefore the analysis does not proceed from the audacious pronouncement that this move is plausible but asks whether or not it is possible and more important, preferable.

Problematizing the Vague Uses of Race

Given the bogus beginnings of race, dismantling race from the inside seems warranted and within the realm of possibilities. The language of race and the racial dimensions of language are a source of much symbolic violence (Bourdieu & Passeron, 1990) the moment that human differences were reduced to skin differences. Although racialized minorities, as skin collectives, may mobilize around the concept of race and find strength (indeed a source of pride) in their survival from and resilience against white supremacy, skin ontologies are not sustainable ways to organize society, even after the demise of racism. What would it mean to dismantle racism but not disband social groups based on skin color? It is possible to discredit race at this level of analysis. However, given race's omnipresence, in US society in particular, the task seems impossible in the Derridean sense. Although race arguably has a five hundred year pedigree, ideologically it feels eternal, just like the unconscious (Leonardo, 2005; Althusser, 1971). That is the space this essay occupies, wedged as it is between the possible and the impossible, between the precept of and a preference for race. It not only requires a language of possibility (Giroux, 1988), but equally a language of impossibility (Biesta, 1998; Cho, 2006). Post-racial analysis is ethically justifiable despite the independent issue of and slim chances for success because whites show such low levels of investment in critical race work (McPhail, 2003). But as I argue later, alongside McPhail, the hope in ending racism trumps the despair in whiteness.

The concept of race and utility of race analysis have been staples of social theory and education for quite some time. One can hardly read or write about the challenges of education without confronting the 'problem of race'. In fact, the ubiquitous language of the 'achievement gap' is inherently a racial gap. That said, the future of the race concept has been left relatively untouched—e.g. in its leading discourses of multiculturalism, critical race theory, and anti-racism. *As a relation*, race is seldom deemed problematic. Questioning race becomes tantamount to interrogating the very existence of racial groups, risking the very self we have come to know. Or worse, sometimes race is elided and dangles as a proxy for the vague identity of 'social group', sometimes conflated with ethnicity, sometimes sliding into nationality. No doubt these concepts are interrelated but they are by no means equatable, at least not without some loss in clarity. For example, it is not uncommon to read treatises on race in education, which comfortably analogize it with ethnicity and leave the educator unsure how culture achieves a color in the process. Racism then becomes a descriptor of any institutional arrangement, as opposed to prejudice, where a group has suffered at the hands of another group because of race's currency in the US imagination. However, there are other sources of injury, such as zenophobia and ethnocentrism, which are related to race but not reducible to it. *In the US, a group's grievance is not recognized until it becomes racialized.* In a literal sense, oppression is not understood before it is expressed in a racial language, tied to racial terms, and does not enter popular cognition until it enters racial reasoning. To repeat Derrida's point, no language, no racism, therefore we must know language in order to know racism. This does not mean that recognition equates with resolution of the problem and nearing 150 years since the fall of slavery, the US is no closer to granting African Americans forty acres and a mule. The upshot is that until the point of insertion into race, a claim to historical reparations only meets with glancing interest.

In the US, race has become common sense and sometimes loses both its specificity and edge. Our attempts to intervene into racism come with difficulties when the language of intelligibility contained in race is not held up to be problematic. The language of race has saturated US society to the point that it loses its strangeness as a bogus social relation. Schools are part of how race is maintained through race's pedagogical dimensions. In other words, educators daily teach young people the naturalized status of race, its foreverness. Educators may question racism, but they rarely interrogate the status of race. The color-blind teacher is perhaps most guilty of this crime as s/he enacts race while denying its reality, but s/he is not the only one who takes race for granted. In general, racism has to end, as the saying goes, but race has a different destiny; it should stay. It acquires a privileged place in history and utopia, an explanation of where we have been but also an apparently inextricable part of our future. Here, I want to recognize that the possibility of race's disappearance does not mean that culture *in toto* goes with it.

The Permanence of Race

To the extent that black culture exists, it is possible that an African American ethnicity endures. A black or brown aesthetics may continue, but within the context of race, one cannot be sure that it is not, in some manner, a form of protection against white racism: aesthetics of color as a kind of weapon. Paul Taylor (2008) argues that within a racial formation, no theory of race is divorced from a theory of aesthetics and no notion of beauty is free from racialization. Such is the case with 'black is beautiful' during the

1960s–70s, when African Americans pushed back against the demeaning images of blackness in US society. As such, this establishes the fact that blackness or otherness may be a source of positivity when it fights against its dehumanization within race relations. The same cannot be said for a White American ethnicity insofar as this is the secret cousin of white raciality, which as Roediger (1994) and other abolitionists remind us is nothing but false and oppressive. Whiteness must go (Leonardo, 2002).[2] Dumas (2008) seems to agree when he admits that he has learned to love and trust certain whites, whereas whiteness is never to be trusted. Here we may notice that as a subfield of race theory, whiteness studies exhibits a tendency to recenter whiteness, even a sense of white fetishism. The Left's derogation of whiteness differs from its valorization from the Right but both recenter it. Whiteness studies disturbs the balance in its insistence on centering whiteness in order ultimately to dislodge it from its seeming permanence. In *A Black Theology of Liberation*, Cone (1990) goes further by arguing that whites can only destroy their whiteness by joining racially oppressed communities, whereby their white being passes into black being. This choice does not follow the usual election of blackness for whites who vicariously experience its benefits without its burdens. To be critical, it must be a simultaneous disidentification with whiteness and identification with otherness. In the end, they become neither white nor black but free.

Regarding racism and the status of race, even Bell's (1992) insurrectionary injunction of the 'permanence of racism' does not suggest that he *prefers* the continuation of racial inequality but in his deployment of racial realism, admits to its stubborn reality. Here he is right as there is more evidence to point to racism's perpetual status than to its eventual demise as white America has proven time and again its fundamental sheepishness toward racial equality. But with respect to race as a future organizing principle for society, Bell is more quiet and, one assumes, more accepting. Race appears permanent as well, and this time without the added irony given to the permanence of racism. What does it mean to clutch onto race but purge racism?

The permanence-of-race-as-skin-color thesis has received some criticism. Loic Wacquant (1997, 2002) interrogates not only the utility of this move, but also the questionable, folk-knowledge status of race that passes as scientific or analytical. Or worse, Wacquant fears that with the reality of US imperialism enacted at the level of theory, 'American' race analysis is exported as a general world analysis rather than a particular set of assumptions. Take the example of the Hutus and Tutsis, where an apparent race war is waged between the slender-constructed Tutsis against the Hutus (Freedman *et al.*, 2008). Although one recalls the traditional skin-based racialization introduced by the Belgian colonizers into Rwanda, this relation has mutated to a complex architecture of non-skin color driven racial distinction today. Slenderness is racialized and associated with Europeanness and therefore represents a higher aesthetics, but it is nominally associated with skin color since both Hutus and Tutsis are practically indistinguishable on this index. On the Brazilian front, a well-known phenomenon goes by the phrase of 'money whitens'. That is, a higher class status affords (pun intended) people of color the power to purchase whiteness, which speaks to the intimate connection between race and capital. For now, I will not make more of these events more than necessary since alternative forms of racialization are outweighed by the more pervasive skin-based racism circulating globally, accelerating through the globalization of racialized beauty industries, such as cosmetic surgery and skin whitening creams (see Hunter, 2005).

With respect to the suggestion of a racial condition absent of racism, Hirschman (2004) observes that this anachronism belies the fact that race has always existed alongside racism. No race, no racism. To be clear on this point, racialization is not the mere recognition of skin color differences *qua* differences but an entire social system founded on a value system designed to elevate lightness (as a sign of godliness, among other things, see Dyer, 1997) and denigration of darkness as sign of an equally dark soul. When the Taíno people of Puerto Rico regarded as beautiful the Spaniards' armor, they were not expressing a preference for racial organization as much as they were enamored by a new form of difference; this event also challenges the otherwise naturalized assumption that human societies inherently fear and desire to control difference. The preference of lightness predates colonization of the Americas when we note that the Bible reminds us, 'there was light and it was good'. Race enters the room precisely when it becomes a justificatory discourse for an entire society. So it is less important to ask whether or not Jesus Christ is white (after all, whites did not exist then) but rather to ascertain the consequences of racializing Jesus and justice, of projecting race back into a raceless past because of a raced present, even to the point of distorting and whitening Christ's racial marking (arguably brown-toned) within current understanding.

As understood here with respect to race and racism, to continue the former while arguing to dismantle the latter is a bit like a Marxist imagining capitalism without exploitation. To the Marxist, no amount of restructuring capital rids it of labor exploitation. Likewise, no amount of resignification will rescue race (Gilroy, 2000). Decoupling race from racism to argue that racial hierarchy is the problem and not racial difference is a bit like suggesting that tracking practices that are hierarchical in schools can be reimagined *sans* the stratification. If that were to happen, it simply would not be called tracking anymore. By definition, tracking *is* hierarchical (see Oakes, 2005). Of course, we are tempted to imagine tracking as the lynchpin of racial oppression in schools but Oakes, Joseph, and Muir (2004) remind educators of a more pervasive differential access to high status knowledge that, while exacerbated by tracking practices, recalls the near complete racial segregation of society, with the US as exemplar. Supported by Massey and Denton's (1993) *American Apartheid*, segregation studies explain the simple fact that in a racialized social system most blacks attend school with other black children, tracked with respect to one another rather than with whites.[3] In the same vein, race without racism simply would not be race as we know it. In all likelihood, it would be a society without race. With the arrival of post-race studies, new opportunities for analysis, insights, and recent ambivalences have made it possible to ask fundamental questions about the status of race.

On Race Ambivalence

Admittedly, a post-race analysis is not a simple task and is liable to make one an intellectual punching bag of critics from left to right. Currently, few spaces in the academy exist where a progressive discussion of a society beyond the color line can attract a sympathetic ear because it has been associated with color-blind pundits, like

Dinesh D'Souza, reactionary politicians, like Ward Connerly, or conservative intellectu-als, like Shelby Steele. Or, it attracts the wrong attention and becomes co-opted. In fact, one may be able to cite post-race tendencies in Martin Luther King, Jr.[4] or Frantz Fanon (see Gilroy, 2000; Nayak, 2006) but there is always the real and public fear that their message will be interpreted without its spirit, as Connerly once attempted when he appropriated King's platform in order to launch the 'Racial Privacy Act'.[5] Had it not been convincingly defeated in California, it would have outlawed any public institution's ability to gather racial data. It would have made it difficult—near impossible—to track racial discrimination in education, the health industry, and labor market. One treads on soft ground when it comes to engaging a post-race language.

But it is important to consider the implications of post-race in order to continually re-examine long-held beliefs about race and whether the ultimate existential choice of disappearing is warranted in order to reappear as something else we would rather prefer. But as Graham (in press) has noted elsewhere, in terms of identity this involves the risk of death in order to become a recognizable subject, of giving up certain identities to become something else. For subjects who have very little power to fall back on, it is understandable to desire holding onto current, but problematic identities in light of an unknown (and perhaps not better) option. Race sits strategically at a crossroad that demands scholarship that is attentive not only to its declining or rising significance but to its very future as a system of intelligibility.

Race Theory becomes Aware of Itself: The Case for Abolition

On one hand, race scholarship that forsakes a conceptual engagement of its own premises takes for granted the naturalized status of race. Questioning its solidity now seems unreal, caught up in unnecessary solipsistic arguments about the ostensible and unquestionable fact of race. After all, race groups exist and race history is indisputable. Race is real. End of story. There are several limitations to this approach. First, race was an invention and its matter-of-fact existence today should not be confused with its objective reality without the daily dose of reification. It is worthwhile intellectually to debate the conceptual status of race if racism significantly depends on the continuation of a *racialized mindset*. This is perhaps what James Baldwin was referring to, when he claimed that as long as white people think they are white, there is no hope for them (cited by Roediger, 1994, p. 13). After all, it is difficult to imagine white racism without the prior category of race that is responsible for white *perception* concerning which groups deserve a blessed or banished life. The challenge for whites is to unthink their whiteness because race trouble arrived at the scene precisely at the moment when white bodies began thinking they were white people. The birth of white people allows for the first premise of racism: put simply, that whites are better than people of color. This is a simplified reduction of a rather complex process but it captures the basic operation of racial superordination and subordination. If a group is simply better than another group, then the former in religious terms is saved, in episte-mological terms represents the true knower, in aesthetic terms constitutes the beautiful, and in ontological terms plainly exists. This is not just the genesis of whiteness but of the very domain we know as race. Whiteness and race are the large and small arms of a clock that began over five hundred years ago. But if I (2002) am correct to announce the coming of *late whiteness*, their hours are numbered.

The abolitionist opposes encouraging an overt racial language and discourages greater awareness on the part of whites so common to racial pedagogy. Instead he asks them to forget their racial rootedness. The caveat is that it is a form of white privilege to even ponder 'giving up' one's racialization, a luxury that people of color simply do not possess. That established, it does not contradict the idea that this is the preferred collective path that abolitionists believe we should follow. The abolitionist assumption is that whites already know intimately their whiteness, which is different from suggesting that they understand their whiteness. Whiteness is the default position of the human and it is unnecessary to qualify one with the other. A white person need not describe his whiteness because it goes without saying. Toni Morrison (1993) says as much when she asserts that characters in novels are assumed to be white until the text explicitly writes them into the story as people of color. Writing 'white' into narratives can actually be jarring for whites whose self-identification with an unnamed whiteness exposes their racial investment. Increasing racial recognition is built on the faulty premise that whites are ignorant of their racial world, when in fact it does not take much of a threat to whiteness for whites to erect barriers around what Cheryl Harris (1995) calls 'whiteness as property'. In short, whites know they are white and do not need to be made aware of this first fact. More important, they know from whom they are set apart: people of color. Therefore, the common suggestion in education that teacher education programs ought to teach white pre-service teachers a heightened awareness of their whiteness misses the target. Becoming aware of one's whiteness is one thing but acknowledging how one's whiteness translates into political and social structures responsible for racial domination is quite another.

Or worse, education programs construct whites as passive observers of race, who must be taught to recognize their raciality. To the abolitionist, this move further embeds their whiteness. Everyday, US educators teach white children that they are white: from curriculum selection that prioritizes Western epistemology, to cultural classroom practices that bridge the home-to-school divide for whites and maintain the distance for students of color, to apparently race-neutral policies like No Child Left Behind, which make a casual, rather than causal, pass at race (Leonardo, 2007). Opposite racial awareness, whites must now forgo their whiteness, disowning it before they even own up to it. Although the abolition movement faces grim prospects about success, they are correct to challenge this oft-unquestioned premise of white ignorance. Said another way, post-race is intimate with post-white discourses. The abolition of whiteness is at the same time the abolition of white people, an invention that must now be forgotten. This move is not without ironies and waiting for whites to forgo their whiteness is like waiting for Godot (see also Ibrahim, this issue).

Second, conceptualizing race is intimately tied to performing it. Perceiving race as real is then tied to acting on it. The upshot is that taking up the race concept asks the primary question, 'What is race?' without which race analysis proceeds commonsensically rather than critically. For example, the question of which collectivities constitute a racial group is still unsettled in the US. Is race a black-white skin phenomenon that *implicates* other groups, like Asians and Latinos, which are quasi-races? If this is true, then it seems racial progress in the US will only result when the modern contradiction between whites and blacks is resolved.[6] One could call this model the modernist racial discourse of race-as-skin-color, a binary spectrum with whites and blacks at two poles and other races incorporated ambiguously along the continuum. Or are there multiple racial projects, each articulating itself in specific ways for different groups? For instance, in the US race has affected each group differently, such as the significant history of citizenship status for Asians, sovereignty and land rights for Native Americans, documented immigration for Latinos, and enslavement for African Americans. If this is true, then it necessitates a postmodern racial perspective (not always synonymous with a post-race philosophy) that decenters skin color from the focus of racial analysis and places it alongside other physical markers (as distinct from culture), such as Eastern eyes and Latino looks. In all, the obviousness of race is becoming increasingly strange.

Big Bang Race Theory versus Steady State: Setting the Parameters

In both of these scenarios, racism maintains its distinction from cultural imperialism by emphasizing somatic relations as proxies for deciding human worth. Race is a relation of bodies and culture only enters the process when it is recruited, as in the case of 'new racism', which replaced the biological basis of racism with its cultural cognate (Barker, 1990). In this transformation, people of color are inferior to whites based on the former's cultural, rather than genetic, make up. Moreover, in both of these offerings, the post-race imagination is mobilized as a mode of possibility after the glow of race relations. Although still surrounding us like the primordial warmth of the Big Bang, the heat of racialization will reach its end point and the possibility of a Big Squeeze ultimately develops, causing an eventual implosion. In contrast to a Steady State theory of race, which provides a portrait of racialization as changing but ultimately eternal as a social relation, a Big Bang theory posits a definite beginning and possible end of race as we know it. But this implosion, as in the field of physics, is not only catastrophic, but provides the elements necessary for life. Just as we are composites of the iron and other heavier atoms left over from supernovas, future generations will be comprised of debris gathered from the ashes of a racial involution. Like planets and stars, which result from gravity's ability to collapse material into a sphere, post-race society will represent the gradual accretion of race material from a time when race used to matter. Life does not start anew *per se* but a new history begins.

Without broaching these definitional debates and directional issues about the destiny of race, critical race analysis ceases to have a future because it cannot imagine a situation that makes it obsolete. For if, as an intervention into racist formations, race analysis is to realize its goal, it may eventually have to disappear as a condition of its own success. Marx predicted as much when it came to class and capitalism, which sowed their own seeds of destruction. This is different from the desire to organize around skin politics in order to end it altogether. A post-race perspective is not the attempt to elide and evade race in order to imagine its disappearance. Quite the opposite. Post-race discourse makes race visible, maps its operations, and enters its interpellations. It is not ambivalent about these commitments but on the issue that racial distinctions should be an endless ride without a destination. *If all good things come to an end, surely bad ones ought to.* One may be tempted to brand the inability to deal critically with the future of race as evidence of a certain anti-intellectual tendency. But that would be inflammatory and in the end does more harm than good. For a post-race project is not only an intellectual project but equally political, conceptual on one hand but actional on the other (see Fanon, 1967).

Reducing the problem of racism to the conceptual status of race comes with its own difficulties, as if racism were caused by a concept rather than racially motivated actions, such as educational segregation and labor discrimination. For Guillaumin (1995), nothing short of dismantling the race concept can rescue us from racism. A concept not white supremacist institutions, like slavery. Not the attempt to exterminate Native Americans, to limit of Asian American mobility by curtailing their citizenship rights, or the constant attacks on Latino autonomy in the US. Not the forced removal of 'half caste' Aboriginal children from their family and communities to 'breed out' the indigenous peoples of Australia. Not the social engineering called 'whitening' in Brazil through selective immigration from Europe in the early decades of the 1900s. Not the South African social incarceration of Blacks. We could go on but it seems apparent that racism is not ultimately the problem of people who think there are races 'out there' but the materially coordinated set of institutions that result from people's actions. Certainly these actions have their root in the concept of race but a whip in the hand seems as responsible for racism as an idea in the head.

Creating a Racialized Society

These arrangements do not continue merely by virtue of our investments in a concept but through historical contestations over power within a racialized field of understanding. We may go a long way with Marxists' distinction between ideas and substance but this makes it all the more ironic that for all their materialist analyses, they would rather emphasize race as an idea rather than a set of material practices (see Bonilla-Silva, 2005). It is not just that people *think* they are white, but that they *act* on it. Like language, white is not reducible to a concept or idea but a social practice. As Appiah (1990) notes, counter-nationalisms may be a form of *intrinsic racism* insofar as they assume a family resemblance among people of color but *extrinsic racism* differs in the way that it enforces a group's assumed superiority on an(other). Just as we do things with words (Austin, 1962), we do things with whiteness, which is a performative, rather than an inert, identity (Youdell, 2004; Giroux, 1997). It is constituted through acts of whiteness, whose articulations are found in segregation in the housing and social spheres, and policies that reinforce black deviance through harsher expulsion and disciplinary actions against them (Gillborn, 2005) as well as blacks' over-representation in special education in the school sphere (Artiles, 2008). Deserving to be quoted at length, Gillborn (2005) writes,

> [T]he English education system appears to be a clear case where the routine assumptions that structure the system encode a deep privileging of white students and, in particular, the legitimization, defence and extension of Black inequity. In terms of policy priorities race equity has been at best a marginal concern, at worst non-existent. In relation to beneficiaries the picture is more complex than usually recognized (some minoritized groups do relatively well), but the most consistent beneficiaries are white students and, in key respects, Black students' position is no better than it was when the whole reform

movement began in the late 1980s. Finally, an examination of outcomes clearly shows that central reform strategies (such as the use of selection and hierarchical teaching groups) are known to work against race equity but are nevertheless promoted as 'best practice' for all. These reforms are known to discriminate in practice (regardless of intent) and are, therefore, racist in their consequences. These [examples] establish the education system's active involvement in the defence and extension of the present regime of white supremacy in the contemporary British state. (pp. 4496–497)

Gillborn's study of the British educational system finds that whiteness is constituted through both informal, naturalized assumptions of white superiority as well as formal policies that solidify white advantage. Whiteness is not so much an identity, if by this we mean something of an essence that whites are born into, but the constellation of acts (beyond their intentions) that constitute whites as always an identity in the making.

Race does not disappear because we alter conceptualizing each other as post- or non-racial *if we act on the world in a racial way and with racial consequences*. Brazil is a case in point, where the concept of a post-racial democracy is compromised by the stubborn reality of racial stratification (see Caldwell, 2007; Telles, 2006; Warren & Twine, 2002). Whether or not we conceptualize Brazilian power relations as racial in the US sense of it, there is a clear color line among those who lead the country and those who follow. Brazilians may think through class, but they appear to act through race. This is not to argue that people of color in Brazil are worse off than those in the US, which is a legitimate argument. This is an empirical assertion with much veracity but is besides my point. The problem of racism cannot be reduced to the concept of race as much as religious warfare fails to be explained by divergent interpretations of sacred texts. Rather, racial contestation is decided by internal concepts (reified as they may be) externalized through social behavior and institutional arrangements. To racial realists, placing the word-race in scare quotes (i.e. 'race') appears as unduly intellectualist, particularly when other social relations that are socially constructed are not put under a similar, bracketed scrutiny (Warmington, 2009). It appears they have an axe to grind against racial analysis. To racial realists, for all the realness that Marxists claim, in the end they ultimately fail to 'get real' about race. Be that as it may, what does race relations look like after the innovation of a race ambivalent analysis?

As we have seen, in Marxist theory race retains its ideological status and a racial cosmology inevitably subverts a clearer understanding of social relations and the basis of an educational apparatus where race is reified through social practice. For example, in education people of color are dogged by racialized notions of intelligence, the most obvious and cruel forms of which were witnessed in the eugenics movement but whose legacy continues today in the knowledge apartheid that derogates minority students and scholars' experiences (Bernal & Villalpando, 2005: see also Stanley, 2006). Its everyday and almost universally accepted practice is tracking, where students are divided by curricular and instructional levels within subjects areas, particularly in high school (Oakes, 2005). Absent some critical race awareness, these intellectual currents and tracking assignments reify race as real, spurring on countless school reforms to 'fix the intelligence gap'. This does not mean that Marxism outright rejects race struggle but questions its scientific status and praxiological implications for change. They help us differentiate between the real and real-like. In sociology, Robert Miles' (2000) work proves instructive; in history, Barbara Fields (1990) assumes prominence; and in education, Darder and Torres (2004), and McLaren and Torres (1999) have taken the lead. Here, post-race is taken literally to mean *after* the usefulness of race analysis, something that may have had utility in 18th century US as a justification of plantation forms of capitalism used to convince whites of all class positions.

Post-race as an Opportunity

Instigated by cultural studies, post-race discourses distinct from Marxist orthodoxy provide an opportunity to ask new questions about race through studies in the politics of representation, language being one of its privileged mechanisms. According to Gilroy (2000), post-race discussions signal an opportunity rather than something to be feared insofar as race understanding may be advanced in order that race may not remain standing. Like Marxism in the current conjuncture, post-race analysis is a politics that proceeds without guarantees, with race under possible erasure (see Hall, 1996, on Marxism). It is, as Gilroy (2000) punctuates, a politics of race abolition. It is a 'crisis of raciology', enabled by 'the idea that "race" has lost much of its common-sense credibility because the elaborate cultural and ideological work that goes into producing and reproducing it' takes more than it gives, that race 'has been stripped of its moral and intellectual integrity', that 'there is a chance to prevent its rehabilitation', and that race 'has become vulnerable to the claims of a much more elaborate, less deterministic biology' (pp. 28–29). Earlier, Gilroy (1993) argued for a Black Atlantic perspective that would link historical continuities among the four continents of Africa, Europe, and South and North America to counter the bombastic claims of European enlightenment. Since then, it appears that Gilroy's ambivalence toward race thinking, or raciology, has increased, leading him to pronounce his position 'against race'. Gilroy finds that the amount of race work that goes into anti-racism fails ultimately to provide a positive alternative beyond the negation of racism. At the end of the day, absent the fight against racism, race becomes an empty vessel. In effect, Gilroy transitions from a trans-Atlantic racial argument to a trans-racial Atlantic argument.

Signifying the 'Post' in Post-Race Theory

As Paul Taylor (2008) has suggested, the innovation of post-race analysis does not signal the end of race as we know it. Rather, like the 'post' in post-analytic philosophy, the same 'post' in post-race analysis signals an opening made possible by a conceptual ambivalence, not the closing of race scholarship. It allows new questions, as products of intellectual and material development, to surface. Like the 'post' in many schools of thought among extant theories, post-race is the ability of race theory to become self-aware and critically conscious of its own precepts. It signals the beginning of the end of race theory proper, which becomes near impossible to continue in the same vein. A race theory that becomes self-aware of its own constitutive activity enters the next stage of development in a dialectical movement of the thought process. Race theory becomes post-race precisely for the same reasons that modern thought is compromised by postmodern theory. Modern theory still exists but only after it reckons with the postmodern (Lyotard, 1984). Likewise, race theory emerges as something different, if not new, through the filter of post-race. It alters the politics of race scholarship.

I believe Taylor is right to frame the discussion in this manner. It avoids the otherwise vulgar suggestion that we are 'beyond race' or have 'transcended race' for usually unsubstantiated reasons. It acknowledges the debt owed to race analysis proper but propels it forward without jettisoning it. What do we make of society as we remake race in a daily way? Like one might ask about modern theories after the postmodern moment, what does race analysis look like after the arrival of post-race thought? For all of Baudrillard's ranting against modern teleologies and determinisms, he did not succeed in making them irrelevant before his death (see Leonardo, 2003). However, he forced a response from modernist thinkers. As a carbuncle on their theories, Baudrillard and other postmodernists pushed social theory and their intellectual adversaries into differ-ent directions, if not forward. Post-race analysis accomplishes a similar move, forcing a hard and sometimes difficult look at race theory.

Race understanding stands at the uncomfortable street corner where our bodies meet their socially constructed racial identity and where we leave the same intersection unsure of what we have just become as a result of race. Gilroy (2000) writes, '[W]e always agree that "race" is invented but are then required to defer to its embeddedness in the world' (p. 52). Nayak (2006) laments, 'The problem that race writers encounter, then, is how do we discuss race in a way that does not reify the very categories we are seeking to abolish?' (p. 415). If race was a figment of the Occidental imagination, it is one of life's deepest ironies that people of color hang on dearly to a concept created in order to oppress them. Many centuries later, US minorities find it hard to imagine a post-race society, either because they suspect that color-blind whiteness is up to its old tricks again or they are invested in a hard fought sense of an oppositional identity, the giving up of which means a fundamental loss of meaning. Of course, it goes without saying that many whites cannot imagine a post-race society either. As Nayak (2006) observes, '[F]or minority ethnic groups the erasure of race may equate with the obliteration of an identity and shared way of life ... the concept of race, however tarnished it may appear, has provided an important meeting place for political mobilization, inclusion and social change' (p. 422). Although Nayak commits the usual slide between ethnicity and raciality, something he misrecog-nizes when he asserts that 'whiteness is not homogeneous but fractured by the myriad ethnic practices', (p. 417), he is correct to note that race (not only racism) is a source of problem as well as a resource of meaning for racially despised groups. Yet he misses an opportunity. Whiteness is precisely homogenizing, wiping out ethnic differences in favor of racial solidarity. This is whiteness' *modus operandi* and emphasizing myriad (white) ethnic practices misrecognizes white raciality. This does not suggest that ethnic differences are not relevant for whites as the Irish-English, German-Jewish, or Turk-Greek Cypriot relations make plain (see Zembylas, 2008). This fact notwithstanding, in places as diverse as the US and Australia white ethnic differences play second fiddle to whiteness because white ethnicity is a demotion whereas white raciality becomes a promotion because the former makes whites concrete while the latter keeps them abstract. For people of color, race is a condition of their being and to dispute its centrality in their lives violates their perceived right to be, and usually without the profitable returns that white ethnics gain as they shed their identity to ascend to white raciality. As a result, race takes away from, more than it gives to, people of color. It certainly benefits whites more than non-whites, even as whites give up their ethnic language, custom, and identity (see Ignatiev, 1995).[7] The upshot is that these losses were well worth giving up for whiteness. In fact, hanging on to ethnicity, which makes whites visible and concrete, decreases whites' ability to guard the invisibility and abstraction called whiteness.

This does not mean that whites are eager to give up race but there is less of an ironic return for them. This point extends Nayak's (2006) claim that 'It is precisely because whiteness is seen as an unmarked racial category that the loss of race for white theo-reticians can appear inconsequential' (p. 422). We might distinguish between whiteness' discursive sleight-of-hand to conjure up a post-race reality and whites' general unwill-ingness to relinquish race privilege. Giving up race is consequential for whites for it is responsible for the lightness of their being, a sense of existential lack of tethers. Their sense of freedom and mobility is a direct and negative correlation with the restrictions people of color face. Their post-race attitude is belied by their racial behavior. A post-race situation is a threat to whites' very existence and can only come at a great loss for them, which may be greater than the loss of meaning for racial minorities. Racial recollections for minorities do not vanish with a post-race reorganizing, such as the South African case, but white domination and privilege may be eradicated structurally, which does not suggest that whiteness does not continue in the form of ideology. Arguably, race memory serves as the constant reminder against the return of white supremacy just as Jewish remembering of the Holocaust guards against its repeat. Race comes with advantages for whites and it is precisely the lack of guarantees that accom-panies post-race analysis that threatens white privilege for it unsettles expectations on which many whites have counted. To the white race abolitionist, the antidote includes acting against whiteness as if it were an affront to one's humanity (see Ignatiev & Garvey, 1996). To be sure, people of color have relied on race as a stable system of meaning on which to base their self-understandings but this process occurs as a response to the first fact of white domination. Without white domination, there is little need to assert black, brown, red, or yellow self-love, whose history is a defense against the imposition of white power. Race ambivalence is intended to challenge white supremacy before it is designed to threaten its victims. Although post-race scholars do not underestimate this loss of meaning, they consider it worth the risk for it is a system of meaning that creates more problems than promises. This loss, as Nayak suggests, can be turned into a gain.

Making Sense of the Crisis in Raciology

To dispel further any notions that this model mystifies the innerworkings of race, education under post-race assumptions makes it clear that it is made possible precisely by testifying to the inhuman tendencies of a racialized humanism. Gilroy (2000) con-tends that his '[planetary] humanism is conceived explicitly as a response to the suf-ferings that raciology has wrought' (p. 18), not its obfuscation. To Gilroy, the crisis in raciology represents less a crisis of identity and more the uncertain status and preferable (rather than inevitable) demise of race, not only at the level of signification but also at the level of social organization. Sweeping global changes in the economy and diasporic movement complicate and compromise racial worldmaking, stripping it of previous guarantees and predictive value as an autonomous relation. New events in history disturb our race-as-skin-color expectations, such as the apparent racial contest undetermined by skin color but mediated by somatic politics between Hutus and Tutsis in Rwanda. In Australia, one may look white but identify as indigenous, or whites with black features are not accepted as authentically indigenous. Of course, in the US there is a long tradition within communities of color regarding the colorism that affects their lives (Hunter, 2005). Although the Rwandan case should not be overinterpreted as proof of the waning effect of skin color difference, for which we have more worldwide evidence, the Rwandan situation brings new insights to race analysis by introducing the reinterpretation of bodily differentiation through primary markers besides skin color. Even the multiracialization of beauty images, which includes increasingly more black and brown faces, signals new anxieties about race, but this time by disturbing clear lines of racial demarcation rather than their enforcement. Whereas race thought was revolutionary in its own right, this new stage of development represents a revolution of the revolution, or the dynamic continuation of that transformation. To the extent that raciology introduced white subversion of the humanity inhered in people of color, post-race represents the attempt to subvert the subversion, to negate the negation. Race changed some subjects into people of color; it may be time to change again. This does not suggest that racism or racialization fails to exert its dominant imprint on social processes, subject formation, and State-sponsored policies. However, it means that both race struggle and raciology may begin the day but in no way end it, giving way to the era of race ambivalence.

I have no desire to overstate the case. Made clear by the stubborn standard of whiteness—from Tyra Banks, Halle Berry to Beyoncé Knowles, to Jennifer Lopez and Selma Hayek—light skin still, according to Hunter (2005), approximates white beauty standards. But as colonized peoples challenge white supremacy across the globe and gain access to networks of power monopolized by whites, counting on race stratification becomes ironically ambiguous and upsets racial expectations. This is a condition not to be deplored ultimately as a sense of loss, at least not in the manner that one grieves the passing of a seemingly endless war that has given this life much meaning. Putting race to peace may open up possibilities for other ways of being, other ways of knowing that have been heretofore limited or closed, particularly for people of color. The loss should not be minimized but countered by a sense of clarity concerning the neuroses of race about which Fanon (1967) spoke so forcefully and which Gilroy calls the 'rational absurdity of "race" ' (p. 14). But like the absurdity of life as we know it, which existentialists and phenomenologists alike argued, we can avoid racial dread by fully committing to our choices. Gilroy taps a certain post-racial tendency in Fanon whose attempts to restore blacks in their proper human place represent black analytics, or negritude, in order then for blackness to vanish under its own weight (see also Nayak, 2006). Just how the problems of humanism fold into the refashioning of the human in a post-race condition remains contested, opening the door for Gilroy's pragmatic, planetary and postanthro-pological humanism. Blackness, for example, may remain a culture and disappear as a racial category. Gilroy clarifies, 'There will be individual variation, but that is not "race" ' (p. 42). Gilroy is quite clear that race does not equate with 'group' and his goal is not to deride human difference. This last point is worth elaborating.

Human differences continue but whether or not skin color variation should form the basis for social organization is the question. As a modern principle, race is a particular grouping of individuals into social groups. As embodied collectivities, these social groups could very well continue intact as we enter a post-race society, but they will no longer be considered skin groups once the race principle has been discredited. The bodies remain but they will be conceptualized differently as post-racial subjects. African Americans may continue as an ethnic group so blackness as a form of cultural practice may thrive in the absence of race where 'skin, bone, and even blood are no longer the primary referents of racial discourse' (Gilroy, 2000, p. 48). African Americans will neither sever completely their relation with blackness as a racial experience, which is historical, nor be reduced to it. Racial solidarity will be liberated from the 'cheapest pseudo-solidarities: forms of connection that are imagined to arise effortlessly from shared phenotypes, cultures, and bio-nationalities' (Gilroy, 2000, p. 41). Of course Gilroy is speaking of both non-whites and whites who desperately cling to identity as a visual confirmation of one's politics.

On one hand, it is whites who, in their fetish of color, clearly profit from racial politics as a form of interest consolidation than people of color who mobilize identity movements as a form of defense against white supremacy (see Lipsitz, 1998). On the other hand, although clearly necessary at this juncture, race-based identity politics brings with it essentialized forms of belonging that may be secondary concerns to the problem of white supremacy but smacks of what Appiah earlier called intrinsic racism. As much as race politics may bring people of color together in a common struggle against white supremacy, it also becomes a source of division when it comes to that elusive grail of authenticity in one instance and the assumption of sameness that denies people of color their uniqueness in the other. They are literally thrown into some situations where the only possible commonality they have with others is the fact that they are people of color. These cheap forms of 'pseudo-solidarities' among minorities of which Gilroy speaks, are tyrannies that remain even after we write the obituary of racism, where race continues to encourage 'ready-to-wear racial identities' (St. Louis, 2002) or what Pollock (2004) calls 'lump sum' identities. It is hardly conducive to progressive politics. In the end, race creates emotional investments that lead to what Cheng (2001) calls 'melancholy', a sense of loss, for both whites and people of color.

Towards a New Day

As race relations enters its late phase of development, its contradictions become more ripe and obvious. Its logics hang desperately onto a worldview that becomes more anachronistic. This does not mean that race struggle becomes obsolete. On the contrary, post-race condition is reached precisely by exposing the myths held up for so long by a pigmentocracy that is whiteness, which people of color both love and hate because they have been taught for so long to admire the white and hate the black. Self-love in this instance is always uncertain for it is bound up with self-doubt. The possibility of ending race is the task of bringing back clarity to a situation that for so long has been clouded with the miseducation of racialized humans. This is the challenge of post-race thinking.

We live in a time when race is under intense questioning. Color-blind race discourse challenges the invocation of race analysis even in its most mainstream versions. However, progressive scholarship has taken this situation and reversed people's normal expectations. Like Judo, post-race analysis takes the otherwise reactionary implications of color-blindness and uses its momentum against itself. For color-blindness is often the performance of feigning indifference to race while enforcing its practice. In a complicated dance with hegemony, post-race scholars strike a compromise that upsets the head-to-head confrontation that usually results in racial antagonism. There is something subversive in this move. Arguing for the moribund status of race, post-race proponents do not rehabilitate race but argue against it. Where they differ from color-blind pretenders is their ability to go *through* race instead of *around* it. They are able to speak to race rather than about it.

Hope in Post-Race versus Optimism of Whiteness

Ultimately, a post-race perspective enables educators to distinguish between hope and optimism. Whereas color-blindness is usually associated with a white mindset or lived experience, post-race is a theory of color, which does not mean that scholars of color are always its author. A bright student of mine once suggested that 'hope is white'.[8] By this she meant that whites exhibit an abundance of hope concerning racial progress when compared to a rather pessimistic black prognosis of the same problem. I took it to mean that even hope is racial and subject to its rationality. It struck me as insightful and I would like to end this essay with a commentary on hope and optimism. I would refine the insight this way: while whites are optimistic about race they are not hopeful, whereas people of color are precisely the opposite, hopeful but pessimistic. When it comes to race progress, whites show much optimism because small increments of improvement are taken as signs of white tolerance. It produces the psychological advantage of focusing on 'how far we have come' instead of the more loaded 'how far we still have to go'. For if whites compare present inequalities with past cruelties, not only do black lives look that much better but white tolerance looks that much greater. Whereas Gramsci (1971) once distinguished between the 'pessimism of the intellect and the optimism of the will', *whites show an optimism of the intellect and pessimism of the will*. In short, we cannot equate white optimism with real hope, which takes a certain will that whites have shown themselves to lack. They are prone to exaggerate racial progress because focusing on the continuing significance of racism indicts their collective inability to end the problem once and for all. They feel good without necessarily having to make good. For all the optimism they express toward racial progress, they lack hope in its actional sense. For whites, hope is abstract. This is hardly post-racial.

In contrast, if people of color have represented anything in the history of race relations, it is hope. It is one of the few 'advantages' that people of color have over whites. Hope is built into the experience of people of color as an ontological part of their being (see Freire, 1993). How else does one explain their ability to withstand centuries of racial oppression? It is premised on the hope that it will one day end despite the fact that they are disappointed by whites' ability to converge racial progress with their own interests (Bell, 1992). Time and time again, people of color cling on to hope as the force that prevents them from despair and resignation. It is historical and allows them to see setbacks as opportunities for defiance. In fact, they project hope onto whites more than they sometimes deserve, a surplus hopefulness that whites underappreciate because they would rather emphasize people of color's animosity over their grace.

We have seen Barack Obama's campaign was built on the audacity of hope and Reverend Jesse Jackson's battlecry was 'keep hope alive'. Even Derrick Bell's apparent bleakness is contradicted by his early endorsement of Obama for president, as evidenced by his public support of him many months preceding Obama's victory over his then favored opponent, Senator Clinton.[9] Hope is what propelled Bell to support change. As Obama accepts his Nobel Peace Prize, we recognize that it was made possible by his going to war with a unilateral decision-making process turned into a science by eight years under the Bush regime. As a concrete possibility, peace will be approached by people of color through a critical, honest appraisal of racialization. Their hope attenuates the otherwise realistic pessimism they feel about race relations, which may keep them bitter. A language of hope is concrete for people of color because it is not just a projected ideal but a way to exist in the present. It is a dream, not a fantasy. It is not an abstract feeling but a concrete emotion, or better yet, an emotional praxis (Chubbuck & Zembylas, 2008).

Post-race thought is ultimately hopeful. It may be a form of surplus hopefulness in light of the formidable presence of race and the fact of racism but people of color have always relied on a certain distortion of reality as someday better than itself, also called utopia. As part of emotional praxis, post-race perspectives allow racially oppressed minorities to recognize anger as part of history without it cementing into a form of indignation (Hattam & Zembylas, 2010). Like post-indignation, post-race analysis does not allow race to cement more than necessary. It recognizes race thinking as historical, and, like anger, is a natural consequence within a condition of racialization without graduating to the victimhood that can result from both indignation and raciology. In effect, post-race analysis is the sublimation of racial anger into a form of hope because 'investing in anger cannot form a particularly skillful political/pedagogical strategy for responding to colonization, racism or nationalism' (Hattam & Zembylas, 2010, p. 25). Post-race analysis is the recognition that the language of race has been necessary in order to understand what we have made of race and what it has made of us. But race is ultimately insufficient and shows its weakening grip over us. Post-race opens up our ambivalence in our search for a more humane and humanizing language.[10]

Notes

1. Below, I discuss the relationship among race, ethnicity, culture, and nation. These concepts are related but often used interchangeably in the literature. In this essay, my main concern is with the concept of race.
2. White abolition sees no redeeming aspects of whiteness, which articulates white bodies with the ideology of whiteness in order to create white people. The results of this partnering have been consistent and predictable: racial violence. In contrast, a pedagogy of white reconstruc-

tion forges a new whiteness, a resignified subjectivity that is not hopelessly stuck in the quicksand of racist understandings. For an extended discussion regarding the merits and problems of both white abolition and reconstruction, see my (2009b) essay, 'Pale/ontology: The Status of Whiteness in Education'.

3. Massey and Denton's treatment of undeclared Apartheid in the US is very convincing and sound on many fronts. In terms especially of housing, the extreme isolation of blacks in US society explains their lack of access to 'good' (read: white) schools, neighborhoods, and social networks; this affects their ability to secure decent jobs and ability to acquire wealth (see Oliver & Shapiro, 1997). However, since Massey and Denton's argument rests on the value of integration as the antidote to the problems of segregation, their argument that the US was more integrated at the turn of the 20th century contradicts their basic premise since no one credible would argue that African Americans fared better in more or less racially integrated neighborhoods during early 1900s. Something else may explain the life chances of African Americans despite the fact that integration (in its true sense of an entire social system) is defensible. Moreover, Chapter Six of *American Apartheid* is positioned awkwardly within an otherwise rigorous sociological study of white supremacy. Revisiting the culture of poverty arguments extant from the 1960s on, Massey and Denton argue that ghetto culture, once a coping strategy for structural conditions, achieves *autonomy* and becomes an independent entity. Besides the fact that black culture from diverse class experiences is reduced to 'black street culture' (i.e. it would sound strange to evoke its counterpart in 'white street culture'), at *what point* it became autonomous is never explained. Furthermore, the authors rely on some questionable sources of evidence when they engage the song 'A Bitch iZ a Bitch' by NWA and its follow up by HWA of 'A Trick Is a Trick', as true expressions of black culture rather than what is more likely: embellishments through artifice like most songs.

4. We must recall here the observation that Martin Luther King Jr (and for that matter Malcolm X) was assassinated precisely at the moment when he broadened his mission to include the struggles of poor whites. In a white-oriented society, MLK Jr's nod to post-racial organizing represents a concrete threat against white supremacy *and* raciology.

5. In 2003, Ward Connerly of the University of California Regents drafted the 'Racial Privacy Act', which would remove data involving identity, including race, from official governmental documents in the state of California, USA. The initiative was voted down by the public, perhaps largely due to the mobilization of the medical and educational community, because it would make tracking of health disparities and school inequality based on race virtually impossible.

6. Admittedly, this is a US-centric point of view regarding race relations. Racial classifications differ across contexts, such as Brazil or Australia, where racial categories are more literal and reflect actual skin color and where miscegenation has created a larger group of mixed-race people in the former, and where Asians and Aboriginals occupy a higher percentage than Blacks among populations of color in the latter.

7. Alternatively, rather than loss, Arturo Cortez (personal communication) substitutes the concept of 'trade'. That is, whites did not lose ethnic practices as much as they traded them for white language, custom, and identity. This tack is preferable to the notion of 'white loss', which quickly degrades into a 'me tooism' (see Dyer, 1997).

8. Thanks goes to Rachel Lissy (personal communication) for provoking me to think critically about the distinctions between hope and optimism.

9. Professor Derrick Bell gave an address at the 2008 AERA in New York, USA, pronouncing his support for Obama.

10. I would like to take this opportunity to acknowledge and thank Linda Graham for putting together this excellent special issue, and for her gracious and critical commentary on my essay. In addition, much appreciation goes to the blind reviews of engaged and helpful colleagues. I have never seen such deep, sustained, and insightful critiques of my work. A simple thanks.

References

Althusser, L. (1971) *Lenin and Philosophy*. B. Brewster, trans. (New York, Monthly Review Press).

Appiah, K. (1990) Racisms, in: D. T. Goldberg (ed.), *Anatomy of Racism* (Minneapolis, MN, University of Minnesota Press), pp. 3–17.

Artiles, A. (2008) Special Education's Changing Identity: Paradoxes and dilemmas in views of culture and space, *Harvard Education Review*, 73,2, pp. 164–202.

Austin, J. L. (1962) *How to Do Things with Words* (Oxford, Oxford University Press).

Barker, M. (1990) Biology and the New Racism, in: D. T. Goldberg (ed.), *Anatomy of Racism* (Minneapolis, MN, University of Minnesota Press), pp. 18–37.

Bell, D. (1992) *Faces at the Bottom of the Well: The permanence of racism* (New York, Basic Books).

Bernal, D. D. & Villalpando, O. (2005) An Apartheid of Knowledge in Academia: The struggle over the 'legitimate' knowledge of faculty of color, in: Z. Leonardo (ed.), *Critical Pedagogy and Race* (Malden, MA, Blackwell), pp. 185–204.

Biesta, G. (1998) Say you want a revolution ... Suggestions for the impossible future of critical pedagogy, *Educational Theory*, 48,4, pp. 499–510.

Bonilla-Silva, E. (2005) Introduction—'Racism' and 'New Racism': The contours of racial dynamics in contemporary America, in: Z. Leonardo (ed.), *Critical Pedagogy and Race* (Malden, MA, Blackwell), pp. 1–36.

Bourdieu, P. & Passeron, J. (1990) *Reproduction in Education, Society, and Culture* (Thousand Oaks, CA, Sage).

Caldwell, K. (2007) *Negras in Brazil* (New Brunswick, NJ, Rutgers University Press).

Cheng, A. (2001) *The Melancholy of Race* (Oxford: Oxford University Press).

Chesler, M., Peet, M. & Sevig, T. (2003) Blinded by Whiteness: The development of white college students' racial awareness, in: A. Doane & E. Bonilla-Silva (eds), *White Out* (New York, Routledge), pp. 215–230.

Cho, S. (2006) On Language of Possibility: Revisiting critical pedagogy, in: C. Rosatto, R. L. Allen, and M. Pruyn (eds), *Reinventing Critical Pedagogy* (Lanham, MD, Rowman & Littlefield), pp. 125–141.

Chubbuck, S. & Zembylas, M. (2008) The Emotional Ambivalence of Socially Just Teaching: A case study of a novice urban school teacher, *American Educational Research Journal*, 452, pp. 274–318.

Cone, J. (1990) *A Black Theology of Liberation* (MaryKnoll, NY, Orbis Books).

Darder, A. & Torres, R. (2004) *After Race* (New York, New York University Press).

Derrida, J. (1985) Racism's Last Word, *Critical Inquiry*, 12,1, pp. 290–299.

Dumas, M. (2008) Theorizing Redistribution and Recognition in Urban Education Research: 'How do we get dictionaries at Clevelend?', in: J. Anyon (ed.), *Theory and Educational Research* (London, Routledge), pp. 81–108.

Dyer, R. (1997) *White* (London, Routledge).

Fanon, F. (1967) *Black Skin White Masks*, C. Markmann, trans. (New York, Grove Weidenfeld). Originally published in 1952.

Fields, B. (1990) Slavery, Race and Ideology in the United States of America, *New Left Review*, I,181 (May-June), pp. 95–118.

Freedman, S. W., Weinstein, H., Murphy, K. & Longman, T. (2008) Teaching History after Identity-based Conflicts: The Rwanda experience, *Comparative Education Review*, 5,4, pp. 663–690.

Freire, P. (1993) *Pedagogy of the Oppressed* (New York, Continuum).

Gillborn, D. (2005) Education Policy as an Act of White Supremacy: Whiteness, critical race theory and education reform, *Journal of Education Policy*, 2,4, pp. 485–505.

Gilroy, P. (1993) *The Black Atlantic* (Cambridge, MA, Harvard University Press).

Gilroy, P. (1998) Race Ends Here, *Racial and Ethnic Studies*, 21,5, pp. 838–847.

Gilroy, P. (2000) *Against Race* (Cambridge, MA, Belknap Press of Harvard University).

Giroux, H. (1988) *Teachers as Intellectuals* (Westport, CT, Bergin & Garvey).

Giroux, H. (1997) Rewriting the Discourse of Racial Identity: Towards a pedagogy and politics of whiteness, *Harvard Educational Review*, 67,2, pp. 285–320.

Gotanda, N. (1995) A Critique of 'Our Constitution is Color-blind', in: K. Crenshaw, N. Gotanda, G. Peller & K. Thomas (eds), *Critical Race Theory* (New York, The New Press), pp. 257–275.

Graham, L. J. (in press) The cost of opportunity, in: J. Marshall & L. Stone (eds), *Handbook on Poststructuralism in Education* (Rotterdam, Sense Publishing).

Graham, L. J. and Slee, R. (2008) An Illusory Interiority: Interrogating the discourse/s of inclusion, *Educational Philosophy and Theory*, 40,2, pp. 277–293.

Gramsci, A. (1971) *Selections From Prison Notebooks*,Q. Hoare & G. Smith, ed. and trans. (New York, International Publishers).

Guillaumin, C. (1995) *Racism, Sexism, Power and Ideology* (London, Routledge).

Hall, S. (1996) The Problem of Ideology: Marxism without guarantees, in: D. Morley and K. Chen (eds), *Stuart Hall* (London, Routledge), pp. 25–46.

Harris, C. (1995) Whiteness as Property, in: K. Crenshaw, N. Gotanda, G. Peller & K. Thomas (eds), *Critical Race Theory* (New York, The New Press), pp. 276–291.

Hattam, R. & Zembylas, M. (2010) What's anger got to do with it? Towards a post-indignation pedagogy for communities in conflict, *Social Identities*, 16,1, pp. 23–40.

Hirschman, C. (2004) The Origins and Demise of the Concept of Race, *Population and Development Review*, 30,3, pp. 385–415.

Hunter, M. (2005) *Race, Gender, and the Politics of Skin Tone* (New York, Routledge).

Ignatiev, N. (1995) *How the Irish Became White* (New York, Routledge).

Ignatiev, N. and Garvey, J. (1996) Abolish the White race: By any means necessary, in: N. Ignatiev and J. Garvey (eds), *Race Traitor* (New York, Routledge), pp. 9–14.

Lather, P. (2003) Applied Derrida: (Mis)reading the work of mourning in educational research, *Educational Philosophy and Theory*, 35,3, pp. 257–270.

Leonardo, Z. (2002) The Souls of White Folk: Critical pedagogy, whiteness studies, and globalization discourse, *Race Ethnicity & Education*, 5,1, pp. 29–50.

Leonardo, Z. (2003) Resisting Capital: Simulationist and socialist strategies, *Critical Sociology*, 29,2, pp. 211–236.

Leonardo, Z. (2005) Through the Multicultural Glass: Althusser, ideology, and race relations in post-Civil Rights America, *Policy Futures in Education*, 3,4, pp. 400–412.

Leonardo, Z. (2007) The War on Schools: NCLB, nation creation, and the educational construction of whiteness, *Race Ethnicity & Education*, 10,3, pp. 261–278.

Leonardo, Z. (2009a) *Race, Whiteness, and Education* (New York, Routledge).

Leonardo, Z. (2009b) Pale/ontology: The status of whiteness in education, in: M. Apple, W. Au, and L. Gandin (eds), *Routledge International Handbook of Critical Education* (New York, Routledge), pp. 123–136.

Lewis, A. (2003) Some Are More Equal Than Others: Lessons on whiteness from school, in: A. Doane & E. Bonilla-Silva (eds), *White Out* (New York, Routledge), pp. 159–172.

Lipsitz, G. (1998) *The Possessive Investment in Whiteness* (Philadelphia, PA, Temple University Press).

Lopez, I. H. (2006) *White by Law* (New York, New York University Press).

Lyotard, J. (1984) *The Postmodern Condition*, G. Bennington & B. Massumi, trans. (Minneapolis, MN, University of Minnesota Press).

Massey, D. & Denton, N. (1993) *American Apartheid* (Cambridge, MA, Harvard University Press).

McLaren, P. & Torres, R. (1999) Racism and Multicultural Education: Rethinking 'race' and 'whiteness' in late capitalism, in: S. May (ed.), *Critical Multiculturalism: Rethinking multicultural and antiracist education* (Philadelphia, PA, Falmer Press), pp. 42–76.

McPhail, M. L. (2003) Race and the (Im)possibility of Dialogue, in: R. Anderson, L. Baxter & K. Cissna (eds), *Dialogue: Theorizing difference in communication studies* (Thousand Oaks, CA, Sage), pp. 209–224.

Morrison, T. (1993) *Playing in the Dark: Whiteness in the literary imagination* (New York, Vintage Books).

Miles, R. (2000) Apropos the Idea of 'Race' ... Again, in: L. Back and J. Solomos (eds), *Theories of Race and Racism* (New York, Routledge), pp. 125–143.

Mills, C. (1997) *The Racial Contract* (Ithaca, NY, Cornell University Press).

Nayak, A. (2006) After Race: Ethnography, race and post-race theory, *Ethnic and Racial Studies*, 29,3, pp. 411–430.

Oakes, J. (2005) *Keeping Track*, 2nd edn. (New Haven, CT, Yale University Press).

Oakes, J., Joseph, R. & Muir, K. (2004) Access and Achievement in Mathematics and Science: Inequalities that endure and change, in: J. Banks & C. Banks (eds), *Handbook of Research on Multicultural Education* (San Francisco, John Wiley & Sons), pp. 69–90.

Oliver, M. & Shapiro, T. (1997) *Black Wealth, White Wealth: A new perspective on racial inequality* (New York, Routledge).

Omi, M. & Winant, H. (1994) *Racial formation in the United States: From the 1960s to the 1990s*, 2nd edn. (New York, Routledge).

Pollock, M. (2004) *Colormute* (Princeton, NJ, Princeton University Press).

Roediger, D. (1994) *Toward the Abolition of Whiteness* (New York, Verso).

Stanley, C. (ed.) (2006) *Faculty of Color* (Bolton, MA, Anker Publishing).

St. Louis, B. (2002) Post-race/Post-politics? Activist-intellectualism and the reification of race, *Ethnic and Racial Studies*, 25,4, pp. 652–675.

Taylor, P. (2008) The Racial Stance: Pragmatism and post-analytic race theory. Paper delivered at the New Perspectives on Race Theory Conference, University of San Francisco, CA, April 26.

Telles, E. (2006) *Race in Another America: The significance of skin color in Brazil* (Princeton, NJ, Princeton University Press).

Wacquant, L. (1997) For an Analytic of Racial Domination, *Political Power and Social Theory*, 11, pp. 21–234.

Wacquant, L. (2002) From Slavery to Mass Incarceration: Rethinking the 'race question' in the United States, *New Left Review*, 13, pp. 41–60.

Warmington, P. (2009) Taking Race out of Scare Quotes: Race-conscious social analysis in an ostensibly post-racial world, *Race Ethnicity & Education*, 12,3, pp. 281–296.

Warren, J. & Twine, F. W. (2002) Critical Race Studies in Latin America: Recent advances, recurrent weaknesses, in: D. T. Goldberg & J. Solomos (eds), *A Companion to Racial and Ethnic Studies* (Malden, MA, Blackwell), pp. 538–560.

Youdell, D. (2004) Identity Traps or How Black Students Fail: The interactions between biographical, sub-cultural, and learner identities, in: G. Ladson-Billings & D. Gillborn (eds) *The Routledgefalmer Reader in Multicultural Education* (New York, RoutledgeFalmer), pp. 84–102.

Zembylas, M. (2008) *The Politics of Trauma in Education* (New York, Palgrave MacMillan).

Index

References are to page numbers and their footnotes indicated by 'n' e.g. 121n

The Power In/Of Language, First Edition. Edited by David R. Cole and Linda J. Graham.
Chapters © 2012 The Authors. Book compilation © 2012 Philosophy of Education Society of Australasia.
Published 2012 by Blackwell Publishing Ltd.